THE
TECHNOLOGY
PAYOFF

How to Profit with Empowered
Workers in the Information Age

THE TECHNOLOGY PAYOFF

How to Profit with Empowered Workers in the Information Age

Gerald M. Hoffman

IRWIN
Professional Publishing
Burr Ridge, Illinois
New York, New York

© RICHARD D. IRWIN, INC., 1994

Sponsoring editor:	Jean Geracie
Project editor:	Gladys True
Production manager:	Bob Lange
Designer:	Heidi J. Baughman
Art manager:	Kim Meriwether
Art studio:	ElectraGraphics
Compositor:	BookMasters, Inc.
Typeface:	11/13 Palatino
Printer:	Arcata Graphics/Kingsport

Library of Congress Cataloging-in-Publication Data

Hoffman, Gerald M.
    The technology payoff : how to profit with empowered workers in the information age / Gerald M. Hoffman.
       p.   cm.
    Includes bibliographical references and index.
    ISBN 1-55623-838-X
    1. Management information systems. 2. Strategic planning.
    3. Information technology—Management. I. Title.
HD30.213.H63 1994
658.4'038—dc20   93-38369

To May Weber

Who has helped me learn about people, how and why they change, and the strength, pride, and creativity that accompany individual freedom.

Preface

This book will help you and your organization achieve competitive success in the marketplaces of the 1990s. It shows how information technology can support your company's strategy and business processes, and how it can increase worker productivity. It shows you how to use information and information technology to improve your bottom line.

We focus on the relationships between business activities and information technology. Thus, we reexamine basic business issues only to the extent that they affect information technology activities, and we analyze information technology issues only as much as necessary to understand their effects on the business as a whole. We make excursions into technology from time to time, but only to the extent necessary to understand the managerial issues surrounding it.

In addition to new insights into the relationships between information technology and business, nearly every reader will find some material that is familiar, even elementary. If you are a line executive, most of the business issues will be well known to you, but the information technology issues may be unfamiliar. If you are an information technology executive, the opposite will probably be true. We discuss both because each of you must understand what happens on the other side of the boundary between business activities and information technology if your company is to gain maximum benefits from this powerful business tool. The very things that are elementary to you may be foreign to your counterparts on the other side of the business/technology boundary. Be prepared to help them understand what drives your activities as you strive to learn what drives theirs.

The most important message of this book is this: whether you are a line executive or an information technology executive, you must become personally involved in integrating information technology into your business. If you are the chief executive, you must take an active role in integrating information technology strategy with business strategy, and you must support information technology organizationally and financially. If you are the chief information officer, you must understand your company's strategies and operations and take a proactive role to ensure that no technological opportunities are missed, even as you resist any temptation to use technology for its own sake.

You should read this book if you are a senior manager or other policy maker, because it shows you how to integrate your information technology strategy with your corporate strategy and how to evaluate your information technology expenditures. You will learn how to use information technology to improve your competitive position, by redesigning business processes and organization structures and by empowering workers to manage their own work.

You will learn what kinds of information systems you need to be competitive in the 1990s, what questions to ask of your information systems executives and your line managers, and what actions you and they must take to ensure that your organization gets the benefits that information technology can provide. You will learn why deep user involvement is essential to successful information systems and how to achieve that involvement.

You should read this book if you are an information systems executive because you must understand the expanded needs for information in the organization of the 1990s and the new kinds of information systems necessary to meet those needs. You will learn new ways to design work processes and information systems to support them. And you will get a glimpse of society in the 21st century and the role of information technology in it.

You should read this book if you are involved in any way in the design of business processes, information systems, or organization structures, whether you are a user of information systems or an information systems professional. You will learn a new approach to business process design and how to support business processes with information technology to achieve maximum efficiency and effectiveness.

You should read this book if you want to live comfortably and work productively in the information age, because you must understand the implications of information technology as it relentlessly penetrates our lives.

Our philosophy, reflected in the structure of the book, is that business needs determine information needs, which in turn determine what kinds of information systems are required to meet those needs.

Part 1 explores the changing business environment. We see how the increasing intensity of competition and new societal demands on business are changing the very meaning of business success, and why advances in information technology will encourage ever greater changes in the future. We see why these changes require a new form of corporate organization, and we examine what that new organization will look like and how it will operate.

Part 2 investigates ways these changes in business affect the needs for information to support business activities. We show how business strategy and information technology strategy are related and how to evaluate information technology expenditures. We discuss ways to modify business processes to improve results and the implications for information needs. We analyze both evolutionary change (in the tradition of continuous process improvement) and revolutionary change (business process redesign), and we develop criteria for choosing between them.

The subject of Part 3 is delivering the information identified in Part 2. With current technology, this means building information systems. We discuss the reasons that users must participate in the system building process and what they must do. We learn the importance of order and consistency in the design and deployment of information systems over an enterprise and how information technology architecture can help create that order. Finally, we look at the practical constraints—technological, organizational, and human—on what you can actually achieve with today's information technology.

Part 4 explores the needs and possibilities for information systems as we enter the 21st century. It seems likely that competition will continue to be vigorous and workers will continue to demand more and more control over their work and their workplaces. The only certainty is that changes in business (and hence changes in information needs) will continue, and that rates of change will increase. We investigate some new ideas about information and information systems that have the potential to help us deal with the rapid changes in needs for information.

Finally, we examine some of the effects of the expanding use of information technology on society as a whole. This must be an essential part of the perspective of every executive because societal attitudes will become increasingly important determinants of what can and cannot be done with information technology, regardless of business benefit or technological capability.

Read the entire book. Don't look only at the sections dealing with your specialty or your immediate interests. One of the most important messages of this book is that all the elements must be considered together: customer demands must affect business processes; organization structure depends on business processes and influences information needs and information system design. And all of these things depend on the people in and around the enterprise.

The opportunities and methods I describe are suitable for all kinds of organizations: for-profit companies, not-for-profit corporations, governmental entities, and educational institutions. In fact, you can use these ideas in any setting that involves people interacting with one another in purposeful ways. I use the lexicon of business (customers, profits, etc.) because it is convenient, but the ideas apply to all kinds of enterprises. The needs of the customers of a business are very similar to the needs of the patients in a hospital or the clients of a social service organization; financial performance is at least as important in a not-for-profit organization as in a for-profit company, if not more so.

Every idea in this book is being used successfully today in some company. I know of no single company using all of them, but you don't need to use all of them to give your company an advantage over most of your competitors. These ideas apply to small enterprises as well as large ones. We shall see uses of information technology that give small companies the same kind of competitive advantage that billion-dollar systems (such as airline reservation systems) provide for corporate giants.

These words are being written in mid-1993. Information technology is changing so rapidly that some of the specific things described here will undoubtedly be obsolescent by the time you read this. Don't be put off by this. The principles will remain the same even though the technology employed may be different.

As you read this book, you may get the impression that I am recommending information technology as the solution for all problems. I am not. Other technologies are important as well: manufacturing technology, marketing technology, financial technology, and so on, but those are topics for another forum. However, it is worthwhile to note that many of the problems of making effective use of information technology are similar to problems that arise with other technologies, and some of the same methods can be used to solve them. Of course, many of our problems are not problems of technology at all; they are problems of management.

This book is about American companies and American workers. Its examples and its ideas draw on our current situation, on our national experience, and on our culture. While its recommendations could be used anywhere, they are most likely to be adopted by American companies, and Americans are most likely to be successful using them.

This is an optimistic book. It asserts that people can control this powerful technology and use it to their individual and collective benefit. It is grounded in the knowledge that most people are independent but cooperative, caring about the importance of what they do, ambitious for success and willing to work for it, selfish but giving, and proud of an important job well done. If you do not believe these things, stop reading now and get your money back. This book has nothing to offer you. If you do believe them, read on. You will be well rewarded.

Gerald M. Hoffman

Acknowledgments

I am grateful to the people who took the time to share their ideas and experiences with me and allowed me to publish some of our discussions:

Thomas J. Barrett
Linda L. Brennan
Raymond Dash
Donald N. Frey
Donald R. Hollis
William La Macchia
R. David Moon
Albert H. Rubenstein

I am particularly indebted to these people for their help and support in preparing this book:

To Richard L. Swanson for his review of the manuscript and his insightful comments both about the book and about information technology in general.

To Mark S. Hauf and Gerald D. Tang who brought the idea of Information Without Information Systems to my attention, and helped me to understand and elaborate it.

To Curt H. Hartog for many discussions about the technology and its impact on our lives.

To Raymond C. Bell, Jr., James C. Felli, Milton H. Paul, and Shelley Schneider-Bello, who helped with the research and other necessary chores.

To the many professional colleagues and personal friends who have helped me shape my ideas over the years.

The thoughts, perceptions, and ideas are derived from many sources. The predictions, opinions, and mistakes are my own.

The discussion in Chapter 9 of the analogy between information technology architecture and building construction architecture is adapted, with permission, from material that appeared in *Information Management Forum*, July 1989, published by the American Management Association.

Contents

Chapter Ten
VALIDATING YOUR INFORMATION
TECHNOLOGY STRATEGY   169

Chapter Thirteen
REVERBERATIONS INTO SOCIETY   231

A Note to the Reader

This book is addressed to chief executive officers and other senior executives who make information technology policy for their organizations. They are the "you" in the summaries at the end of each chapter ("What you must know" and "What you must do") and elsewhere throughout the book.

The book also speaks to those who implement information technology policy and those who are the beneficiaries (and the victims) of it: line managers, workers, information technology managers, and information technology professionals. It shows them how information technology policy looks from the executive suite, so that they can influence it and apply it properly as it touches their jobs.

BUSINESS IS DIFFERENT IN THE 1990s

Business is intrinsically different in the 1990s from what it has been in the past. Competition is becoming more intense as markets become global in scope and as we move toward an economy dominated by services rather than goods. Information technology is one of the major drivers of these changes, and the technology itself is changing so rapidly that we can be certain that changes in business and in our economy will continue for a long time to come.

One of the most profound changes in business is that there is a new definition of success. Success means meeting the needs of all the stakeholders of the enterprise: customers, workers, suppliers, and the community at large, as well as owners. The only way to meet the demands of all stakeholders is to enlist the full efforts and talents of every worker, and that can be done only if every worker has all of the information he needs to manage his work and do his job.

The hierarchical organization structure with its management by command and control, the norm in American business for more than a century, cannot meet the needs of the 1990s. It discourages the very initiative and creativity that are needed. Management based on employee empowerment—information, resources, and authority to make decisions in the hands of every worker—and a new organizational structure called the federated organization can help your company achieve competitive success in the 1990s.

Chapter One

The Business Environment of the 1990s

The business environment of the 1990s is vastly different from the environment of the 1980s, and the new environment is itself changing. Recognizing these changes and their causes is the first step toward meeting the challenges they present. The most difficult challenge is that change will continue. We are not moving from one stable state to another. We are moving from a condition of relative stability to one of continual change, and we need new ways of thinking about organizations and people if we are to prosper in this new world.

New demands are being made on organizations of every kind: for-profit and not-for-profit, public and private. Customer demands for high-quality products and services must be met in the face of increased competition and global marketplaces. At the same time, organizations face increasing demands by other stakeholders: employees, shareholders and other sources of funds, suppliers, and the community at large.

Information technology is at once a cause of many of these changes and a potential solution for some of the problems it generates as it relentlessly penetrates our organizations and our lives. The costs of computing and telecommunications are decreasing drastically, capabilities are increasing, and the sizes of components are shrinking. Workers, customers, and suppliers are becoming more computer-literate and more computer-demanding. All these trends will continue at least for the next decade.

To understand the interactions between information technology and business, we must look first at how business is being forced to change by increasing competition, by societal pressures, and by advances in information technology.

EVERYTHING IS DIFFERENT IN THE 1990s

American business is in a state of change bordering on chaos. You see the signs everywhere you look.

The structure of our economy is undergoing drastic changes.

Of the 500 companies on *Fortune* magazine's 1990 list of the largest industrial companies in the United States, only 414 appeared on the 1992 list. Some were displaced by other companies with higher total revenues. Others disappeared in mergers, acquisitions, or bankruptcies.

There are new leaders in many old industries. On January 21, 1993, the stock market capitalization of Microsoft exceeded that of IBM.[1] Nucor Steel is now the low-cost producer (in the United States) of reinforcing rods and other specialized products. In 1992 it earned more money in the steel business than did United States Steel.[2] Nucor recently formed a joint venture with Oregon Steel to produce cold rolled sheet, which is one of the mainstays of the old line integrated steel companies.[3]

Many companies find that the core of their business has changed. USX, the holding company for U.S. Steel, has generated more revenue in recent years from its petroleum business than from its steel operations.[4]

Staid old electric utilities, once classic investments for widows and orphans, are attacked at every turn. Some find themselves forced to become common carriers, moving power owned by others. Many are compelled to buy power from any independent company that chooses to connect to their distribution systems. Virtually all are under public pressure to encourage their customers to buy less of their product rather than more.

Some multibillion-dollar companies (and some multibillion-dollar industries) did not even exist 10 or 15 years ago: Federal Express and Microsoft come to mind.

The structure of individual companies is changing as well. Restructuring, downsizing, and outsourcing are the fashions of the day.

The most important factor affecting corporate structure is the abandonment of the 1970s conglomerate as a model, in favor of a strategy of focus on a small number of core competencies. Companies are selling, spinning off, or closing businesses that are peripheral to their main mission. IBM sold its low-speed printer business to Lexmark, even though low-speed printers are essential accessories to personal computers and workstations, products that are important components of IBM's corporate strategy.[5] (The distinction between personal computers and workstations is fuzzy at best; both are types of microcomputers. We will use these terms interchangeably.)

Organizations are being made flatter as well as smaller. IBM, General Motors, and AT&T have laid off both production workers and middle managers by the tens of thousands. In August 1991, Alcoa eliminated two levels of senior management—four division presidents and three group vice presidents—leaving 25 business unit managers reporting directly to the CEO.[6] Many smaller and less visible enterprises are taking similar actions.

The envelope of ownership is changing.

Companies are hiring outside contractors to provide services formerly provided by their own employees—from running the mail room and the cafeteria to designing, building, and operating information systems. In 1989, Eastman Kodak hired IBM to run its data center operations for 10 years. Kodak expects to reduce its computer operations costs by 40 percent to 50 percent.[7]

Some companies are entrusting core activities to business partners: National Semiconductor has hired Federal Express to act as its warehouse and distribution arm.[8]

Automatic teller machines have become a competitive necessity in the retail banking business, but in most cases the banks do not own the communications networks that allow the machines to function. Some networks are owned by consortia of banks. In other cases, individual banks sell network access to other banks.[9]

The primary productive force in our economy is now knowledge, rather than land, raw materials, or physical labor, as in earlier years. This will affect the products and services that companies offer in the marketplace, and it will affect individuals as the nature of their work changes.

The lives of individual workers are being changed in deep and lasting ways.

Many jobs are disappearing as a result of better organization of work or automation. The remaining jobs are becoming more demanding as staff sizes are reduced, and more difficult as managerial supervision decreases.

In years past, workers in some companies could reasonably aspire to spend their entire working lives with one employer. Today there are virtually no large companies in the United States in which this is a realistic expectation for the majority of workers.

It is no longer realistic for most workers to look forward to working in a single profession or trade throughout their working lives. The pace of technological and business change is so rapid that lifelong continuing education is becoming essential for long-term individual success. Even in cases where an individual remains in what is nominally the same profession throughout her working life, the intellectual content of that profession is likely to be almost totally different at the end of her career than at the beginning. Compare the work of an electronic engineer in the 1950s with the work of the 1990s. In the 50s, she (there were a few women in engineering in those days) finished college and went to work designing radios and TV sets with pencil and slide rule, sets that used a dozen or so individual vacuum tubes and perhaps a hundred other components as their main circuit elements. Today that same engineer designs circuits at a computer workstation, working with semiconductor chips that contain tens of thousands of circuit elements.

Everything is in a state of flux: individuals' work and careers, companies, and the economy as a whole, to say nothing of massive social and political changes throughout the world. If we are to deal with these changes effectively, we must have some sense of what is driving them and how these drivers are evolving.

INFORMATION TECHNOLOGY AND THE DRIVERS OF CHANGE

Information technology is at the root of many of these changes, either as a cause or as an enabler. The most obvious change is the increasing intensity of competition in almost every facet of business. But we must look beyond the intensity of competition to understand what is happening. The very nature of competition is changing as we move into a service economy and into the information age. Furthermore, new demands are being made on businesses by employees and by society at large, in addition to the traditional demands of customers and shareholders.

Fortunately, the same information technology that drives change often contains the seeds of solutions to the problems it begets. The crucial point is this: Change will continue and the pace of change will accelerate because information technology will continue to evolve at a rate unmatched by any other technological change in human history.

Information technology is not the only driver of change. Advances in manufacturing, changing patterns of transportation, and social and political changes all contribute to changes in businesses and other organizations. We focus on information technology because it underlies many of the other drivers, because it is changing more rapidly than any of the other drivers, and because its use is expanding into every area of our lives.

The Increasing Intensity of Competition

Competition is more intense than ever. The global village has arrived for virtually everyone who sells goods or services. A decade or so ago, American companies (and American workers) competed mostly with one another, within the American cultural and political framework. More recently we have been forced to compete with companies from all over the world, companies with different economic incentives, based in different political and economic systems, whose workers have different backgrounds, abilities, and goals. We are relearning what Adam Smith taught us 200 years ago: that different countries and different regions within the same country have different talents and abilities, and that specialization based on these differences is good for everyone.[10]

Information technology, particularly the marriage of computing with telecommunications, is one of the things that has made this specialization particularly attractive in recent years. Examples abound.

- AT&T, forcibly separated from its local telephone operations, is struggling to learn to compete in the long-distance business, where its competitors are regulated much less than it is. The operation and administration of multiple long-distance carriers working with the individual regional bell operating companies (RBOCs) would be a physical impossibility without the computer-based central office switches the RBOCs are now using.

- The RBOCs themselves, which a decade ago seemed secure in their monopolies of local service, are being attacked on all fronts. These attacks, mostly in the political arena, would not be possible without modern information technology.

  The Federal Communications Commission, as a matter of policy, has licensed competitors of the RBOCs to operate cellular phone systems in every region of the country, and it requires the RBOCs to allow these competitors access to their networks.

  Metropolitan Fiber Systems and other independent companies have installed fiber optic networks in the downtown areas of New York, Chicago, Los Angeles, and other cities, allowing businesses to gain access to long-distance carriers without using any RBOC facilities, thus depriving the RBOCs of significant revenues. [11]

  In September 1992, the Illinois Commerce Commission granted permission to Teleport Communications to provide local switched service to businesses in Chicago and 28 surrounding communities, allowing competition in the most important market remaining to the RBOCs.[12] Other states seem likely to follow suit. In June 1993, Time Warner filed for permission to offer similar service in San Diego.[13]

  And to add insult to injury, in November 1992, AT&T announced plans to purchase a one-third interest in the largest cellular telephone company in the United States, with an option to acquire a larger share later.[14] If a business combination should result, AT&T will once again be in a position to provide complete end-to-end telephone service over much of the United States. Where does this leave the RBOCs, which are prohibited from offering long-distance service outside of their own designated service areas?

- American Airlines located a major data-entry facility in Barbados in the 1970s to take advantage of lower labor costs and greater worker productivity. It ships used flight coupons to Barbados by air, where data from the coupons is entered into computers and transmitted by satellite to American's main computers for further processing.[15]
- Ford Motor Company has established electronic links with its major parts suppliers that allow the suppliers to monitor Ford's inventories and production schedules. This results in closer coordination of production and shipping schedules, saving money for all parties. Both Ford and its suppliers gain a competitive edge in the marketplace.[16]
- Levi Strauss has linked its factories and warehouses directly to the inventory systems of some of its major retailers to minimize inventories at every level, while still meeting changing customer demands for its products.[17]

The global village is here for consumers as well as for producers. Worldwide satellite-based television means that consumers everywhere know about products and services from everywhere else, and worldwide direct-dial long-distance telephone service means that anyone anywhere can order any product. I recently had occasion to use a USA-issued credit card in Ürümci in Chinese central Asia. The transaction was as quick and easy as using it in New York City. On that same day, I watched one of the 1992 presidential campaign debates live on local television. No one has yet built a worldwide television home shopping network, but it is only a matter of time. The technology exists today.

The Changing Nature of Competition

The very nature of competition is changing. Many manufactured products are becoming commodities, as manufacturing skills and technologies spread throughout the world. As this happens, producers have two options: compete in the commodity market on the basis of price alone, or differentiate their products from their competitors' by customizing the products or the services that surround them.

There are literally hundreds of different brands of IBM-compatible personal computers being marketed in the United States, all of which have essentially the same capabilities.

Many small vendors compete solely on the basis of price. Dell Computer, a catalog company, began by competing on price. It now stresses quick delivery of custom configurations and hardware repairs on customer premises (rather than requiring the customer to ship defective equipment back to the seller, as do most other mail order companies). Dell has become a $2 billion company in just 10 years.[18]

Information technology has made it easier than ever to purchase merchandise without going to a store. The "mail order" catalog companies such as Lands' End make up a $50 billion industry, in direct competition with conventional retailers.[19] They are, of course, not "mail order" companies at all; they are "mail a catalog, take a telephone order, deliver by UPS, Federal Express, or mail" companies, supported at every point by sophisticated information systems.

New Demands of Other Stakeholders

In addition to the new global competitive arena for producers, and the demands of customers and ultimate consumers, competition is further changed by the increasing demands of stakeholders beyond owners and customers. Workers demand stable and satisfying jobs, suppliers seek ongoing relationships, and the community demands that environmental concerns and workers' health be factored into every business decision and every transaction.

United Services Automobile Association, a large writer of automobile insurance, reorganized its claims department in 1988 using electronic images of paper documents instead of the documents themselves. The new system enriches the jobs of claims representatives by enabling one individual to handle an entire claim from start to finish, rather than having each employee work only on one part of a transaction. Customers are getting quicker service, and productivity has increased significantly.[20]

Public health authorities have identified workplace hazards such as passive smoking and repetitive stress syndrome by using sophisticated statistical techniques to analyze massive employee health databases.

Information technology has played a central role in each of these major business changes, as well as in others too numerous

to mention. As the technology advances, it will open new opportunities and create new imperatives for every organization and
every individual. And the technology will advance, rapidly and
relentlessly, as we shall see in the next section.

THE CHANGING WORLD OF
INFORMATION TECHNOLOGY

We now take a brief excursion into information technology itself
because this technology is crucial to business change and to business success. My goal is not to make you a technical expert; rather
it is to give you an appreciation of the rate and magnitude of advances in the technologies that underlie information systems and
a sense of why these changes will continue.

It is worth a moment to define what we mean by information
technology (IT) and to distinguish information technology from
information systems (IS). **Information technology** is an all inclusive term that encompasses computers and telecommunications
in all their forms, whatever their use. It includes mainframe computers, supercomputers, microcomputers, and the $5 computer
chips that control your VCR and your washing machine. IT includes the public telephone network, television and radio broad-
casting, credit cards (because of the magnetic stripes), radio
paging systems, facsimile machines, and cellular telephones, as
well as the software that controls them all.

An **information system** is a combination of information technology and other things, organized to support or manage a
business process. These other things usually include business
procedures, paper forms, and human effort. The distinction between information technology and information systems is important because advances in information technology change the
economic trade-offs between the technological parts of an information system and the nontechnological parts, as well as the
trade-offs among the technological elements. These changing
trade-offs are among the main causes of the organizational disruption that accompanies the introduction of every significant
new information system.

The personal computer revolution is a direct consequence of
changing cost and capability relationships between microcom-

puters and mainframe computers. But the changes have gone far beyond merely moving computing work away from the mainframe. The PC has generated profound business and organizational changes, as well as major changes in the way many people do their work.

A parallel though less visible revolution is occurring in telecommunications, as cellular telephones and communications satellites make it possible for anyone anywhere to communicate with anyone else at modest cost, and as optical fiber communication links make rapid transmission of massive amounts of data practical and cost-effective in the everyday conduct of business.

It is not possible within the confines of this book even to list the important technologies that are changing, much less to describe the changes. Instead, we will discuss two pivotal technologies on which many others are based: the microprocessor and optical fiber. The descriptions that follow are necessarily incomplete and imprecise. But they are accurate as far as they go, and they go far enough to make the point: Information technology will improve enormously in capability and in price/performance for at least the next 10 years, and probably much longer.

The Microprocessor

A **microprocessor** is a piece of silicon, about one-quarter of an inch square and one-fiftieth of an inch thick, containing all the electrical circuit elements (a million or more) that perform the computations and data manipulation that are the essence of every computer.

These little pieces of silicon, called *chips* or *microchips*, can be fabricated to do other things, most notably to serve as "main memory," storing programs and data while the microprocessor is using them. The underlying manufacturing technology is the same for all kinds of chips, so that advances in one kind are quickly reflected in others.

The evolution of the microprocessor is almost unbelievable. Table 1–1 shows the history of Intel's "86" series of chips, which are used in IBM and compatible PCs. (Some variants have been omitted.)[21] Power, measured in millions of instructions per second (MIPS), has increased by 340 times in just 15 years. Motorola

TABLE 1–1
The Evolution of Microprocessors

Date of Introduction	Name of Chip	Number of Transistors	Power in MIPS*
June 1978	8086	29,000	0.33
February 1982	80286	134,000	1.2
October 1985	80386DX	275,000	6.
April 1989	486DX	1,200,000	20.
March 1992	486DX2	1,200,000	40.
May 1993	Pentium™	3,100,000	112.

* Millions of instructions per second

has made similar progress with its 68000 chips, which power most Apple computers. The price of each type of chip at the time of its introduction has been in the same general range: $500 to $1,000. Typically, prices have fallen to 15 percent to 25 percent of initial price by the time the successor chip reaches the market in significant quantities.

One of the key factors in determining the speed of a microprocessor is its physical size: The smaller it is, the faster it can operate. In everyday life, we tend to think of the transmission of electrical signals as instantaneous: we turn a switch and a light goes on, for all practical purposes, immediately. In the context of a microprocessor, which operates at speeds measured in billionths of a second per cycle, this is not true. In fact, one of the main limitations to the speed of a microprocessor is the time required for a signal to move (at the speed of light) from one part of the chip to another. Thus, the quest for a faster chip is in large part a quest for a smaller chip.

A chip is made by a process similar to making a photographic enlargement. A piece of silicon is coated with a light-sensitive material and an image of the desired circuits is projected onto it. The image is "developed," giving a stencil that is used to etch a pattern of lines into the silicon. These lines are filled with whatever materials are required to do the electrical job: conductors, insulators, resistors, and semi-conductors—the active elements.

This set of electric circuits is then covered with an insulating layer. The process may then be repeated up to a dozen times with other stencils and circuit elements, until the desired configuration is achieved.

Circuit elements can be moved closer together in a number of ways so that signals do not have to travel so far. One way is to make the lines thinner. Line width is limited by the laws of physics to no less than three times the wavelength of the light used to project the image, which means about one micron (one one-millionth of a meter) wide with current technology. No one can modify these laws of physics, but computer scientists and engineers have been incredibly successful in working around them.

Work is now under way in various laboratories to use X rays rather than visible light to etch the patterns onto the silicon chips. X rays have a wavelength of one-tenth to one one-hundredth of the wavelength of visible light, which means individual lines could be from 10 times to 100 times thinner. Early experiments indicate that the use of protons as etching tools can yield lines 10 times finer than X ray-generated lines.

Another approach is make the chip surface three dimensional rather than two dimensional. Circuit elements can be placed on the vertical parts of the surface as well as on the horizontal parts, thus packing the elements more tightly.

Simply making the chips smaller is not enough, of course. Many other problems arise, including getting rid of the heat generated by the chip as it does its work and connecting these complex devices to the outside world. These problems too are being solved.

There many other possibilities for making faster microprocessors, in addition to merely making them smaller. One is to change the base from silicon to another material in which electrons move more rapidly, such as gallium arsenide or germanium. Another way to make faster chips is to use light rather than electricity to carry information within the chip.

The point is this: In this one limited part of information technology—reducing chip size to achieve faster computations—improvements of 100 to 1,000 times compared with current commercial products have already been achieved in laboratory prototypes. Production models will follow. Comparable improvements are also being made in other factors contributing to computational speed.

Optical Fiber

An **optical fiber** is a strand of glass about one one-thousandth of an inch in diameter, not very different from the glass in your windows except that it contains far fewer impurities. Information is transmitted through the fiber by means of pulses of light representing the zeros and ones that make up computer code, just as pulses of electricity carry information through wires. Each zero or one is called a **bit**—short for binary digit. In the most common computer coding scheme, eight bits taken together (called a **byte)** are used to represent one character, say a letter of the alphabet. Thus, a standard telephone circuit that can be switched on and off 4,800 times per second can transmit 4,800 bits or 600 characters of data per second (also called a capacity of 4,800 **baud**).

The information-carrying capacity of any medium depends on how fast the pulses can be started and stopped. In electrical circuits, this speed is limited by certain intrinsic characteristics of the circuits (inductance and capacitance, to those of you who remember your college physics). These limits are severe in telephone lines, but there are no such limits inherent in optical fibers. Switching speed is limited only by the capabilities of the external electronics, which are very great.

The numbers tell the tale. An ordinary telephone circuit can transmit a single human conversation or carry digital data at a rate of 2,400 to 9,600 baud. Devices that connect computers to phone lines can increase transmission rates to 56,000 baud in some cases. The coaxial cable that carries the video signal between a cable TV supplier and your TV set has a capacity of 1.2 million baud, which is the equivalent of 500 ordinary telephone circuits or one video signal. A single optical fiber has a capacity of 500 video signals, equivalent to 25,000 telephone circuits. Typically, optical fibers are installed in cables consisting of 12 to 26 fibers, giving a total transmission capability of 6,000 video signals or 150,000 voice conversations. Put in other terms, one optical fiber has the capacity to transmit the entire *Encyclopaedia Britannica* in less than three seconds.

The economics of optical fiber are very attractive. As of this writing, optical fiber is competitive in cost with copper wire and coaxial cable for many high-volume applications such as busy local area networks and long-distance telephone networks. Costs are decreasing as manufacturing economies are achieved and as installers become more familiar with the material.

This is not to say that optical fiber is always the right transmission medium to use. Just as chip designers are finding innovative ways to make chips smaller and faster, electrical engineers are finding ways to move information through copper wires more quickly. Computer scientists, meanwhile, are inventing ways of conveying information with fewer bits. This is called data compression.

You can get a feel for the way data compression works by watching your fax machine. Transmit a document that contains a large empty space in the middle of a page. The machine moves over the empty space much more quickly than it moves over typewritten text. Here is what happens. When the scanner detects the beginning of a white space, it transmits the location of the beginning and then seeks and transmits the location of the end of the white space. This requires transmission of about 100 bits of information, compared with the over 650,000 bits that would be required to cover a two-inch strip if the data were transmitted in full. A more complex version of this technique can be used to compress voice and video transmissions, reducing the data transmitted by 50 to 90 percent.

Data compression can be applied to optical transmission as well as electrical transmission, and it will be whenever there is need for it. Once again we see vast increases in capability—this time in telecommunications—at little increase in cost.

For the past 20 years, overall information technology capabilities and cost/performance have improved at an average rate of about 30 percent per year. There is every reason to think this rate will be sustained for at least the next decade, based on inventions that have already been proven in the laboratory and the voracious demands of the marketplace. Changes of this magnitude and duration will inevitably change the organizations that use this technology, which is to say every organization.

SUMMARY

What You Must Know

- The business environment of the 1990s is intrinsically different from that of the 1980s, and it is continuing to change.
- Cost and capabilities of information technology are improving dramatically and will continue to do so into the foreseeable future.
- Business practices and organizations will change, continuously and drastically, driven in part by changes in information technology.

What You Must Do

- Monitor your business environment so that you will be the first to detect changes, instead of the last.
- Learn the possibilities that information technology offers to your organization.
- Have someone monitor advances in information technology so that you can get the benefits of them before your competitors.
- Plan on the basis that everything in your enterprise is subject to change and that information technology will be a central force in causing it.

Chapter Two

New Paradigms for Business

Business success means meeting the needs of all stakeholders: workers, suppliers, customers, and the community at large, in addition to the needs of the owners of the enterprise. It is paradoxical but true that placing other stakeholders on a par with shareholders will improve results for the shareholders as well as for everyone else.

You must take a new look at corporate vision and corporate strategy to assure that both support this broad new definition of success. The corporate vision must include meeting the needs of all involved with the enterprise, and the corporate strategy must be sharply focused on those few things at which the organization excels.

Successful execution of strategies in today's highly competitive environment requires a sharp focus on customer needs and on new ways of managing that make full use of the talents and energies of everyone in the organization. This means moving authority outward, from the administrative center to the edges of the organization, where the business meets the world of customers, suppliers, and community. Above all, it means managing for flexibility: flexibility to meet changing conditions, flexibility to take risks, and flexibility to correct mistakes.

Traditional measures of results are not sufficient. You must measure and manage the things that are important to every constituency: profits for the shareholders of course, but also satisfaction of customers, job opportunities and security for workers, success for suppliers, and good citizenship in the community.

Our changing environment requires us to think about the very essence of business in new ways if we are to be successful. Indeed, success itself takes on a new meaning, a meaning beyond the bottom line. New strategies and new methods of management are required and different measurements are needed to understand whether an enterprise is successful in this new way.

SUCCESS BEYOND THE BOTTOM LINE

Many people and many organizations in addition to the owners of a business have a stake in its success. These stakeholders (sometimes called constituents) include customers, employees, suppliers, lenders, and the community at large. Each is essential to the very existence of the enterprise, and with rare exceptions, each can refuse to participate. Employees can seek other jobs, suppliers and lenders can find other customers, and the community can withdraw permission for the business to operate. But getting the stakeholders merely to participate is not enough. To thrive in the competitive marketplace, an enterprise must engage the full skills, efforts, and creativity of every one of them. Employees must be motivated and enabled to improve their work processes and products; suppliers must be encouraged to participate in design, scheduling, and pricing decisions; the community must be induced to provide schools, roads, and a favorable business climate. And, of course, customers must be induced to buy.

The company's need for willing, cooperative participation by all stakeholders gives us a new definition of success. Success is meeting the needs of all stakeholders, not merely the needs of the owners.

Until rather recently, if you had asked business managers the question, "What is the basic purpose of a business?" most would have replied, "To earn a profit for its owners." If you pressed on and asked why then a business should spend money on employee training, or health insurance, or retirement programs, the common answer would have been that each of these things contributes, at least indirectly, to profits.

- A company would train employees because the company needed workers with new or different skills. If the employees got better jobs, that was a side benefit; the point was for the company to make more profit.
- A company would provide its employees with health insurance or retirement benefits in order to keep workers on the

job instead of off sick, to improve morale, or to minimize turnover, thus increasing productivity or decreasing costs associated with hiring new employees.

- A company would contribute to local charities to be a good corporate citizen, in the hope that the community would respond by minimizing taxes and adverse regulation.

Occasionally an executive (typically an entrepreneur who owned his own company) would be heard to say that the purpose of his business was to make excellent products, to provide jobs, or to serve the public welfare. He was usually ridiculed into silence.

I doubt whether most of us really believed in our heart of hearts that profit was the sole purpose of business, but most of us talked that way, and many of us acted that way. No more! One of the most important business lessons of recent years is that customers' demands for high-quality products and excellent service can be met only by a company whose work force is trained, managed, and motivated to make high-quality its primary goal.

Hal Rosenbluth of Rosenbluth Travel takes an extreme point of view. His management credo is, "The customer comes second." He believes that a worker will not be able to provide excellent service to a customer if the worker is uncomfortable in his workplace, unhappy with his supervisor, or worried about losing his job. Rosenbluth's strategy is to put the interests of the employees first so they can concentrate their energies on serving the customers. It works for his company: revenues of Rosenbluth Travel grew from $20 million in 1978 to $1.2 billion in 1990. It works for the workers as well: Morale is high and turnover is very low.[1] The Rosenbluth example is only one of many that show serving interests of employees benefits the owners as well.

Suppliers seek stable relationships, fair prices, and prompt payment. A notorious example of bad practice in this regard was the relationship between the American automobile manufacturers and their suppliers. Until recently, most parts were designed by the auto manufacturers and then purchased from the lowest bidder, usually without regard to the profits of the supplier or previous business ties. Now some manufacturers have begun joint design programs with parts suppliers to take advantage of the suppliers' familiarity with their own manufacturing processes. Suppliers provide design services in exchange for longer-term contracts and a preferred status in the contracting process. The manufacturers get better products and often save money in the bargain.

The community at large demands economic performance so that the enterprise can assume its share of taxes and other public burdens; it demands enterprise stability to maintain jobs; and it demands compliance with law. Although businesspeople always complain about taxes, most of us recognize those taxes that provide good roads and educated workers will in the long run lead to higher company productivity and profitability, as well as to a better community for all.

Success for the enterprise can come only when every stakeholder is a willing and competent participant. This will happen only when the enterprise meets the needs of every stakeholder, as well as the needs of the owners for profits, growth, and stability.

SUCCESS WHEN THERE IS NO BOTTOM LINE

One of the challenges in managing a not-for-profit organization, private sector or governmental, is that there is no generally accepted measure of success to guide decisions, which is one of the important roles profit plays in for-profit businesses. Our new definition of success—meeting the needs of all stakeholders—can help us solve this problem, once we understand who the stakeholders are and what they want.

Employees of not-for-profit organizations have needs similar to those of employees in for-profits. We used to say that employees of not-for-profits or government agencies received less monetary compensation than they would in a for-profit enterprise, but this was balanced by increased job security and, more important, by the intangible rewards of serving their "clients" (not customers). The monetary gap has closed in most instances, and the satisfaction gap is closing. The focus on customer satisfaction and employee empowerment that is central to success in the business world is providing workers in the for-profit sector the same kinds of intangible benefits workers in not-for-profits have long enjoyed.

Suppliers to not-for-profit organizations have the same needs for consistent, productive relationships as do suppliers to for-profit enterprises. The needs may be harder to satisfy because of the vagaries of funding, but they are essentially the same.

There are no owners seeking profits for their private use in a museum, a hospital, or a welfare agency. But there are suppliers of money whose expectations must be met—the private contributors and the public agencies that fund them. Government agencies also have suppliers of money—the legislatures that appropriate it, the bureaucrats who disburse it, and, indirectly, the taxpayers who pay the bills. Except in the case of organizations funded directly from appropriations, the suppliers of money want the organizations they support to seek an excess of revenues over expenditures for the same reasons that owners of businesses seek profits: to provide a buffer against risk and to have the resources to expand activities.

The community at large has a direct interest in the actions of governmental and other not-for-profit organizations, rather than the indirect interest in tax revenues and so on that it has in the activities of for-profit businesses.

Clients or recipients of services are analogous to the customers of the profit-oriented business. Sometimes these clients pay fees and in fact are customers. In any case, meeting their needs is essential to success of the organization. The needs of the customers of not-for-profit or governmental enterprises, like the needs of all customers, are determined by the customers, not the providers. Some not-for-profits have a bad tendency to decide what services and what levels of service the customers should have. (Some for-profit companies do the same things, but the marketplace has a way of dealing with them.) The clinic that keeps patients waiting interminably because it does not have an effective scheduling system is only partially successful, no matter how good the medical care may be.

Success for a not-for-profit organization looks very much like success in a for-profit: It is meeting the needs of every stakeholder. Determining those needs for a specific organization and measuring how well the organization meets them are difficult and subtle tasks.

ENDURING VISION, FLEXIBLE STRATEGY

The business mantra of the day is change—predicting change, coping with change, managing change, causing change. We devoted most of the previous chapter to discussing changes in technology, changes in competition, and changes in expectations. Although some of the trends are clear, the only thing we really know about the future of business is that it will be different from the present. In the face of all this, how can you plan?

You can plan because there *are* things in business that are not changing, or at least are changing very slowly. The problem is that many of the things we had thought to be stable are now proving to be very changeable, and we have not yet clearly identified those things that are constant.

One of the most pernicious statements of recent times is, "The only thing constant is change." You have heard it over and over again. That statement probably makes you nervous, if you believe it. It should make you nervous, because to the extent that it is true, it is an admission that we do not understand our businesses and hence can have no effective control over them. The natural scientists learned 400 years ago that the only useful scientific laws are those that are "time-invariant"—laws that were true yesterday must be true today and true tomorrow. We need to learn to recognize what is time-invariant in business management.

Corporate goals and corporate strategy used to be fairly stable. Corporate goals were usually articulated in industry-specific ways. We will become the most profitable producer of widgets in the country; we will earn 40 percent of our revenues outside of our home country; we will strengthen our position as technological leader of the widget manufacturing industry.

These kinds of statements were useful long-term guideposts in an era when it made sense to subdivide markets by countries, when an industry was defined by existing technology and products, and when worker and community expectations were fixed and well known. But none of these things is true today.

The typical corporate strategic plan specified strategy for five years into the future, with the understanding that the strategy would be reviewed and modified from time to time, but with the assumption that major strategic thrusts would rarely change. Corporate strategies were typically so stable that many executives and managers viewed strategic planning as a sterile exercise, merely confirming what everybody already knew. The final "proof" that the process was a waste of time came when the strategic plan was reviewed, and the reviewers concluded, "The results are not new, but the process was important." Sometimes the first year of the strategic plan became the operating plan for the next year. More often, the plan was adopted, bound into an expensive binder, and put on a shelf until the next planning cycle began.

This was not a bad process in its day; radical change was not in order for most enterprises most of the time. The process served to remind everyone that there was a strategy to guide corporate decisions and actions and to restate its thrust.

Strategies that remain relatively fixed for years at a time simply do not meet today's needs. Today businesses often need to make rapid, fundamental changes in strategy to accommodate changes in competition, technology, regulation, and the expectations of employees and customers.

But if strategies can be made obsolete by external events, what can a manager use for long-term guidance? The gurus of management have suggested the idea of "corporate vision" as something which can be more enduring than corporate strategy because it focuses on things less likely to change than markets and technology. Strategy is about what you plan to *do;* vision is about what you want your company to *be.*

Corporate vision is the specification of what constitutes the essential nature of the enterprise, stated clearly for all to hear. It should be one of the time-invariant pillars of your business. Enterprises without a corporate vision are doomed to be tossed aimlessly on the sea of change. They will either sink into it without a trace or have their corporate wreckage cast up on the beach of the bankruptcy court.

Amoco Corporation provides an example of corporate vision. Vice Chairman Lawrie Thomas tells of the three key objectives developed for the corporation by Amoco's Strategic Planning Committee.[2]

- To develop a corporate mission, vision, strategies, and values that are understood at all levels of the organization.

- To become a major global player in its core businesses and build a winning organization in an increasingly uncertain global environment.
- To create more cohesive and participative leadership teams, including developing technical skills in oil exploration and production, refining, and chemical manufacturing, as well as organizational and interpersonal skills.

Amoco calls these *objectives* rather than a vision for the organization. The name doesn't matter. The point is to have a view of the enterprise and its place in the world that has these characteristics:

- The vision must be an ambitious, far-reaching statement that can guide the company and inspire its workers for years to come. Thus, it must be general enough so that short-term changes in markets or technology cannot make it obsolete.
- It must be focused on a few areas of unique competence. One of the lessons of the 1980s is that no one organization can be the best at everything.
- It must be published for everyone in the company to see, short enough for everyone to remember, and clear enough for all to understand.

An organization need not be a giant to have and make good use of the concepts of vision and strategy. The Mark Travel Corporation is a leisure travel company whose primary business is assembling and selling travel packages (transportation, hotel accommodations, car rentals, etc.) to consumers through travel agencies. It has about 850 employees in seven locations in the United States and one location in England. Mark Travel has a vision, not a very formal one, but one that drives the company none the less. Its vision is of a growing travel company that provides superior service to its customers (the travel agencies) and consumers (the travelers) while treating its people very well. Its strategies to achieve this vision are to diversify into other parts of the travel market, and to use information technology aggressively to cut costs, improve service, and support new product offerings. Founder and President Bill La Macchia works continuously to communicate this vision to everyone in the company and to sell his workers and managers on its value.[3]

It would take us too far afield from our main subject to discuss the process of formulating a corporate vision in detail. But here is an idea that may help you get started. One constant for every organization is the set of stakeholders we discussed above: customers, owners, employees, and the community. Begin your search for a vision by asking yourself what your company wants from each stakeholder and what it can give to each. You must take them into account in any event, so why not start with them?

When your vision is firmly in view, you can begin to think about what you must do to turn that vision into reality, which is what strategy is all about. It will probably not be possible for you to follow a fixed strategy for long, because strategy necessarily deals with the very things that the vision bypasses: changing markets, new technologies, evolving social conditions. In a world of change, it is essential that every strategy allow for the inevitable changes the business will require. For each major strategic thrust, you must ask these questions.

> What are the basic assumptions on which this strategy is based? That is, what assumptions have been made that, if events prove them to be wrong, will make the strategy ineffective?
>
> How can you monitor those assumptions to see whether they are proving to be correct or incorrect?
>
> What will you do if an assumption proves to be wrong?

In a word, your strategy must be flexible, even as your vision is enduring.

THE CUSTOMER-DRIVEN ENTERPRISE

New measures of success and a new view of business strategy are just two of the changes affecting our business lives. You can get a further sense of how our view of business has changed by comparing current management fads with those of the past. In the 1970s, we had management by objectives, optimal use of resources, and motivation by the work itself. Each of these focused on the internal operations of the enterprise. Today we are directing our attention outside of the enterprise to total quality management (TQM), excellent customer service, and strategic alliances.

One thing that makes it difficult to implement a TQM program is that TQM begins with an external focus: High quality is defined as providing what the customer wants. Most of us find it much easier to deal with internal issues such as how to make certain the diameter of each of our widgets is within 0.001 inch of specification, rather than trying to find out what level of accuracy is important to our customers, or whether they are more interested in something else, such as price, delivery, or service.

Competition is the obvious reason to look outside of the enterprise. If our competitors get our customers, we want to know why so we can figure out how to get them back. That's clear enough—but it is wrong. It is wrong because the rhetoric focuses on us, on the seller, instead of on the customers. We cannot "get" customers to buy what we have to sell. We must attract them by offering them what they want to buy.

The seller-centered approach worked fairly well in an era when goods were relatively scarce and when information about the marketplace was scant. Today the opposite is true. Businesses are inundated with publications and vendor representatives offering every conceivable variety of goods and services. Advertisements, mail order catalogs, and television have made every consumer aware of the wide variety of products and services available, and television programming (as well as advertising) almost always shows them in the best possible light. The consumer's expectations are very high, and the producer who doesn't meet those expectations is at a serious disadvantage trying to compete with one who does.

In television programs, products and services are usually perfect except when the plot demands that something go wrong. Cars always start, airplanes are never late, telephone answering machines never malfunction, and the hero always finds a parking place. Customers want things to work just as well in real life. If a vendor does not provide what the customer wants, the customer will seek another vendor.

FOCUS ON EXCELLENCE—YOUR OWN
AND OTHERS'

One of the important lessons of the 1980s was that no company can do an excellent job of all the many business processes necessary to bring a product to a customer. The lesson we are learning in the 1990s is that you don't have to perform all of the business processes yourself, provided you perform a few core processes extremely well and provided you establish appropriate relationships with other companies that perform *their* core processes extremely well. If all the processes are performed extremely well, your product will be a world beater.

Continental Bank of Chicago has contracted with outside companies to provide many staff functions formerly performed by its own employees, including information services and telecommunications. Richard Huber, vice chairman of Continental, says:

My experience in the banking business had taught me that information was a tool clever bankers used to their customers' advantage, but managing it was not a banker's core competency. . . . Continental aims to spend its time and money furthering its central strategy, which can be summed up in a single sentence: serving as a financial intermediary between client needs and the markets.[4]

MaxServ Inc. of Austin, Texas, provides service information to users of Frigidaire™ and Sears Roebuck appliances and to Sears repair technicians. Evidently these companies think MaxServe can handle this work better than the companies could themselves. They have entrusted one of their most important resources—access to their customers—to an outsider. This is not unusual: Some 300 firms operate telephone call-in centers for other companies, performing tasks from providing repair information to taking orders for catalog companies.[5]

This idea of specialists in different companies working together to deliver a product is not new. Real estate developers have long recognized that they can be very successful by conceiving a project and assembling the elements (land, financing, regulatory approvals, design, and construction), while contracting the actual construction work to those who make a specialty of it. The skills of developers are different from those of general contractors, as many have learned to their sorrow when they tried to perform both functions.

Two buzzwords are used to describe these kinds of cooperative efforts: outsourcing and business alliances. They both describe what we have been discussing—different companies with complementary areas of expertise working closely together to meet a market need. The choice of terms seems to be based on how the relationship comes into being. Outsourcing is contracting with another company to provide something formerly supplied by an in-house staff; an alliance is an arrangement you form with a company already doing on its own an activity that you wish to couple more closely with your business. What you call it doesn't matter. What does matter is that the independent company with which you associate your company must itself have a core of excellence in the appropriate area.

EMPOWERED WORKERS

The demands of flexible strategies, intense competition for customers, and close cooperation with business alliance partners cannot be met with the traditional top-down management methods. Listen to Paul Allaire, CEO of Xerox:

> In a functional organization, there is a natural tendency for conflicts to get kicked upstairs. People get too accustomed to sitting on their hands and waiting for a decision to come down from above. Well, sometimes the decision does come down. But sometimes it doesn't. And even when it does, often it comes too late, because market conditions have already changed or a more nimble competitor has gotten there first. Or maybe the decision is simply wrong—because the person making it is too far from the customer.[6]

The typical response of a hierarchical organization to this problem, assuming it were recognized, would be to appoint an expediter or establish a corps of customer service representatives. This might solve the problem at hand, but in the long run it would make the solution of other problems more difficult and more expensive

The companies that will prosper in the 1990s are those that empower their line workers to make the decisions and take the actions necessary to meet business needs. Line workers often know
the needs of the business better than their managers because
they are closer to the customers and the processes by which the
business operates.

You may be dubious about giving this kind of responsibility to
line workers, concerned that they might not use it well. But empowerment means much more than simply delegating authority.
Knowing a business need is the first step, but taking effective action to meet that need requires more. The worker must understand the business and the place of her activity in it. She must be
given the authority to make decisions and the resources to implement them. And she must be provided with the information
necessary to monitor and evaluate the results of her actions, so
that she can make better decisions in the future.

All of this talk about empowered workers may sound impractical to you, if you think your workers are interested only in maximum pay for minimum work. But most workers are not like that.
Most workers are proud of their work, ambitious to succeed, and
caring of their fellow workers and their employers. That is why
empowerment works. We will discuss ways to organize your
company to make it work in the next chapter.

Effective leaders have known this intuitively for centuries. It
was proven by Robert Ford in field studies at AT&T in the 1960s,
and the results were published in 1969.[7] Yet here we are, more
than 20 years later, still debating whether it makes sense to en-
rich jobs and empower workers to manage their own work.

MEASURING RESULTS

Our new definition of success means that we must measure new
things to know whether or not we are successful in meeting the
needs of all of our constituencies. The financial measures remain
of course, to gauge our success in meeting the needs of owners
and other providers of capital. But they must be expanded to help
empowered workers understand the consequences of their decisions, and to explain the enterprise to the community at large.

Let's take a radical approach to determining what we should measure to know whether we are successful in meeting needs of our other stakeholders. Let's ask them! Make a list of your stakeholders and ask each group what it wants from the enterprise. You will probably be very surprised at some of the results.

Many consumers want to talk to a human being rather than a phone answering machine when they call for product information. If your customers are unhappy with the machine, maybe you should redesign the system's operation or perhaps you should reevaluate benefits it provides.

Any employee worth keeping is concerned with the financial health and stability of the enterprise. But do you know specifically what they care about? It may be the prospects for a particular product line or the likelihood of changes in health insurance. Find out, and tell them.

Will collecting these new measurements cost money? Yes. Will they consume some of your scarce time? Of course. Will they upset some of your preconceptions? Absolutely. Can you afford not to keep track of how well you are meeting the needs of your stakeholders? No. We will discuss how to identify the information you need in Chapters 6 and 7.

SUMMARY

What You Must Know

- Success means meeting the needs of all stakeholders.
- You cannot succeed unless you get the benefits of all the talents and all the energies of every worker.
- The better you meet the needs of the other constituencies, the more profit you will earn for your owners.

What You Must Do

- Develop a corporate vision that can guide you for a long time into the future.
- Rethink your strategy to focus on those things at which you excel.

- Systematically listen to workers, customers, suppliers, and the community, as well as to shareholders.
- Develop measures and reporting mechanisms to help you know how well you are serving all your stakeholders.

Chapter Three

The New Organization for the 1990s

The hierarchical organization is dying after a century and a half of success because it cannot meet the needs of the 1990s. A new organizational form is needed for success in the information age, one based on the realities of competition, technology, and people. The old form is dying because it is organized and managed on false assumptions about people: that workers are only "hands," not "heads," that they are lazy, and that they have no concern for the success of the enterprises of which they are a part.

A variety of management fads and quick fixes have been tried in vain attempts to make the hierarchical organization work. They have failed because they treated symptoms rather than underlying causes and because they were not integrated into the fabric of the enterprise.

A new organizational form is evolving, called the federated organization. It is based on more realistic assessments of workers: that they are intelligent, proud of a job well done, and caring about the success of their company. As a result, the federated organization can make full use of the potential of every worker in meeting new customer wants, using new business processes, and responding to the challenges of continual change.

The changing environments of business—social, commercial, and technological—will cause many organizations to rethink the basic purposes for which they exist. They will develop new goals and new strategies to achieve those goals. But they will not be able to reach their new goals or put their new strategies into action unless they make radical changes in their underlying organizational structures. We are concerned with organization structure because it is a major determinant of information needs.

THE FAILURE OF THE HIERARCHICAL ORGANIZATION

For the past century and a half, virtually every large business in the United States has been organized on a hierarchical basis, indirectly modeled after the Prussian Army of Frederick the Great. Orders are issued from on high, passed down the chain of command, and executed in the field. Middle managers and staffs are employed to monitor the enterprise and report successes and failures back to the top.

This structure worked very well for a long time, but recent events require us to question whether it is the right model for success in the 1990s. The failures of many large and famous companies to compete effectively in recent years have been chronicled so extensively that they need not be listed here. But let's take a brief look at two of them and see if we can discern the beginnings of a pattern.

Sears, Roebuck announced in January 1993 that it would discontinue its century-old catalog business, the operation that started the company.[1] It had been unprofitable for seven consecutive years. Yet those same years saw an explosive growth of catalog merchants selling everything from clothing to office supplies to computers. Most of these companies are small compared to Sears and young in years.

Why are Lands' End, Goldberg Marine, and The Sharper Image successful while Sears is not? Instead of trying to be all things to all people, each of these small companies concentrates on a niche market, a market it knows intimately. And each monitors its sales very closely and can modify product and merchandising strategies very quickly as conditions change.

Information technology, among other factors, has made the catalog business easy to enter. To go into business, an entrepreneur needs only a vision of a market, a source of products, and the price of producing and mailing a catalog. Sophisticated 800 telephone service and computer-based order-entry-systems are available at modest cost off the shelf. (Or, as we noted in the previous chapter, the entrepreneur can hire an outside contractor to take the orders.) Package delivery services provided by vendors such as United Parcel Service and Federal Express complete the cycle of promotion, sales, and delivery. The main roadblock is that banks are hesitant to authorize new businesses to accept credit cards. In the past few years, companies have been formed to act as intermediaries between new merchants and banks, guaranteeing credit and processing transactions for a fee. Meanwhile, Sears's catalog warehouse and distribution system, once the wonder of American merchandising and an enormous competitive advantage, has become a burden rather an asset.

IBM adhered to its mainframe-centered view of corporate computing and telecommunications long after the technology made it obsolescent and the market decreed that mainframes were decreasing in importance. This technological and marketing giant was humbled by small competitors with a clearer vision of the market and the willingness to adopt new technologies to meet market demands.

IBM began marketing its personal computers in 1981 through a select group of retail computer stores. Later it added direct selling by its own sales force, but only in 1992 did it start a telephone sales program. 1992 was the year Dell sold nearly $2 billion worth of PCs by phone.

Entire books have been written, and are being written, about what went wrong at Sears and IBM. Obviously there is no one cause for all their troubles. But the hierarchical organization structure was clearly an important contributor. Each company is large and old. Their hierarchical structures kept decision makers so remote from the marketplace that they could not assess it accurately, and those same structures so protected entrenched interests (monetary, physical, and human) that it was impossible for the companies to respond properly even after the market realities were recognized.

You can certainly find hierarchical organizations that are competing successfully today, but so many are unsuccessful that we must ask whether basic changes are needed.

MODIFYING THE HIERARCHICAL ORGANIZATION IS NOT ENOUGH

We have known for a long time that the hierarchical organization is not perfect, and we have tried to improve it in a number of ways. Two kinds of approaches have been tried in recent years. One is to attempt to impose new ideas and methods on the existing structure; the other is to modify the structure, while retaining its basic hierarchical character.

Management by Fad

A cover story in *Business Week* some years ago described popular efforts to change business practices as "management by fad."[2] It listed 14 management fads of the prior 10 years—new management practices that began, moved into prominence, and then faded from view without discernible long-term effects on most organizations that tried them. These included Theory Z, intrapreneuring, corporate culture, managing by walking around, and the one-minute manager. If the article were rewritten today, it would surely include total quality management and empowering employees.

These fads have worked in some companies, but not very often. The reason is clear. Although each of them is based on a sound idea, no technique will work unless it is used; and it won't be used—beyond the initial surge of enthusiasm of the CEO—unless it is integrated into the culture of the enterprise. Most of these fads simply cannot become a part of a hierarchical organization.

Managing by walking around is a good example of an idea that did not take root in hierarchical organizations. Senior managers who walk around the factory and discuss business problems with production workers subvert the command and control philosophy that is central to hierarchy. The hierarchy reacts by rejecting the foreign idea, just as the human body rejects an organ transplant, even though the new organ is essential to survival.

Some of these fads do survive. One of my consulting clients has been using management by objectives (MBO) successfully for many years, although it is no longer called by that name, or any name. But every job description and every performance review incorporates MBO concepts. It is no longer something special. It is just "the way we do things here." For that company, MBO works.

Will total quality management turn out to be a fad and fade away without any lasting benefits? The quality gurus say, "Make quality everyone's job." This is more than a slogan; it reflects the deep reality that a quality program can succeed in the long run only if it becomes so ingrained in the corporate culture that no one would even consider departing from the goal of high quality or ignoring the procedures that produce it.

So far, worker empowerment has not been around long enough for us to judge its overall success, but we must make it work. As we shall see later, it is essential for business success in the 1990s. As with the other fads, the talk will fade away. We must make sure that the reality remains, but the reality of worker empowerment cannot exist for long in a hierarchical organization.

Structural Changes

The most common structural change over the years has been decentralization. One of Alfred Sloan's great achievements of the 1920s was to organize General Motors into product divisions, each serving a different segment of the market for passenger automobiles, while the company as a whole blanketed the market. GM's enormous success over the next two decades encouraged other large corporations to copy its organization, often with excellent results. Some decentralized by geography, others by product lines as GM had done. But in every case, the decentralized divisions were themselves hierarchies, with all of the associated advantages and disadvantages.

Currently, the most popular idea for structural change is "flattening the organization"—reducing the number of layers of management between the top and the place where the work is done. Information technology has enabled many companies to do this and still retain the same degree of control from the top. But a flat hierarchy is still a hierarchy, and a flat one suffers from most of the same ills as those that are not so flat.

Despite structural changes, despite many new and insightful managerial ideas and methods, and despite advanced information systems, the hierarchical organization is not the right structure for today's world.

THE DEATH OF THE
HIERARCHICAL ORGANIZATION

The hierarchical organization is dying because it is based on false assumptions about business and false assumptions about people. These assumptions seem almost grotesque when they are stated clearly, but they form the implicit logical basis on which the hierarchical organization is designed.

What is the purpose of the business?

Assumption: The purpose of the business is to earn profits for its owners.

Comment: As noted above, the business that does not serve all its stakeholders will not succeed, even using profit as the only criterion.

Reality: Unprofitable suppliers or unhappy regulators are just as dangerous to a business as dissatisfied customers.

Who understands the business?

Assumption: The boss at each level knows more about the business than all of her subordinates combined.

Comment: This idea is rooted in two other assumptions: (1) the boss understands the operation she controls, either because she worked her way up through it or because she invented it, and (2) the operation has not changed since she worked in it. Both assumptions may have been true in the past, but are less and less true as businesses become more dynamic and more complex.

Reality: The people who know most about production are the workers on the production line. The people who know most about the market are those in moment-by-moment contact with customers: salespeople and, most of all, people in the service department. These people may not have the perspective to plan for the future of the business, but they know its present needs and problems better than anyone else.

Who should manage the business?

Assumption: The role of managers is to tell their subordinates exactly what to do; the role of subordinates is to do exactly what they are told to do.

Comment: In the early years of this century, we spoke of hiring "factory hands" or "farm hands." You can no longer hire "hands" without getting the "heads" as well. And since you are getting the heads, you might as well use them. Indeed, you will have to use them because employees are demanding and getting more control of their work lives.

Reality: The people best suited to manage an activity are those who execute it, provided they are given the education to understand what they are doing and how it affects the enterprise, the information to monitor the effects of their actions, and the authority and resources to make necessary changes.

Who cares about the business?

Assumption: Workers are interested only in getting the maximum pay for minimum work. The only people who care about the success of the business are the owners and a few senior managers.

Comment: This assumes that workers have no pride in their work and in their company and that they do not understand that their jobs depend on the success of the enterprise.

Reality: When you hire the "hands" and make good use of the "head," you can enlist the "heart," if you do things right. Most workers want to do a good job, are proud of work well done, and want to be proud of the companies for which they work.

If you accept these assumptions, you should build an organization based on command from the top, detailed supervision of line workers, and monitoring and control by middle managers and support staff. You will need a structure in which everyone knows exactly who is to do what and who reports to whom. You will need procedure manuals, work standards, and delegations of authority to support and control all work activities. In brief, you will need a hierarchical organization.

If you reject these assumptions and choose to build your organization based on the realities of today, you will create something quite different.

THE NEW ORGANIZATION: MAXIMIZING THE SPAN OF NO CONTROL

Let's make some new assumptions.

- Assume that success is defined as meeting the needs of all constituents.

- Assume that the enterprise is in a state of constant change (generated by all the forces we discussed earlier).
- Assume that the enterprise is dedicated to a few core competencies and depends on other companies to use their core competencies to complete the product delivery cycle.
- Assume that getting the maximum contribution from every employee is essential to success.
- Assume that the people of the organization—all people at every level—are smart, proud, knowledgeable about their jobs, concerned about results, and committed to the success of the enterprise.
- Assume that the people actually performing the work of the organization know more about that work than their supervisors know.

To make the most of the opportunities offered by this new view of people and their place in the enterprise, you need a different view of control. Unlike the flattened organization based on the idea of increasing the span of control, the new organization must be designed and managed in such a way as to maximize "the span of no control"—the range of actions individuals and teams can take without reference to higher authority.

Here is the kind of organization we might design to maximize the span of no control.

Senior managers would function mostly as leaders, rather than as administrators. They would develop a vision for the company and strategies to bring that vision toward reality. They would muster resources (human, financial, and material), coordinate activities where necessary, and monitor overall performance.

Middle managers would set strategy for their units and coordinate with other units. Their relationships with their subordinates would be mostly that of teachers and coaches rather than supervisors.

The organization would be divided into the smallest possible units commensurate with a complete, identifiable business process.

Each unit would have almost total internal autonomy, subject only to performing the job, which means meeting the needs of all constituencies it affects: earning a profit, serving internal and/or external customers, meeting public needs, and so on. The key to unit success would be teamwork within the unit.

Each employee would have all the information he needed to do a good job—information about his own process, information about the company as a whole, and information about external conditions.

Each employee would have the education and training required to make effective use of that information.

And each employee would have broad authority to expend resources and to do the job as he saw fit.

Some aspects of hierarchy would survive. There would still be senior executives in charge of the enterprise. Just as the line workers have the best view of what is happening on the production floor, senior managers have the best view of the enterprise as a whole. There would still be managers and subordinates. And there would still be reporting and control systems. From the outside, it might even look like a hierarchy.

This is by no means the first proposal for radical changes in organization structures, and I am sure it will not be the last. Paul Allaire, CEO of Xerox, has spoken repeatedly of the need for organizational change. In describing what happened at Xerox, he said it was rather like turning the hierarchy on its side, so that senior managers and staff were on the same level as line workers and could be seen as giving support to operations rather than giving orders. He emphasized meeting customer needs, worker empowerment, and managerial initiative.[3]

Academic and consultant Peter Senge has developed the notion of "the learning organization" as a description of an enterprise that is constantly learning new and better ways to conduct its business.[4] Several people have written recently of the networked organization, a structure where each entity in the organization does its job rather independently of the others, but all are connected so they can work in concert as necessary.

William Davidow and Michael Malone see the "virtual corporation" as the organization of the future; it is called virtual because both its external and its internal boundaries are fuzzy. Their vision is of a corporation so closely tied to its customers and its suppliers that in some cases it may be difficult to tell who is paying a given worker. Internally, workers will move from self-managing team to self-managing team as corporate needs dictate.[5]

Charles Handy suggests the federated organization as a way to balance the need for strategy and direction with the demands of the marketplace and the realities of the workplace.[6] He uses the word *federated* in the same sense we use it to describe the structure of government in the United States: a collection of nearly sovereign states each pursuing its own agenda, subject to limited overall guidance and constraints from the central government.

All these organizational ideas have at their base the new assumptions listed at the beginning of this section and all reach almost the same conclusions about how the organizations would operate. The differences among them are significant and worth examining in detail, but not here.

It is easy to dismiss these names as unimportant—more consultant hyperbole than reflections of reality. But the changes required to create a federated organization are massive and very traumatic. A new name announces to one and all that something new is coming and is worthwhile for that reason alone. I'll use the name *federated organization* because it is descriptive of the structure and evocative of the tensions between central control and operational independence, which will forever characterize these organizations.

Our business in this book is to investigate how to meet the information needs of a federated organization.

SUMMARY

What You Must Know

- The hierarchical organization doesn't work any more, and no amount of tinkering will fix it. The underlying assumptions are no longer valid.
- An organization can be built that will be much more productive because it gets the best from every worker.
- It will require massive changes in jobs and attitudes of everyone, managers and production workers alike.

What You Must Do

- Redefine the needs and functions of your business before you attempt to rethink its organizational structure.
- Implement whatever form of organization meets those needs and takes account of the true nature of workers. It is most likely to be a federated organization.

PART

II

IDENTIFYING YOUR INFORMATION NEEDS

Organizations are becoming increasingly dependent on information technology (IT), making it vital that IT strategy be integrated with corporate strategy. This can be accomplished only if information technology is placed on a par with other corporate activities during the strategic planning process. The imperatives of business and the realities of information technology will nearly always require that some IT facilities be developed in advance of specific business need. Immediate costs will be incurred to make future benefits possible.

Information technology expenditures of most organizations have been growing steadily for years, and that growth is likely to continue because of the many opportunities for IT to create value. IT can be used to reduce costs or to increase profits of existing business processes, it can become an integral part of redesigned processes, and it can support the future of the business. Each of these sources of value must be appraised in its own special way.

To capture the value available through information technology, business processes must usually be changed. They can be changed by evolution, in the tradition of continuous process improvement, or by revolution, as with business process reengineering. An approach to reengineering called *holistic business process design* offers special insights into the structure of business processes and the ways information can be used to support them.

When business processes are changed, either by evolution or by revolution, additional information provided to the workers nearly always yields significant benefits to the enterprise. This information can support routine operations and transactions, nonroutine operations, auxiliary activities that support operations, and decision making at all levels.

Chapter Four

Business Strategy and Information Technology Strategy

The success of any organization depends on the right people having the right information at the right time. This will happen only if the organization's information technology strategy is an integral part of its overall business strategy, particularly for an organization that depends on empowered employees.

Information technology must do more than support current corporate strategy. It must explicitly support the longer-range goals of corporate vision, because the time required to deploy a major information system is sometimes longer than the duration of a business strategy. Corporate vision provides the head start that makes it possible to meet strategic needs on time.

Some elements of company vision and business strategy are common to all federated organizations: the need to serve all stakeholders, the requirements of empowered employees, and the need for quick response to business change. Every company must take account of these common requirements as it defines its own vision and develops its own company-specific strategies.

Development and deployment of an information architecture is an essential part of information technology strategy. Without an orderly and consistent framework within which to implement and manage information systems, a chaos will ensue that will make it impossible to respond to changing needs or to gather the cross-functional information that empowered workers need. Information architecture provides that framework.

All of this costs money. Modifying strategy to accommodate vision nearly always adds costs, at least in the short term. So does designing and implementing an information systems architecture. Benefits accrue later, sometimes much later.

As the organization of the 1990s evolves, information technology will penetrate every aspect of it. IT will be essential to support self-managing workers and self-managing teams. It will become an integral part of nearly every business process, as well as an integral part of many products. Thoughtful, well-planned use of this technology will be critical for success; this can be achieved only when strategic plans for information technology are integrated with the strategic business plans of the company.

WHY BOTHER WITH INFORMATION TECHNOLOGY STRATEGY?

As we observed in Chapter 2, many executives feel that strategic planning is a wasteful, if not a futile, exercise. They are largely correct if the plan remains unused between planning cycles. But there can be a different, more productive, result.

Information technology strategy can support the business by playing three roles. The first is to support current operations by providing the information and systems needed to run the current business effectively and efficiently. The second is to provide support for new strategic thrusts, both for activities inside the company and for whatever is necessary to link the company's operations with customers or suppliers.

The third role of IT strategy is to support the corporate vision, *even going beyond the requirements of the current business strategy where necessary.* Changes in the business environment often force us to change corporate strategies so rapidly that information systems cannot keep up. If information systems are to be able to support the new business strategy of next year, and the newer one of the year after that, the deployment of IT must get a head start. It can take as long as five years to implement a worldwide telecommunications network. Suppose you had a three-year strategy that required telecommunications facilities joining several continents. You would be two years behind before you started, even if your business strategy remained unchanged!

We can get the head start we need by looking to the corporate vision in conjunction with corporate strategy. If our corporate vision is of a worldwide company with a core excellence in processing financial transactions (as might be true for a credit card company), our IT strategy must provide for a highly reliable telecommunications network that can be readily extended around the globe. If our vision limits us to the United States, a more limited telecommunications strategy is better.

Professor Al Rubenstein of Northwestern University has been studying the management of research and technology for many years. He talks about the need to integrate corporate strategy with other long-range business initiatives:

> Information systems is not the only activity which is caught up in the problems of shifting strategy to meet changed business needs. Corporate research has to face the same issue. If its work is really research (as distinguished from product development), the time between starting a project and bringing a product to market will be far longer than any corporate strategy is likely to last. Research too must be guided by vision, not restrained by strategy.
>
> For example, key elements of the vision needed for a long term and robust research (corporate R&D) strategy include recognition that (1) technology is likely to provide substantial competitive advantages to the firm in the future, (2) the firm needs a strong and continuing technology base to be able to exploit new technologies underlying its products, processes, and general business into the future, (3) it is seldom clear at any moment which specific technologies will be needed to support the businesses of the firm in the longer term, and (4) a flexible strategy is needed, which will support a "core technologies" group aware of and skilled in the most likely technology clusters of future relevance for the firm's business.[1]

VISION AND STRATEGY FOR A FEDERATED ORGANIZATION

It is useful for our purposes to think of corporate vision as being made up of two parts, although in practice these two parts may be so intertwined that it is difficult to separate them. Every company should have a specific vision of itself: its products, its markets, the business processes it chooses to emphasize, its place in its industry, and its position in the community. Underlying this company-specific vision is the vision shared by all federated organizations, based on the new paradigms of business we discussed in Chapter 2.

- Our company serves the needs of all its stakeholders.
- Our company performs its core business processes extremely well.

- Our company provides excellent products and services to
  its customers.
- Our company gives workers at every level the maximum
  possible responsibility for their own work lives.

Corporate strategy can also be divided into two parts, mirroring
the two parts of corporate vision. The first part is company specific, driven by the company-specific part of the vision. It reflects current conditions and available resources, together with
company vision and goals. These are typical company-specific
stategies.

1. Commercialize product X and have it in worldwide distribution by the end of year three.
2. Expand distribution of product Y to six Pacific Rim countries by the end of year two.
3. Become the world leader in physical distribution of high
   value, low weight products by the end of year five.
4. Establish programs of regular meetings with major shareholders and with community leaders, by the end of year
   one.

The second part of the business strategy reflects the common
vision of all federated organizations. All aspects of the vision cannot be implemented at one time, nor should they be. (See the discussion of tolerable levels of disruption in Chapter 10.) Company-
specific business vision will identify the core processes in which
the company must excel, and guide us to improve these processes
by empowering workers with better information, training, and
tools. Here is how it might work in conjunction with the four
business-specific strategies described above.

5. Reorganize the distribution function so that line workers
   make most of the decisions. (This supports strategies 1, 2,
   and 3 above, and supports the vision of worker
   empowerment.)
6. Present education programs that explain the fundamentals
   of physical distribution to all workers in the distribution
   function, in conjunction with training programs on operating the new system. (This supports the vision of worker
   responsibility as well as strategy 3.)

INTEGRATING INFORMATION TECHNOLOGY STRATEGY WITH BUSINESS STRATEGY

Information technology strategy should be integrated with business strategy. This probably sounds obvious to you, hardly worth saying. But the statement is more profound than it may seem at first glance. Again, we have a two part issue.

Common sense tells us that information technology exists in a company only to support the company's business objectives, and so IT strategy should be driven by business strategy. As we observed above, there are reasons IT strategy should look both at business strategy and beyond it, to business vision.

Do you believe that most information technology managers are guided by business strategy? Many executives don't, and they don't hesitate to say so.[2] IT people as a group have the reputation of being more interested in their technology than in business needs. There is some truth in this, but not as much as there used to be. I suspect that in many companies IT managers have been guilty of going beyond business strategy to support a corporate vision, but the vision they supported was their own rather than the vision of corporate management.

Integrating IT strategy with business strategy has another dimension: information technology should be able to influence business strategy. Information technology can substantially enlarge the set of business strategies your company can pursue. It is essential that you give careful consideration to these new possibilities. Your competitors certainly will. To paraphrase Joe Louis, you can run from the information revolution, but you can't hide from it.

United Parcel Service (UPS) found this out the hard way. UPS opened its doors in 1907 and grew to become the dominant company in ground transportation of small packages in the United States. Federal Express started its air delivery service in 1973 and quickly began to make inroads on UPS's customer base. For our purposes, the important part of the story is that Federal Express inaugurated its computer-based real-time tracking system in 1980; UPS began its program to automate package tracking in 1986. In the intervening six years, Federal Express made major market gains, based in part on its ability to track customer packages and

FIGURE 4–1
Integrating IT Strategy with Business Strategy

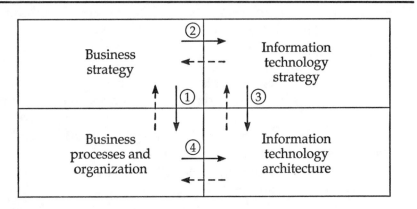

respond instantly to questions about location and delivery. UPS spent more than $1.5 billion between 1986 and 1991 on information technology, and it will have spent another $3.2 billion by 1996. *Yet in 1993, it was just catching up with Federal Express in package tracking and related capabilities.* By 1996, it will have several innovative product offerings based on its information technology, with which it hopes to make significant competitive gains.[3]

At one level, business strategy drove information technology strategy: The business necessity of competing with Federal Express drove UPS to develop a new IT strategy to support its own package tracking system. At another level, that new IT strategy will enable UPS to implement new product offerings as part of its business strategy.

The essence of integrating IT strategy with corporate strategy is captured in Figure 4–1, which illustrates the relationships among four of the basic building blocks of every business: business strategy, business processes and organization, information technology strategy, and information technology architecture.[4]

We will discuss the importance of information technology architecture in detail below. For the moment, think of it as simply the overall design of the company's information systems.

The traditional view of business planning is that business strategy drives business processes and organization (arrow number 1) and it also drives information technology strategy (arrow number 2). Information technology architecture is in turn driven by IT strategy (arrow number 3) and by business processes and organization (arrow number 4.) This is in fact the way most information systems have been designed.

The dotted arrows indicate that for effective strategic planning, the influences should go in both directions. Most important for this discussion, IT strategy should be able to influence strategic planning for the business. Strategic planning for the business and strategic planning for information technology should occur simultaneously, in close interaction with one another. (We could say the same things about integrating financial technology, or marketing technology, or manufacturing technology into the strategic planning process.)

Unfortunately, this seldom happens. Many senior executives simply do not see the potential of information technology to influence business strategy. Instead, they think of it only as support for the primary business of the enterprise, support that will be available when and where it is needed. The only IT strategy they are interested in is one designed to cut costs.

You obviously don't share this opinion or you wouldn't have taken the trouble to read this far. The point of view we take is that information technology may or may not be strategic in a particular enterprise, but its importance has been documented in so many instances that an executive would be shirking his responsibilities if he did not give it thoughtful consideration.

The only effective way to integrate IT strategy with business strategy is to make the senior IT executive a part of the group that creates business strategy. This will happen automatically if the senior IT executive is a part of the senior management team, say a member of the executive committee. Or you can make your IT executive a full-fledged member of the strategic planning committee. The mechanism is less important than the result: he must have an equal voice at the strategy table with the representatives of other functions, such as manufacturing, marketing, and finance.

Perhaps you think that your IT executive doesn't know enough about your business, or about business in general, to make a useful contribution to your strategic planning process. You may be wrong; check him out. If he really doesn't understand the business, educate him. If you can't educate him, get someone else. You must have someone in your senior council who understands both information technology and your company.

Two major pitfalls may trap you on your way toward integrating business strategy and IT strategy. One is that you might become entranced with the idea of strategic applications of information technology and try to invent one. You probably have read how American Airlines used its SABRE[SM] reservation system as the basis for its frequent flyer program, one of the most successful marketing programs in airline history. You may also know that American's parent company, AMR Corp., earned $216 million from SABRE in 1992, while losing $250 million on airline operations.[5]

You cannot invent a strategic application of information technology because there is no such thing separate from a business process. You might be able to identify a business process that could become strategically important with the judicious use of information technology.

The other pitfall is this: there may not be a corporate vision to guide either IT strategy or business strategy. In that case, the best thing you can do is to infer a vision based on what your senior executives say and do. The most useful words are those the senior executives say to securities analysts, followed closely by those they say to government regulators (if you can understand them). The reason these statements are reliable is simple: executives who don't tell the truth to analysts or regulators are subject to severe sanctions. The most important actions to watch are the ones that make major changes in product lines or the organization chart: adding or eliminating divisions or product lines, drastically shrinking or eliminating staff groups, and so on.

A thoughtful analysis of these kinds of events can give you a very good idea of the corporate vision, even in cases where the vision is unstated. If you are a CEO attempting to develop a vision, try it on yourself. Look at your recent public pronouncements (internal as well as external) and your recent organizational changes. See what they imply about what you want your company to be 10 years from now.

INFORMATION TECHNOLOGY VISION AND STRATEGY

The concept of vision is usually reserved for the senior management of a company, as a tool to set the stage for the company's business strategies. But the same idea is useful within an information systems department. Indeed, an IT vision is essential if IT strategy is to fulfill its mission of supporting corporate vision as well as current business strategies. The word *goals* is often used rather than the word *vision*, but it is the same concept under a different name.

Here is an IT vision that supports the corporate vision of a federated organization in today's rapidly changing business environment.

- To serve the needs of our company's stakeholders, we will have available information relevant to our suppliers, our customers, and concerned governmental and community groups, and we will have the ability to connect our information systems to theirs whenever appropriate.

- To support our company's commitment to excellent performance of core processes, we will be able to provide all information and systems necessary for planning, operations, and control, including quality management and other advanced management techniques, and do so in a cost-effective way.

- To support worker empowerment throughout our enterprise, we will be prepared to provide every worker with all information relevant to that worker's job and its effect on the company as a whole.

- To respond to business changes in timely fashion, we will have a technological base that will permit us to respond to minor changes in business needs in a matter of days, to major changes in a matter of weeks, and to new strategic initiatives in a matter of months.

About now, you may be thinking that this is all a wild dream, that no company can do these things. You're right: no company can do these things *today*. But this is a vision, a set of goals. This is where we want to be, and we must say so. If we don't, we will surely never get there.

The point of having the vision—the goals—is to help make certain that what you do today takes you toward where you want to be tomorrow. The vision must influence which strategies you choose and how you execute them.

If your strategy is to achieve lower production costs, this vision tells you to plan to empower your production workers by providing them with access to management reports, and the training to understand them.

If your corporate vision is to continually enter new lines of business, this IT vision tells you to acquire advanced information system development tools and become extremely proficient in their use, so that you can create new systems in the shortest possible time.

If your current business strategy is to expand the distribution of one product line from the United States to Europe and your business vision is a company growing for many years to come, this IT vision tells you to design your communication network to be easily expandable from Europe to the rest of the world, and to be able to accommodate new product lines without major changes.

INFORMATION TECHNOLOGY ARCHITECTURE TO SUPPORT INFORMATION TECHNOLOGY STRATEGY

Historically, we built individual information systems to meet specific needs, usually the needs of a particular department. We would connect a new system to existing systems as best we could, often modifying existing systems in the process. This approach worked well enough in an era of corporate stability. But as organization structures changed in response to increased competition and other business imperatives, we found it necessary for systems to interact with one another in ways not planned for when the systems were built. In nearly every case, it was extremely difficult to get the required interactions. In many cases, it proved to be impossible, leaving us with the distasteful (and expensive) choice of abandoning old systems and building new ones from scratch or doing without important information.

The business strategies of today nearly always include making information widely available to workers, responding quickly to business changes, and minimizing costs without compromising other business objectives. This means we must be able to connect our information systems to one another, quickly and easily.

The idea of information technology architecture was developed to support these strategies and to prevent the recurrence of the problems of connecting old systems with new ones. An information technology architecture is a set of design criteria, implementation rules, and technical standards that governs the design, deployment, and operation of all information technology and systems in an organization.

> *All*, of course, is an overstatement. There will always be a few systems and some technologies that do not conform to the architecture, for good reasons or bad. A well-designed architecture provides an orderly process for making exceptions and for monitoring them.

The word *architecture* is evocative of the construction industry, where it typically refers to the detailed design of a specific structure. It has a somewhat different flavor in the context of information technology, more like city planning than the design of an individual building. We will discuss this and other aspects of IT architecture in detail in Chapter 9. For the moment, we address two issues: why IT architecture is an important component of IT strategy, and how the technical structure of IT architecture creates significant problems in the evaluation of information technology.

An effective IT architecture can help implement business strategies in a number of important ways.

- It can make it easy for information systems to exchange data with one another, for instance, making production data available to the inventory system, the financial system, and the payroll system.
- It can support orderly deployment of new systems, so that they can be installed using standard procedures and so that installation of new systems will not interfere with the operation of existing systems.
- It can provide economies of scale in the use of resources, in a variety of ways. An obvious example is the use of a single telecommunications network to serve the entire enterprise, rather than having a separate network for each

application. Another example is using data collected for one system to serve others. Using the same programming language for many systems saves costs in training programmers and later in maintaining systems.

- It can support rapid deployment of new information systems by making parts of old systems (data, networks, programs, etc.) available for reuse by new systems.

In this kind of architecture (there are other kinds), one of the central ideas is the re-use or multiple use of the same resources to speed deployment of new systems and to achieve economies of scale. We give the name *infrastructure* to the set of resources that are used (or can be used) by more than one information system; the infrastructure includes data, computers, telecommunications facilities, some computer programs, and people. (This definition is broader than the usual one for reasons that will become clear when we address issues of the value of information technology.)

The economic problem of the infrastructure is this: How should you evaluate expenditures for elements of the infrastructure, and how should you allocate infrastructure costs? Should you charge the cost of each addition to the infrastructure to the first system that uses it? Should you allocate the costs according to usage? Or should you simply treat infrastructure costs as burden and not allocate them at all? We will discuss some ways of dealing with these questions in the next chapter.

STRATEGY COSTS MONEY IN THE SHORT TERM

All the things we have discussed in this chapter cost money, at least in the short term. Developing a vision and supporting strategies will consume a substantial quantity of your scarcest resource: the time of your most talented executives. Furthermore, when you modify a strategy to accommodate your long-term vision, you will inevitably increase the cost of executing that strategy. When you developed it, you did it in the most cost-effective way you could think of. Any modification will make it less effective, or more costly, or both. You'll get the benefits later, as the vision is realized. But that will probably be much later, and you have to pay the bills now.

The same things can be said about information systems architecture. Costs surely go up now; they will go down later.

I don't mean to sound pessimistic or negative about this. I deeply believe that you must develop creative visions and effective strategies if your company is to survive. And you must develop an information infrastructure. But you must also be prepared to pay the initial costs.

SUMMARY

What You Must Know

- Information technology strategy must be developed as part of the process of developing corporate strategy.
- Information technology strategy must support corporate vision as well as corporate strategy.
- You cannot predict what information you will need very far in advance.
- Easy and timely access to information is essential if you are to get the maximum benefits from the talents and energies of your workers.

What You Must Do

- Bring your information technology professionals into the corporate strategic planning process.
- Demand that information technology strategy have flexibility and quick response as major goals.
- Commit significant corporate resources to information technology: money, people, and time.

Chapter Five

Focusing Information Technology on the Bottom Line

In most organizations, information technology expenditures are so large and are growing so rapidly that they have become a matter of concern to senior management.

Information technology can bring value to an organization by supporting existing business processes, by enabling new ones, or by enabling corporate strategy and vision. Each of these sources of value must be assessed in its own way. In order to allocate IT resources properly across the organization, the portfolio of IT activities must be considered as a whole, in addition to the analysis of individual items.

A clear understanding of the value of various uses of information technology provides the starting point for evaluating proposals to outsource some or all IT activities. But this is only a starting point; many other issues must be considered before deciding to outsource IT, or anything else.

In our discussion of integrating information strategy with business strategy, we observed that preparing to meet future information needs usually increases current costs. We now look in detail at the question of how to decide whether any expenditure for information technology is worthwhile.

THE IMPORTANCE OF INFORMATION TECHNOLOGY EXPENDITURES

In most organizations, information technology expenditures are large and increasing rapidly, often growing faster than sales or profits. These expenditures are very difficult to restrain even in recessionary times because information technology has become an integral part of so many business processes. A recent survey found that the average respondent was planning to increase its IT expenditures by about 10 percent, as measured against revenues, from 2.2 percent of revenues in 1992 to 2.4 percent in 1993. The survey included organizations of all sizes, in manufacturing, services, and the public sector.[1]

IT expenditures differ substantially by economic sector. Informal surveys I have made recently show IT expenditures ranging from 1.5 to 3.0 percent of gross revenues for manufacturing companies and from 8 to 12 percent for banks and other financial services organizations. These expenditures have been growing from 10 to 20 percent per year for the past decade or more and show no sign of slowing. Furthermore, these numbers probably understate actual expenditures because a significant fraction of IT costs are incurred by operating units rather than IT departments, and these costs are often very difficult to identify.

Any corporate expenditure showing these characteristics—large size and rate of increase exceeding rate of corporate growth—should receive careful management attention.

In addition, issues peculiar to IT often arise within individual companies.

There is a general perception that information technology is a staff function and therefore "burden" that should be reduced to the minimum necessary for corporate survival.

The benefits of information systems are often intangible and thus open to attack by expense cutters.

Many nontechnology executives have had bad experiences with information system development projects: projects completed late and over budget.

The continuing barrage of stories in the business press about failures of system development efforts gives the impression that information technology is not well managed in many companies.

IT executives often do not do a good job of reporting the results of their activities, either to users or to senior managers.

Paul Strassman is a highly respected IT executive who was Vice President of the Information Products Group at the Xerox Corporation and later Chief Information Officer of the US Department of Defense. He analyzed IT expenditures and financial results of US corporations and concluded that there is no overall correlation between level of IT expenditures and corporate profitability. However, he found a wide variation in results among individual companies, even in the same line of business. He speculates that companies already well managed can improve their results by using information technology, but for poorly managed companies, addition of IT only makes things worse.[2]

In addition to these company-level concerns, there is a climate of skepticism about the benefits of information technology in our economy as a whole. Steven Roach of Morgan Stanley has written repeatedly that America's investments in computer technology over the past 20 or so years have not resulted in any economic gains for the country. In 1987 he said, "Technology has quite simply not delivered its long-awaited productivity payback."[3] Recently he has suggested that lack of payback is a result of managerial ineptitude in applying IT where it can do the most good, and that the recent wave of downsizing, restructuring, and re-engineering has enabled American managers finally to achieve some of the productivity gains of IT that have eluded them in the past.[4] The data on which Roach's analyses are based is dubious to say the least.[5] Nevertheless, doubts about the effectiveness of information technology remain widespread.

All of this isn't new. A study published by McKinsey and Co. *in 1968* said:

> As super-clerk, the computer has more than paid its way. For most large organizations, going back to punch cards and keyboard machines would be as unthinkable as giving up the typewriter for the quill pen. Yet in these same companies—including many that pioneered in the mechanization of paperwork operations—mounting computer expenditures are no longer matched by rising economic returns.[6]

The study also examined the ratio of IT expenditures to company sales in 1967 and found only one company (out of 36) that spent over 2 percent of sales on computing. Seventy-eight percent of the companies surveyed reported IT expenditures between 0.25 percent and 1.99 percent of sales.

Twenty-five years and countless billions of dollars later, we are still confronted with the same question: How can we evaluate the contributions of information technology to business performance? Cost reduction is clearly one method, but others are needed.

INFORMATION TECHNOLOGY COMPARED WITH OTHER SUPPORT ACTIVITIES

Information technology is viewed as a staff activity in most companies, and, as such, it is subject to the constraints, biases, and misunderstandings to which all staff activities are prey. Staff activities are seen as overhead, burden, necessary evils (and sometimes unnecessary evils). Each manager wants the accounting reports that she thinks are helpful to her, but views the accounting system overall as too big, too complex, and too expensive. It is common to have an individual manager want special and expensive IT support for her own operation, yet complain bitterly about the overall cost of IT to the company.

The work products of support (staff) activities—reports, analyses, procedures, and so on—are rarely directly related to business results.

A corporate image advertising program may indeed help the company in its relations with government agencies and community groups, but the effects of this help are very difficult to trace.

An information system that supports corporate long-range planning will certainly change the planning process and may improve the results. But by how much? And incidentally, how do you evaluate the work of the planning department itself?

In situations where staff work does contribute directly to business results, it is so interwoven with other factors that it is impossible to quantify the value of the staff contribution.

Market research to understand customer needs contributes to product success, but so do engineering, finance, and many other support activities. How do you apportion the value between the support groups and the groups that make and sell the product? How do you separate, and then evaluate, the contribution of each support group?

Executive information systems provide senior executives with up-to-date information about company operations and the ability to determine the causes of variations from plan. How much do these systems contribute to the bottom line?

Over the years, most organizations have developed reasonably effective ways of managing staff support activities and resolving the inevitable tensions between line and staff. Some of these methods work for information technology; others do not. To understand why this is so, we need to look at the ways in which IT is different from other support activities.

- The sustained high rates of growth of IT expenditures are unique among support functions. This rapid growth carries with it the connotation of an activity possibly out of control, one that needs better internal management and close outside monitoring. As we have noted previously, IT has a well-known history of disasters, weakening the credibility of its predictions of costs and benefits. In addition, the long time required to develop and install a major new system adds to the perception of mismanagement, even where this perception is not justified.

- IT is intrinsically disruptive to the organization. Any worthwhile information system changes individual jobs and business processes, and sooner or later requires organizational changes. No part of a company is immune from upheaval caused by IT, as it casts an increasingly wide net over the organization and invades individual operations ever more deeply.

- The power base of many managers and administrators is the information they control. New information systems often result in wider availability of information, undermining the positions of those managers. They may fear that their jobs are in jeopardy. They may be right.

- The rate of change of information technology is far greater than the rate of change of any other technology that is central to business success. Users who feel threatened by information technology are intimidated even more by rapid changes in it: just when they think they understand some aspect of IT, it becomes obsolete. Worse, just when they begin to enjoy the fruits of past investments in IT, they are asked to fund a new generation of technology.

- Many senior executives and senior line managers are un-comfortable dealing with IT issues. Most of them have little or no direct experience with information systems, whereas many have had significant tenure in other support activities, particularly finance and human relations. As a result, they have developed a base of knowledge about these other activities and an intuition about what makes sense and what does not. Very few senior executives have this same kind of intuition about IT issues, so they are uncomfortable making IT decisions even when they are supported by a substantial base of facts.

There is another way in which IT is similar to other support activities. It is very dangerous to base management decisions on the overall amounts and trends of any staff expenditures. It makes exactly as much sense to say, "We are going to cut our expenditures on information technology by 15 percent" as it does to say, "We are going to cut our expenditures on human resources management by 15 percent." Either or both may be necessary for survival in extreme cases. In a more normal world, the question is which information technology expenditures (or which human resources expenditures) should be reduced and which should be increased in order to enhance the organization's performance. These questions can be answered only after we understand how information technology adds value to the company.

SOURCES OF VALUE OF INFORMATION TECHNOLOGY

Information technology can add value to an enterprise in three basic ways.

- It can help reduce costs or increase profits of an existing activity.
- It can be an integral part of a redesigned business process.
- It can support the future of the business, which is to say business strategy and business vision.

Each of these sources of value has its own unique characteristics, and each must be analyzed by a method appropriate to those characteristics if we are to understand the contribution of each to the overall cost/benefit equation.

Reducing Costs or Increasing Profits

Reduced costs or increased profits resulting from automating an existing activity have historically been the primary way in which information systems expenditures have been justified.

In the simplest case, an information system displaces clerical labor, and the cost of the system (development plus operation) is less than the costs associated with the people who formerly did the work. A small retailer, Frank's Nursery and Crafts, reduced staff time spent monitoring and reordering inventory by 75 percent by installing hand-held scanners to check stock.[7] The United States Air Logistics Center rebuilds jet engines in a facility at Tinker Air Force Base near Oklahoma City. After the installation of a new inventory tracking system, management was able to eliminate 75 expediters and work-in-process inventory decreased by $100 million.[8]

Sometimes a new information system can directly generate profits. A cash management system can increase profits by using lockboxes and wire transfers to speed the collection of customer remittances, providing investable funds or decreasing borrowing requirements.

Cost/benefit analysis of this kind of use of information technology may be complicated, but it is straightforward. All costs and benefits associated with a new information system are identified as to amount and timing. The cash flows are then merged into a single stream and analyzed by whatever technique the company uses for other capital projects, such as net present value, payback time, or internal rate of return.

Costs and benefits of IT are relatively easy to identify when the only changes to the business process are those directly associated with the new automation. However, there are some traps you should watch for.

You will be able to get quite accurate estimates of IT expenditures for a new system if you wait until the system is fully specified. But it is unlikely that you will get good estimates of the costs of user participation in the development process. These estimates will almost always be low, which means that you will consistently underestimate total information system development costs (see Chapter 8).

You may underestimate operations costs because users will tend to incorporate system operations activities into the rest of their work (as they should) and will therefore be unable to say with any precision how much time they expect to spend on operating the system.

The costs of the IT infrastructure must be allocated among different systems, and the allocations will always be somewhat arbitrary.

Your accountants and your tax lawyers may require you to capitalize costs of purchased software but treat costs of internally developed software as current expenses. Whatever they say and do for their purposes, from the point of view of economics, an information system is a capital asset and should be evaluated accordingly.[9]

Redesigning a Business Process

Information systems that are created as part of a new business process design cannot be analyzed in the same way as systems that automate existing processes.

A telemarketing activity with an information system embedded in it is intrinsically different from a manual process to which IT is appended. You cannot evaluate the separate contribution of the embedded information technology because if the information technology is removed, the entire business process disappears.

In theory, one could determine the value of the information technology that is part of a new process design in the following way. First, do the best possible process design using information technology; next, do the best possible design without using IT (if you could create a workable design); then compare the expected costs and benefits of each design. The difference between the two would be the value of the information technology. In practice, this would be a wasteful and empty exercise: wasteful because the time and talents of competent process designers are too valuable to squander, and empty because it addresses the wrong issue. The business issue is not the costs and benefits of information technology *per se*; it is the costs and benefits of the new business process compared with the old one. The question of where and how much information technology to use to achieve the best possible process is a question for the process designers. Value can be assigned only to the process as a whole, not to any individual part of the process.

Supporting Business Strategy and Vision

The value of information technology that supports business strategy—without also serving some current business need—is that it enables strategy to be executed in timely fashion. The company is in a position to take advantage of business opportunities that would otherwise be closed to it or to generate entirely new opportunities.

As we discussed in Chapter 4, possession of a telecommunications network that can be expanded quickly to include additional countries or continents might well be essential to a business strategy of rapid worldwide expansion. In a similar vein, an internal information network that provides everyone in the company with access to production and marketing information can provide powerful support for a corporate vision of empowered workers.

The value of being able to take advantage of future opportunities cannot be captured by net present value or any other method of analysis based on the time value of money. The new business ventures we are talking about are years away, and some of them may never come into being. It is impossible to make realistic estimates of returns so far in the future. And even if good estimates could be made, discounting at any reasonable rate of interest would result in net present values close to zero.

A better approach is to view this kind of strategic investment as the purchase of an option to go into some new business in the future. Consider a real estate developer in a major city. Suppose his strategy is to build a major office building in the area of most rapid growth. He might construct a number of scenarios and conclude that rapid growth will occur in one of three corridors, but have no way of predicting which one. He would purchase options on land in each corridor, intending to exercise one of the options and let the other two expire. The total cost of all three land purchase options would be the cost of being able to participate in the best opportunity.

Or suppose you were running a consulting engineering company and your strategy were to provide unbeatable service to your construction customers at their field sites. This could involve any of a number of different services: providing analysis of structural engineering problems, providing working drawings reflecting changes in specifications, interpreting building codes, and so on. Whichever services you ultimately chose to offer, it is likely that you would want to provide communications capabilities at each site. A strategic IT investment would be to begin converting part of your telecommunications network to wireless transmission and training some of your staff to support it. The costs would be immediate, and the benefits nebulous and far off. What you would have received for your investment is the option to offer these services, when it became appropriate for your business to do so.

MANAGING YOUR INFORMATION TECHNOLOGY PORTFOLIO

With so many ways to get value from information technology, demand for new information systems exceeds supply in nearly every enterprise. There is a bit of folklore in the information systems world that every company has a two-year backlog of systems waiting for development. Whether the number is two years or not, it is indisputable that there are large unmet needs for information systems.

Supply cannot catch up with demand for several reasons. One is that new opportunities for profitable use of IT are constantly being discovered and created. Another is money. There are limits to how much money any enterprise can allocate to IT, no matter how valuable the opportunities, because IT is nearly always a support activity rather than a direct generator of profits. In some cases, a shortage of people with the required experience and talents will be more of a constraint than limited funds. You may be able to hire the IT expertise you need in the open market, but the people who really understand your company are probably in it already, and they are likely to have other important duties. Finally, there is a limit to the disruption that any organization can tolerate at a given moment. If your company is near that limit, you probably should postpone installation of more new systems, even if you can muster the resources to build them. We will return to this topic in Chapter 10.

Managing your IT expenditures requires a view of the overall effects of IT on the company, in addition to evaluations of the profitability of individual projects. Think of your IT expenditures as a portfolio of activities designed to achieve a number of different goals simultaneously.

You manage your securities portfolio in this way. You keep a certain amount of cash or cash equivalents for emergencies. You allocate a fraction of your assets to government bonds to safeguard a portion of your capital and assure a basic amount of income. You allocate some capital to common stocks to try to achieve capital appreciation. You seek to choose the best investment within each category, but you do not reduce your safety net of bonds because some common stock may yield a greater return than the bonds. A recent study of security industry advisory letters shows that asset allocation is a more reliable road to investment success than selection of individual securities.[10] It is likely that the same thing is true about investments in information technology: A thoughtful allocation of IT resources across the different ways of generating value may be more important than picking the single new information system that shows the greatest return on investment.

There is no theoretically correct way to decide how much of your IT expenditures to allocate to each type of value generation any more than there is a correct way to decide how to divide an investment portfolio among cash, bonds, and stocks. Let's take a different approach. Let's look at the current allocation of funds, determine what corporate purposes that allocation supports, and then decide whether or not it reflects corporate goals.

In order to understand the effects of IT activities on the company, we must disentangle IT expenditures from the budget categories in which they are usually displayed and reaggregate them in terms of the purposes they serve.

Let's look at a hypothetical example, the Widget Corporation, a manufacturing company with about $100 million in annual revenues. Its information services department (ISD) budget is shown in Table 5–1. (The numbers are reasonable estimates of what they might be for a real company.) The first three columns of Table 5–1 show the budget as it would normally be presented: subdivided into expenses for each of the organizational units of the IS department. These columns show the activities on which the department's resources are expended, but not the reasons for those expenditures.

The remaining columns show an allocation of the cost of each activity to the corporate purposes ISD serves: supporting current operations, improving current operations, supporting specific corporate strategies, and supporting corporate vision.

You will find the process of making these allocations very enlightening. Some of them, such as computer and telecommunications operations, are relatively straightforward: The operations staff typically knows what resources each activity consumes. On the other hand, it will be very difficult to allocate costs of a new system that serves several functional departments. Indeed, the allocation may be impossible to make on any totally rational basis, but you can make reasonable approximations. As we shall see below, we are interested in the thrust and direction of expenditures, rather than precise amounts.

Widget is planning to devote 87 percent (53 percent + 34 percent) of its IT budget to supporting or improving its current operations, a total of 10 percent to three specific strategies, and 3 percent to supporting its long-term vision. Is this an appropriate breakdown? Should more money be spent on preparing for the future, or less? If Widget sees a period of relative stability ahead, this may be about right. If it is looking forward to major changes, perhaps it should transfer some money from improving existing operations to supporting new strategies. Perhaps it should increase or decrease its IT budget.

Look at the three strategies. Only 1 percent of the budget, $60,000, is allocated to the new product focus strategy. Is that enough? Perhaps it is, or perhaps this allocation reveals that Widget is not really serious about this strategy. To address this question, Widget will have to examine total expenditures on this

TABLE 5–1
Widget Corporation IT Budget Strategic Allocation (Thousands of Dollars)

	Budget Amounts	Percentage	Support Current Operations	Improve Current Operations	Strategy: Global Marketing	Strategy: New Product Focus	Strategy: Excellent Customer Service	Support Vision
Operations								
Computers	$1,250	25%	$1,038	$ 188				$ 25
Telecommunications	500	10	375	50	$ 50			25
Data administration	150	3	120	23			$ 8	
Help desk	100	2	100					
Total operations	$2,000	40	$1,633	$ 260	$ 50		$ 8	$ 50
Application development								
Maintenance	1,000	20	200	800				
New systems								
Marketing	450	9	90	180	113		68	
Manufacturing planning	350	7	175	140		$35		
Human resource management	150	3	53	75				23
R&D management	50	1				25	25	
Total new systems	$1,000	20	$ 318	$ 395	$113	$60	$ 93	$ 23
Total application development	$2,000	40	$ 518	$1,195	$113	$60	$ 93	$ 23
IT planning	250	5	425	50			125	75
IT administration	500	10	75	75				
Training	250	5	75	100			50	25
Total budget	$5,000	100	$2,650	$1,680	$163	$60	$275	$173
% budget	100%		53%	34%	3%	1%	6%	3%

Note: Totals may be inconsistent because of rounding.

strategy, rather than just IT expenses. What this analysis of IT expenditures does is raise the question.

In the preceding discussion, we implicitly assumed that the information services department budget is the entire information technology budget of the company. There are almost no companies for which this is true today. In many organizations, IT expenditures outside the ISD constitute more than 25 percent of all IT expenditures; in some companies, the number approaches 50 percent.

IT activities outside the ISD are often called end-user computing. End-user computing can be divided into two categories. The first is utility computing: computing done within a department solely to support the activities of that department. There is much less of this kind of computing than you may think, and as time passes, more and more utility computing takes on companywide significance. Expenses for utility computing should be controlled at the departmental level, with the department manager deciding how to allocate his resources among people, computing, and the other facilities available to him to do his job.

The other kind of end-user computing is computing that interacts with other information systems in the company. If the systems plan requires the end users to write queries to retrieve data from a database, the costs associated with this activity should be included in the economic calculations we have described above. These costs will be hard to estimate and almost impossible to monitor after the system is in operation, but it is important to include them because they are a large and growing segment of overall system costs.

In some instances, end users develop complete application systems on their own, without involving the information services department. In looking at the economics of user-developed systems, it is important to note that cost estimates for this kind of system often exclude infrastructure costs, either because the systems rely on the infrastructure supplied by the information services department or because the systems simply do not provide for such things as data administration, security, or disaster recovery. As we shall see below, these costs often amount to about one-quarter of all ISD costs.

COSTS AND VALUE OF THE INFRASTRUCTURE

In our previous discussion of the Widget Corporation, we focused mainly on the costs of building and operating individual application systems and sets of application systems (the portfolio). We looked at the infrastructure only in terms of its support of individual systems or other companywide objectives. But as we saw in Chapter 4, the infrastructure has functions that transcend individual applications. These functions are increasing over time in both scope and cost. The costs of these functions should be related to their effects on IT activities as a whole, just as the costs of individual applications are related to their effects on the business as a whole.

We can use the same kind of logic to analyze infrastructure expenses as we used to analyze system costs: allocate the costs of the individual components of the infrastructure among the purposes that the infrastructure serves and then decide whether the expenses are reasonable. As in Table 5–1, the first three columns in Table 5–2 show the budget in conventional form. The other columns allocate the budget across the various ISD purposes: supporting applications, system security, disaster recovery, system flexibility (ease of making changes as future needs become known), and support of corporate information technology standards.

The bottom row in the table shows that direct support of application systems consumes 73 percent of the budget of the information services department; the other 27 percent is to be spent on activities that support applications and strategies as a whole and that help the ISD function smoothly and efficiently.

As with the allocations across corporate purposes in Table 5–1, these allocations raise policy questions.

- Is it worthwhile for Widget to spend $335,000 per year for system security and $277,000 for disaster recovery capabilities? One way to look at system security and disaster recovery activities is as insurance policies. Analyze your potential losses from theft of data or failure of your computer systems, and see if the risks justify the premiums.
- There are many benefits of having technical standards: lower training costs, easier modification of existing

TABLE 5–2
Widget Corporation IT Budget Allocation By Its Purpose (Thousands of Dollars)

	Budget Amounts	Percentage	Support Applications	System Security	Disaster Recovery	Support Flexibility	Support Standards
Operations							
Computers	$1,250	25%	$1,000	$125	$50	$75	$25
Telecommunications	500	10	375	25	50	25	15
Data administration	150	3	75	30	15	15	15
Help desk	100	2	90				10
Total operations	$2,000	40	$1,540	$180	$115	$115	$50
Application development							
Maintenance	1,000	20	1,000				
New systems							
Marketing	450	9	270	45	45	45	45
Manufacturing planning	350	7	210	35	53	18	35
Human resource management	150	3	90	15	15	15	15
R&D management	50	1	40	10			
Total new systems	$1,000	20	$ 610	$105	$113	$ 78	$ 95
Total application development	$2,000	40	$1,610	$105	$113	$ 78	$ 95
IT planning	250	5	350			125	125
IT administration	500	10		50	50		50
Training	250	5	175				75
Total budget	$5,000	100	$3,675	$335	$277	$317	$395
% budget		100%	73%	7%	6%	6%	8%

Note: Totals may be inconsistent because of rounding.

75

systems, easier integration of new systems with existing ones, and so on. Are these benefits worth the $395,000 per year that these standards cost Widget?

- Making systems flexible enough to accommodate unplanned changes costs $317,000 per year. Is it worth it? Think about how fast your business is changing and the costs in both money and disruption if entirely new information systems are needed.

Again, there is no mechanical way to answer these questions, but posing them clearly can help lead to useful insights.

OUTSOURCING

The concept of outsourcing is simple enough: contract with another company to perform activities currently being performed by your company's employees. Most information services groups use outside contractors from time to time to build software, supply telecommunications services, do program maintenance, and so on. This kind of routine subcontracting is different from outsourcing, as the word is commonly used, in that outsourcing usually refers to situations where all or a major part of the information technology activities are transferred to an outsider. That kind of transfer generates a whole new set of problems and opportunities.

Information technology outsourcing is big business. A recent study estimates total outsourcing volume of $3.5 billion in 1992, growing to $9 billion or $10 billion in 1995.[11] Obviously, many companies think outsourcing makes sense for them. Does it make sense for you?

Reasons to Outsource

The strongest motive to outsource is money. It is not uncommon for an outsourcer to offer to take over a company's existing IT operations at a price 15 percent to 25 percent less than current costs, with a commitment to limit the rate of price increases to the rate of inflation plus adjustments for increased volume of work.

Eastman Kodak began a major outsourcing effort in 1989. In July, it signed a $150 million agreement outsourcing PC procurement to Businessland, Inc. Later that month, it outsourced its information systems operations (data centers) to IBM.[12] Two months later, it was negotiating to outsource its application development work.[13]

Sometimes there is a cash incentive for outsourcing as well. The outsourcer may purchase the customer's data center or other assets as part of the transaction.

In addition to saving money, outsourcing frees management to concentrate on the core activities of its business, rather than diverting attention to the technical and operational tasks of managing information technology. Even outsourced IT requires substantial managerial attention, as we shall note below, but it is of a different and more congenial kind.

Of course, you do not have to outsource all your IT activities. One strategy is to outsource the routine IT tasks such as building an accounting system or operating a data center, leaving your own skilled IT people available to support strategic IT initiatives. One of my consulting clients concluded that it needed new systems for several of its core activities. It outsourced the maintenance and operation of its existing systems, while using its own people to build the new systems that will support the company for the next decade.

Another reason to outsource is to obtain a higher level of performance in IT activities. Outsources often claim they are more competent than most companies at operating data centers, building information systems, and so on, because IT is their main line of business, rather than being a support activity. There is some justification for these claims in the experiences of outsourcing clients.

Reasons Not to Outsource

There are arguments against outsourcing that are also worth considering.

The monetary savings are not as clear-cut as suggested above. You will incur the costs of negotiating the outsourcing contract and, more important, the ongoing costs of monitoring the outsourced activities. This is not merely a matter of handling paper and issuing checks. Monitoring means being sure that service level agreements are kept, that changes are made in timely fashion, and that in general the outsourcer meets the changing needs of your business and charges you a fair price for doing so. You must also have people within your own organization who are able to evaluate the outsourcer's technological plans and capabilities to assure you that your long-range IT goals can be met.

You cannot delegate complete responsibility for the effective use of information technology in your organization to an outside contractor any more than you can delegate all responsibility to an internal information services department. In either case, users must spend substantial time on IT issues. It is reasonable to assume that more user time will be required if the IT services are obtained from an outside supplier rather than from an internal department. When Continental Bank of Chicago outsourced its entire IT function, which employed about 500 people, it kept about 20 of the people on its staff, half to administer the contract and half to set IT strategy for the bank. It leaves the specification of user requirements to its operating departments.[14]

There are more subtle, and perhaps more important, problems than money. Profitable use of information technology requires extremely close working relationships between IT professionals and the business users of the technology. Their joint work focuses on business needs, with careful balancing of value received and costs incurred. That kind of relationship is much harder to establish and maintain with contractors than with company employees.

Your company may lose a competitive advantage by using an outsourcer. If you have a strategic business process that incorporates information technology, or are planning to implement one, you necessarily must disclose it to your outsourcer. This in turn may make it available to your competitors. An outsourcer seeks to learn what its client company is planning and doing for two reasons: to meet its obligations to the company and to obtain an intellectual base for obtaining contracts with other companies. Indeed, one of the chief advantages the outsourcer brings to a client relationship is its knowledge of the activities of other companies.

After you have outsourced a major portion of your IT activities, it may be very difficult to bring them back in house. You will have lost many experienced people, and the transition from the outsourcer can be difficult.

None of this is intended to impugn the integrity of those in the outsourcing business. It is simply a recognition of two basic facts of life: the interests of buyers and sellers of any product or service are fundamentally in conflict; and it is impossible for any human being to partition his mind so that what he has learned in one place does not influence his actions at another.

Negotiating a fair and effective outsourcing contract is extremely difficult. The intrinsic conflicts described in the previous paragraphs are only part of the problem. The rates of change in both the technology and the way it is used make a fixed price contract impossible. For existing activities, a fixed price plus adjustments for volume and inflation can work. Radically new activities—redesigning a business process or implementing a new strategic initiative—pose a serious dilemma to the company. It can attempt to negotiate a fixed-price contract for the new activity, but it does so at a substantial disadvantage because the current outsourcer is often the only viable bidder. The alternative is to handle new activities on a cost plus basis, which presents major cost control problems.

One final point about the contract: It is essential to provide for an orderly transfer of activities from the outsourcer to either an in-house group or another outsourcer, if you should wish to terminate the outsourcing agreement.

Other Effects of Outsourcing

In addition to economics, there are two other issues to consider when you are evaluating an outsourcing proposal: the effects of outsourcing on your IT activities and its effects on your organization as a whole.

Let's look at the effects of outsourcing on IT activities in the same way we analyzed the ISD budget of Widget Corporation: in terms of the corporate purposes IT serves.

Outsourcing can work very well in support of existing operations. Fair and effective contracts can be negotiated based on current activity levels and projected growth. There are norms against which to measure performance and evaluate quality.

One way to improve current operations is to modify or rebuild the information systems that support them. Working with an outsourcer to do this is not very different from working with an in-house systems department. Needs and costs can be specified with reasonable accuracy once the functional specifications have been developed, and fixed-price contracts can be negotiated. The process of constructing and implementing a new system is largely the same whether it is done by a contractor or an in-house group.

A major business process redesign is a different and much more complex matter. Even if you can negotiate a fixed-price contract, it may not be in your interest to do so. A fixed-price contract may limit the ability of your design team to follow up promising ideas that were not under consideration when the contract was negotiated. Cost plus, with all of its hazards, may be your best option.

The biggest problem with outsourcing is the difficulty of supporting the future of the company: its strategies and its vision. The whole idea of strategy is to change the company in significant ways. This is difficult enough for company employees to do well; it is far harder for outsiders, no matter how close their relationship with the company.

The organization as a whole is seriously affected by an outsourcing decision, beyond the direct effects on IT activities.

Outsourcing is intrinsically disruptive to the organization. The informal network of working relationships that make things run smoothly is disturbed. The new relationships with nonemployees are different in kind from the old ones.

Morale can be hurt. Outsourcing IT is often seen by the entire company as an effort to eliminate and/or downgrade jobs, whether or not the outsourcer offers jobs to the company employees who are no longer needed. Outsourcing IT may be viewed as the harbinger of things to come: outsourcing distribution, or even manufacturing.

You may be mortgaging your future. Outsourcing may leave you without a sufficient base of IT knowledge and experience to recognize and take advantage of new IT opportunities, opportunities that your outsourcer cannot recognize.

An Outsourcing Checklist

Here are some things to do as you make an outsourcing decision.

- Analyze the economics, making certain you include the costs of contracting, transferring the activities to the outsourcers, monitoring the contract, and terminating the arrangement.
- Plan to maintain a core of IT expertise to monitor the outsourcer and to work on strategies for the future.
- Analyze the effects of outsourcing on your various IT activities. Stable and predictable activities are good candidates for outsourcing; others are not.
- Analyze the effects of outsourcing on your vision and strategies for the future, particularly with respect to flexibility to respond to changes in your business.
- Analyze the effects on the rest of the company, in terms of relationships and morale.

COMMUNICATING INFORMATION TECHNOLOGY RESULTS IN BUSINESS TERMS

Earlier in this chapter, we described ways to evaluate the potential contributions of information technology to corporate performance. If these contributions are to be realized, two things must happen: (1) the business goals to be achieved using information technology must be clearly articulated by line management, and (2) progress toward meeting those goals must be measured and reported by IT management *in clear, understandable business terms.*

You may think that the members of your IT management team understand your business goals, but there is a good chance that they do not. Survey after survey of chief information officers show that one of their major problems is the lack of effective communication with senior management. Looking in the other direction, a recent survey of CEOs and CFOs showed that only about half (55 percent) of the respondents felt that information technology in their companies was linked to business strategy "very well."[15]

The process of measuring and reporting is easy to describe and hard to execute. Just as top management must articulate strategic goals to guide the IT planning process, so must line executives work with information system designers to identify those aspects of each operation that are crucial to its success and to define metrics for them. Procedures for collecting data about these metrics should be designed as the system is designed and executed as a regular part of system operation.

Mark Travel has a product database of about 29 million elements representing rates and availabilities of travel, hotels, and other services that it packages for customers. There about 1.4 million rate changes per month. Mark Travel's marketers offer new products nearly every week of the year, each based on a combination of elements in the database. If the data is not entered in a timely fashion, opportunities to sell new products are lost. If the data is wrong, products may be mispriced and/or travelers may be inconvenienced.

David Moon, vice president and chief information officer of Mark Travel, relates Mark Travel's experiences in improving the process.

> The concerted opinion throughout the company was that the data in the product database was not accurate and not timely. That was just an observation; it didn't give us a basis [for action] until we could measure how untimely it was and how inaccurate it was.
>
> We sent some of our data-entry people to a quality seminar and established a quality group of workers that met weekly. The group developed metrics based on the number of complaints about data quality which it received each week, and the nature of each complaint. Three numbers are now tracked: number of complaints received, number of complaints resolved, and turnaround time to resolve complaints. Weekly reports are issued showing the three-month trend of each metric in graphical form. The same reports go to management and to the workers.
>
> The same kind of informal assessment which had been bad before showed that things have vastly improved. Our turnaround time on new products has decreased, and our rate of pricing errors on tickets has decreased by 92 percent.[16]

Three things in this anecdote are worth emphasizing. There was no way of responding to the dissatisfaction in the organization until measures of quality were defined. The metrics themselves were developed by the workers, not by management. And the collection and reporting of the metrics have become a routine part of operations.

The specifics will be different for each business process and for each system, but it is always possible to establish useful measures. Sometimes they will be objective, and sometimes they will be subjective, but you can find measures. If you cannot measure the outputs of business process, or if the rate of production is not important, perhaps you should not bother with the process at all.

SUMMARY

What You Must Know

- Your information technology expenditures will continue to increase.
- The value of all information technology expenditures can be assessed in terms of corporate purpose, but only some of them can be evaluated by conventional cost/benefit analysis.
- Outsourcing is a viable alternative for predictable IT activities.

What You Must Do

- Resist the pressure to constrain IT expenditures merely because they are increasing, but demand analysis by business purpose before approving them.
- Prepare to spend money on information technology to support your corporate vision and strategy, money that will show no immediate return.
- Demand that all IT activities be monitored and reported in business terms.

Chapter Six

Holistic Business Process Design

Effective and efficient business processes are central to the success of every enterprise. When a company grows significantly or when its business or its markets change, it must change its business processes. Small changes in business needs can often be accommodated gradually, by a process of evolution; large changes may require revolutionary changes in the way business is conducted.

Conventional process design techniques sometimes miss important opportunities because they deal with one facet of the design at a time. Holistic business process design provides a way to deal with all aspects at once, rather like the concurrent engineering coming into prominence in manufacturing industries. It seeks out the reasons the process is important to the company and applies all relevant concepts and technologies, old and new. It considers the criteria of maximum local control, flexibility in operations, and ability to accommodate change.

Teams of people who understand the entire process from many different points of view can do the best job of business process design provided they understand the underlying purposes and philosophy of the business and provided they focus on a business process rather than on an organizational unit.

In an earlier chapter, we discussed vision—what we want our company to be —and strategy—the large-scale things we plan for our company to do to achieve our vision. In this chapter, we get down to the gritty details of the daily operations that make it all happen, the activities and the "business processes" that make a company work. Who opens the mail? Which products should we schedule for production next week? When is a sale booked? Where do we store the raw materials? How do we respond to a customer complaint? Deciding how these things should be done and how they should be connected to one another is called *business process design*.

Formally, a business process is a coordinated set of activities that produces a specific, identifiable output. The concept of specific, identifiable output is crucial; if a process produces no identifiable output, there can be no criteria to judge its effectiveness for the enterprise as a whole.

Business process design should be a voyage of discovery, rather than another trip down a familiar path. Design is a creative activity. There are two or twenty different ways to perform each activity; there are a hundred or a thousand different ways to combine them. We have no time-tested recipes for success. Every company is different from every other company, and every company is different this year than it was last year. What works in one case may not work in another. Fortunately, there are some widely applicable principles that can be used to guide the design process and help us avoid some common pitfalls. These principles and pitfalls are the subject of this chapter.

REASONS TO CHANGE YOUR BUSINESS PROCESSES

Many business process were never actually *designed* in the first place. In a startup operation (a new company or a new operation in an existing company), that is how it should be. The goal of a startup is to get started. Elegant, or even thoughtful, process design is a luxury that most startups cannot afford. They begin with something that works and go on to pursue their real goal: serving customers. After the startup has become stable, a fresh look at business processes is in order.

This is one reason that franchised businesses are attractive. One of the most important things that the purchaser of a franchise gets for his money is a set of proven business processes developed by the franchiser. The franchisee is free to deal with issues of marketing and staffing, knowing that the basic business processes are in place.

Normal growth also requires changes in business processes. Venture capitalists have learned that as a company grows, it requires changes in management style, from entrepreneurial (visionary and risk taking) to administrative (a focus on order and control). This change and the many others associated with corporate growth inevitably require fundamental changes in business processes.

David Moon of Mark Travel tells how one of its process redesigns came about:

> It was initiated by the IS department. That has typically been the story. The company historically had growth rates in the 1980s of 20 percent or so. You had people who were responsible for a process, like distributing brochures or getting the tickets out, who had to grow their capabilities each year. The answer that we were usually getting was something like this. "Well I had 100,000 tickets to produce, I had 10 people on staff to do that. Next year I must do 120,000, I need 12 people. Let's go out and hire." This linear growth idea has been a tradition with a lot of our middle-management people. It has been a struggle to look at those areas where we had the greatest opportunity to reengineer a process and make that process completely different from what it was before. Eventually, some of these things become so obvious that everybody looking at them says we are never going to get to where we are going unless we do this a completely different way.[1]

The new business environment we discussed in Part 1 forces us to take a fresh look at our business processes even if our business has been operating profitably for a long time and is not suffering growth pangs. (Perhaps out-of-date business processes are one reason we are not "suffering" those pangs.)

- Business requirements change as competition intensifies and as business and markets increase their geographic scope. Business alliances change the structure of business processes and the information needed to support them.
- The new paradigms of business—meeting the needs of all stakeholders and empowering employees—force us to take a new look at the ways we do things.
- The meteoric advances in information technology demand that we give careful consideration to how it can help make

our operations more efficient and more effective. (We again note that other important technologies are changing as well: manufacturing, finance, etc. They too must be taken into account, in the same ways we deal with information technology.)

Maybe your business processes are working fine now and you really don't need to change them. Maybe not. It might be worth your while to take a fresh look at them using some of the design principles described below.

EVOLUTIONARY CHANGE OR REVOLUTIONARY CHANGE

Your corporate vision and strategy should identify your core competencies—those things at which you must excel in order to succeed in the marketplace. The business processes that support these competencies must have priority in your thinking.

The first question to ask when you are considering changing a business process is whether you *should* change it. Even when a process is less than perfect (as most are), some other process may be more in need of help. As we shall see in Chapter 10, changing business processes is disruptive, and there is a limit to the amount of disruption that any organization can tolerate.

There are two very different ways to modify a business process: evolutionary change and revolutionary change. Evolutionary change means keeping the existing process in place, looking for flaws, difficulties, and inefficiencies, and fixing the problems one at a time as they are discovered. This approach is called by a variety of names, including *continuous process improvement.*[2]

Continuous process improvement lies at the heart of many total quality management programs. It is so well documented in that context that we will spend only enough time on it to make two points relevant to information systems.

First, much of the information system activity called *maintenance* is in fact continuous process improvement. Most maintenance of information systems involves minor changes in the system to accommodate minor changes (hopefully improvements) in the business process that the system supports. Maintenance goes on throughout the life of an information system, in the aggregate often costing four to five times as much as the original cost of developing the system.

Second, most new information system development is closely akin to continuous process improvement, except on a larger scale. The standard system development process begins with an analysis of the existing business process, including asking those who participate in it what changes and improvements they see as desirable. This analysis becomes the basis for the design of the new process and the information system to support it. It is based on two unspoken assumptions: that the existing business process is reasonably close to the best possible one, and that incremental improvements can improve it significantly. The result is usually a large number of relatively small changes in the business process, supported by a completely new information system.

Revolutionary change means a complete redesign of a business process from the ground up. It means discarding all your previous notions about what things should be done, how they should be done, and who should do them. As we shall see, it is difficult, expensive, and disruptive. You should only undertake it in the expectation of major benefits in your competitive posture.

Xerox Corporation began its revolution in business processes when it found that some of its competitors were offering certain photocopiers at retail prices less than Xerox's own cost of manufacturing comparable products. At that point, the need for revolutionary change became clear. Nothing less than totally new ways to design, manufacture, and market would enable Xerox to compete successfully.[3]

Evolution is always easier, less expensive, and more pleasant than revolution. If evolution will do what you need done, use it. If not, revolution may be your only choice. Use these guidelines to help you decide which method is appropriate for your situation.

- If a business process has been redesigned fairly recently, if the business demands on that process haven't changed much since its last redesign, and if there is no technological breakthrough (in any technology, not just information technology) that could make a major improvement in the way it is conducted, choose continuous process improvement and information system maintenance as the way to keep it up to date. Seek minor improvements in effectiveness and efficiency.

- If a process is meeting the company's needs fairly well but could benefit from a major infusion of information technology, consider building a new information system to support the existing process, with whatever changes are needed to take advantage of the technology. Seek a payback of two to three years on your investment.

- If a process is clearly inadequate as determined by benchmarking or competitive considerations (as in the Xerox example), and if it is a core process on which your business success depends, redesign it from the ground up. Seek a new process that is at least five times as effective as the old one. (If it is not at least two or three times as effective, the results won't be worth the effort.) Gains of this magnitude can be achieved. Ken Freeman, CEO of Corning Asahi Video Products Company, reports that the targets of its process improvement efforts for its order-fulfillment process were "up to a 97 percent decrease in work time (44 hours to 1.2 hours), a 93 percent reduction in elapsed time (165 days to 11 days), and a 96 percent reduction in the number of tasks (230 to 9)." The company achieved a $2 million positive impact on the bottom line.[4]

These guidelines will not always give you a definitive answer to the question of which method to use, but they should give you a start.

The evolutionary processes of building new information systems and the maintenance of old ones is discussed in Chapter 8. We will devote the balance of this chapter to revolutionary change: business process redesign.

CONVENTIONAL BUSINESS PROCESS DESIGN

Let's take a brief excursion into history to understand how we arrived at our current ways of planning work. We will follow the description by Professor Martin Starr of Columbia University, grossly oversimplifying his analysis to emphasize the ideas that are germane to our current problems.[5]

In 1798, Eli Whitney forever changed the way of producing mechanical devices when he devised and implemented the idea of using interchangeable parts to manufacture guns for the United States Army. Expensive, time-consuming custom fitting of each part into each gun gave way to simply taking one part from a supply of identical parts and putting it in place.

A century later, Frederick Winslow Taylor worked to improve individual production processes by identifying and experimenting with process variables to learn "the one best way" of doing each individual operation, such as cutting metal or shoveling coal. He began by studying machines and tools, but soon realized that the people who operated the machines were as important as the machines themselves. He moved into planning in detail the work of the people who ran the machines, eventually considering the people to be extensions of the machines.

With Whitney's interchangeable parts and Taylor's efficient production processes, only one more thing was needed to make possible mass production as we now know it: an orderly way to manage the *set* of production processes necessary to produce a finished product.

Henry Ford invented the assembly line—bringing the work to the workers rather than having the workers go to the work—for precisely this reason: to decrease costs and gain better control of the set of processes required for final assembly of an automobile. At about the same time, Henry L. Gantt was developing charts and other analytical tools to help production planners design efficient production lines of various types.

Each of these ideas began in manufacturing plants, then gradually migrated into offices as ways to improve performance of repetitive clerical tasks. As computers came into use, work flow studies necessarily identified information as an item of importance, distinct from the paper on which the information was recorded, transferred, and stored. This analytical process, which came to be called *information systems analysis*, is remarkably similar to work flow analysis on the factory floor or in the nonautomated clerical office.

Factory work flow analysis and conventional information systems analysis have exactly the same design goals:

- A process that produces large quantities of identical products at low cost.

- A process that requires minimal skills of the people who operate it, hence minimal training.
- A process that is easy to supervise, once it has been designed and installed.

The two kinds of analysis share many ideas and techniques.

Both are based on interchangeable parts. All customer orders are forced to be alike to an information system, just as all gun barrels were made to be alike by Eli Whitney. (In fact, all customer orders are not alike, or rather, they should not be. We will discuss the consequences of this later.)

Following Taylor, both break each operation down into its basic parts. This is even more important in information systems analysis than in conventional work flow analysis because computer programs must specify business processes in such excruciating detail.

Both kinds of analysis are dedicated to the idea of *one best way*, although not explicitly. (This idea is one of the things that alienates users of information systems from the professionals who build them.)

Both acknowledge Gantt's idea of a process made up of a sequence of operations, and both attempt to simplify flow—work flow or information flow—and eliminate redundant activities.

Both are based on the assumption that the whole of a process is equal to the sum of its parts.

Both factory work process analysis and information systems analysis are carried out by specialists: industrial engineers and systems analysts, respectively.

Both work flow analysis and information systems analysis regularly achieve their goals of work simplification and efficiency. Unfortunately, the systems that result also have some undesirable characteristics.

They are usually defined in terms of internal function (accounting, manufacturing, etc.) instead of being defined by the outputs of a process. They often miss opportunities because the specialists who design them do not get sufficient input from nonspecialists—workers, managers, customers, suppliers.

They usually require large capital investments.

They tend to be very inflexible in operation and to require substantial time and expense to modify.

Work flow systems make efficient use of the physical labor of workers, and information systems make efficient use of workers doing "mental manual labor," but neither leaves much room for worker initiative or creativity.

Many highly automated, computer-enabled systems have carried the ideas of Eli Whitney and Frederick Taylor to their end point. They have made workers interchangeable parts of the process of producing information, each worker performing a small task in a completely predetermined way.

A NEW APPROACH: HOLISTIC PROCESS DESIGN

The same forces that require us to make radical changes to our business processes require us to make radical changes in the way we design them, because if we design them the old way, we will get the old kind of processes—the kind that don't work anymore.

The new design process is called *holistic design*. It starts with the basic ideas and tools of earlier business planning methods, but it makes important additions and modifications to each.

- It accepts the concept of breaking a process into component parts, but rejects the idea that every process must be divided into the most elementary possible operations.
- It accepts work flow analysis and work flow diagrams as tools, and extends their use to other flows, such as flows of information and flows of people.
- It accepts the idea of business processes driven by business needs, but defines those needs in terms external to the business (serving customers, etc.) rather than in terms of internal organization (e. g., the accounting department).
- It accepts the idea of asking line workers and supervisors to describe the process as it exists, and adds the idea that they should participate in the design of the new process.

Holistic design adds these new ideas to the design process:

- Improvements of 500 percent and more may be possible if a business process is completely redesigned.
- Some parts of a business process are best carried out by human beings using their own knowledge and judgment about how the business should operate, provided they have the information necessary to assess the consequences of their actions.
- Support of business vision and strategy is a paramount design goal.
- Needs of all stakeholders must be taken into account during process design.
- Business needs will change after the new process is installed, and the design must allow for orderly modification of the new process to meet those needs.
- Design of all facets of the process is carried on concurrently.

The strategy for holistic process design has three parts. First, use all available resources in the design effort. Use the workers who will execute the process, the managers who will supervise it, the suppliers of inputs, and the customers for whose benefit the process is carried out. Use industrial engineers, management scientists, information systems analysts, and other technical specialists. Use our new knowledge of people, teams, and organizations. Use anything or anyone who can help the process.

Next, execute the design process concurrently rather than sequentially. Think about information flow while you are thinking about how to receive inventory and whether to use forklift trucks; don't wait until after the warehousing scheme is complete. If you do the warehousing scheme first and then automate it, you may create a good manual business process supported by automation. But you are likely to create a much better process if you have information technology available as one of your basic building blocks instead of as an afterthought. (In any given case, you might not use information technology, but it should always be available.)

The benefits you can obtain from this method of design will astound you. Boeing Company's traditional aircraft design process had three steps, each carried out by a separate engineering group. The first group designed the overall shape and style of the aircraft and specified its major components. After this task was completed, the designs were transferred to manufacturing engineers, who planned production and assembly. Finally, the design was sent to tooling engineers, who designed the production machinery, tools, and jigs necessary to build the plane. Boeing is using a new process, called *concurrent engineering*, in the design of the cargo version of its 767. All the design processes are carried out at the same time, so that errors are found earlier in the process, before subsequent design work has been completed. Boeing expects to reduce its design costs by 25 percent by reducing redesign.[6]

Finally, make sure that the business process design reflects all the aspects of the business that the process touches. It must support business strategy, meet the needs of all stakeholders, and empower employees to support the process. At the same time, the process must meet the ongoing corporate requirements of functional management, auditability, control, accountability, and so on, but in new ways.

I have named this method *holistic business process design* because it acknowledges and takes advantage of the fact that the whole of a business process is more than merely the sum of its parts. (Holism is the name of a philosophic viewpoint that asserts that every entity, animate or inanimate, has a reality of its own in addition to the realities of its components.) Do we really need another management buzzword? Perhaps not, but I have chosen to invent this one because it is important that we continually remind ourselves that we are doing something that is intrinsically different from what we have done before. The word *holistic* characterizes our new approach quite well.

Describing holistic design in words presents a dilemma to an author. The essence of the process of holistic design is that all aspects of a problem are considered simultaneously, tentative decisions are made and revised, and the final product is intrinsically different from and more than merely the sum of its components. But words are linear: they necessarily describe one thing at a time, in a fixed sequence. I have chosen the sequence below to make the descriptions easy to understand. Don't interpret this to be the sequence in which the design tasks are to be executed. In fact, most of them should be done concurrently.

For descriptive purposes, we divide the design process into three parts: (1) selecting and defining the business process, (2) forming the design team, and (3) creating the design. But the separation is not as neat as this listing implies: the "later" parts can affect the "earlier" ones, and often do. We postpone consideration of information needs to the next chapter, not because it should be the last thing considered in business process design, but rather because it is the primary topic of this book and as such deserves special attention.

As you read, remember that everything affects everything else and all aspects of the business process must be considered simultaneously.

SELECTING AND DEFINING THE BUSINESS PROCESS

You should not embark on a program of process design or redesign without a good business reason. It is expensive, it consumes the time and energies of some of your most valuable people, and it is very disruptive to the organization. You should be driven to redesign a business process—driven either by a problem or by an opportunity.

The problems will come to your attention more or less automatically: our competitors are beating us in the marketplace, costs are up, the manufacturing department is in disarray, administrative expenses are rising much faster than sales, the regulators are after us.

Some of these problems can be traced to specific processes rather easily; others cannot. If our problem is that manufacturing costs are up, we should look both to the process by which our product is made and to the process by which costs are computed. Things are not always what they seem: unit costs of manufacturing may be going up because the manufacturing process is deteriorating or because raw material costs are rising. Or it may be that the apparent rise in manufacturing costs is an artifact of the accounting system: declining unit volume causing a larger amount of overhead to be allocated to each unit. In that case, the problem is not in manufacturing; it is in marketing.

Rising administrative costs are a different matter. Some administrative activities produce identifiable outputs such as regulatory reports and financial summaries for senior managers. Sadly, other administrative activities produce no specific outputs, or outputs of no value, such as the summary report that no one reads.

Sometimes there is an opportunity for reengineering a business process when an existing information system must be modified or replaced. Tom Barrett is director of the Information Services Division of Bemis Company, a manufacturer of flexible packaging materials and related products. He tells how deficiencies in an information system led to the reengineering of a major business process:

> Our operating divisions had been complaining about the accounts payable system. It was inflexible, and people in the plants were spending a lot of time and effort trying to get around the system to get things done. The system was about 26 years old, and it contained more changes and enhancements than original code.
>
> We soon realized that the accounts payable system was really a cash disbursement system, which is logically a part of the purchasing process, which also includes receiving goods from suppliers and putting them into inventory. We reengineered the purchasing process and built a new information system to support it.[7]

It is more fun to exploit opportunities than it is to solve problems. You will find your opportunities in your strategies. A strategy to expand marketing to the Pacific Rim is a mandate to design at least three new business processes: one to market in that region, another to deliver the products, and a third to handle accounting in a variety of currencies. You might be tempted to modify existing business processes and information systems to meet your new needs, but this may not be a good idea. A better idea might be to design new processes which take into account existing needs as well as new ones, and then abandon the old processes when the new ones are in place.

Senior management must select the business processes to be redesigned. The effort will be doomed by the bureaucracy unless the initiative comes for the top.

Which processes you select will depend on your company, your industry, your strategy, and your vision of your future. A rapidly growing company would probably choose to spend most of its efforts on opportunities: designing processes to support its strategic objectives. It would work only on problems serious enough to demand immediate attention. A company with mature markets might find its strategic options so limited that its best choice is to fix existing processes that are causing problems.

Bemis redesigned one of its business processes after it was approached by a customer that was engaged in a program to reduce the number of its suppliers from over 50 to just 2. Bemis was invited to negotiate to become one of the two suppliers. At that time, Bemis was selling this customer just one product, at the rate of about $6 million per year. The new arrangement would yield revenues to Bemis of about $70 million per year, with the prospect of increasing to over $100 million per year. Tom Barrett explains the new process:

> The relationship you get with these customers is completely different from what we are used to. . . . Yes, they want quality, they want price, and they want service. What we do now is meet with them a couple of times a year. They tell us what we are doing that we should change to help them cut their costs. Maybe we're not packaging things properly; maybe we are shipping full truckloads when they want half truckloads. We change those things. Then we tell them what they can do to cut *our* costs. And in each case, we share the savings.[8]

After you have selected the business process in general terms (e.g., all activities necessary to deliver the product to the customer), you must set boundaries to assure that the design task is feasible. There are three types of boundaries: scope, breadth, and size.

Scope refers to the segment of the value chain you include in your definition. Is selling a part of the process? How about purchasing? Do you include after-sale support? What about activities conducted by the customer on the customer's premises? The rule is: Initially include everything it takes to make the product valuable to the customer. A distribution company that does not include the supplier in its analysis runs the risk of missing opportunities to drop ship merchandise; one that excludes the customer is unlikely to create a design that allows the customer to enter orders by computer from the customer's site.

Breadth refers to the boundaries between the process under study and other business processes. Does the product delivery process include order entry? It probably does. Selling and sales administration? Maybe. Marketing accounting? Probably not. The rule for breadth is similar to the rule for scope. When in doubt about whether an activity is part of the process, include it.

If you follow the rules for scope and breadth, you are likely to define a process much too big to handle. After you have taken this all encompassing view, you must ask yourself how many people you can realistically assign to the design task, how much money you can afford to spend, and how much disruption your organization can tolerate. The level of tolerable disruption will narrow the breadth of the process, and the availability of money and effort will shrink its scope.

Don't worry too much about the details of your process definition. The design process will adjust scope and breadth many times before it is finished. The main point is to give the design team enough guidance to get started in the right direction.

THE PROCESS DESIGN TEAM

The power of holistic business process design lies in the design team. The team is itself an example of the holistic principle: The skills and abilities of the team as a whole are greater than the sum of the skills and abilities of the individual team members. As a result, a well-formed and well-managed design team will inevitably create a better process design than separate groups of specialists, each going about its own work.

The members of a design team must have a wide diversity of knowledge and experience if the team is to be effective. They must understand in detail how the business process actually works, and how the process affects others, both inside and outside the organization. Thus, the team should include people who participate in all aspect of the business process: workers, suppliers, customers, and any other stakeholders concerned.

The people who work in and around the process can make two kinds of contributions to the process design. They can specify in detail what needs to be done to execute the process, and they can make informed judgments about what to specify in the process design and what should be left to the discretion of the workers who execute the process. One of the most important benefits you will get from including some of the people who will operate the new process is that they will become emotionally committed to the success of the process. You won't have to get them to "buy in" or to "take ownership" when the new process is installed. The process will already be theirs because they helped design it.

The team should include people with technical expertise as well as business experience. Some team members should understand whatever technologies underlie the process, such as manufacturing, marketing, finance, and so on. In addition, the team must have expertise in one of the "integrating disciplines," the disciplines that study how to make disparate things work together. These include operations research, systems design, information systems analysis, management science, organization development, and industrial engineering.

Finally, every team needs a champion: a senior executive committed to the success of the effort. This executive should not be a regular member of the team, but rather should serve as a coach and as a buffer to the rest of the organization.

All of this may seem as though you need a cast of thousands. You don't. What you do need is a diversity of views and a diversity of interests. The team will recognize any need for additional information or help with technical problems as it goes about its work. You need, above all, good people—your best people.

The team must be empowered to do its job. That means providing training, access to people, and access to information. It means giving the team the resources it needs: money, equipment, and, most important, the time to do the job right. I'm not suggesting a blank check. What I am suggesting is that in so far as possible you should free the team from bureaucratic constraints. Team members should be able to visit work sites or other companies without long journeys up and down the chain of command to get permission. They should be able to talk freely with customers and suppliers. And they should have access to senior management when necessary.

FIGURE 6–1
Holistic Flow Diagram

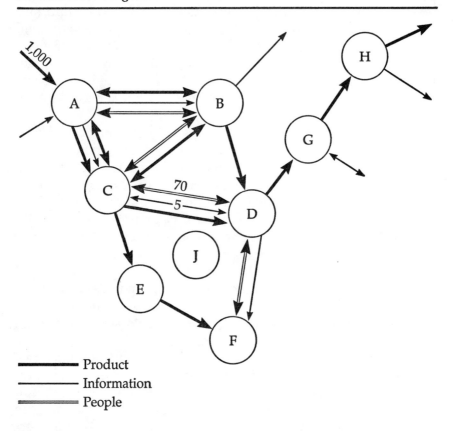

Product
Information
People

CREATING THE DESIGN

There is an analytical tool called flow analysis that you should understand because you will need it to evaluate the team's recommendations. Flow analysis is a way of describing movements between activities. It can be applied to flow of physical work such as materials being fabricated in a factory, to information, and to people such as airline pilots or design engineers. In fact, flow analysis can be applied to anything that moves.

The results of a flow analysis are usually displayed in the form of flow diagrams such as the one in Figure 6–1. The circles represent activities (receiving, machining, packing, shipping, accounting, etc.). The lines represent flows: thick for physical objects, thin for information, and double for people. The numbers are rates of flow, in whatever units are appropriate.

Let's start by looking at the flow of physical work. The process begins with an input of 1,000 units of raw material to activity A for fabrication. After it is processed by A, it is passed about among A, B, and C for further processing. Ultimately the work is sent on to D or E. D ships to G, and E ships to F. The business process ends when H sends the product to some other process or to a customer.

Information flows into the process at A and G, and out of it from G, H, and B. People move back and forth between C and D, between D and F, between A and B, between A and C, and between B and C.

We can learn a lot by examining this diagram.

- The bounds of the process are appropriate. There is a single input of material (the output of another process), and a specific output, from H. If we want to reduce the scope of the process, we can exclude H, or G and H.

- A, B, and C are very closely coupled. We should determine whether the two-way flows of product make sense. Perhaps we should combine A, B, and C into a single activity.

- Look at F. It receives inputs of material and information. It sends people back and forth to D, but it produces no output. F is clearly a candidate for elimination. (At this point, it is only a candidate because there may be other flows we have not yet mapped.)

- Nothing flows into J and nothing flows out. This activity turns out not to be part of the process, even though we initially thought it was.

- Activity E is not receiving any information from anybody. Perhaps this is appropriate, perhaps not.

- Look at C and D. Suppose C is a manufacturing plant in Hong Kong and D is a design center in Chicago. The flow of people is high, 70 trips per month. Information flow is minimal, just 5 units per month. Perhaps we should increase the information flow and decrease the people flow.

It is convenient to think of the process of creating the design as being divided into a number of discrete tasks, as described below. But keep in mind that these are tasks, not steps to be performed in a prescribed sequence: we are engaged in a holistic process, where all aspects are considered simultaneously. The task list is useful as a guide to the skills needed on the team and as a checklist to assure you that nothing is overlooked. The team can use the list as a way to get started, but be sure the team does not follow the sequence slavishly, using it as a crutch to avoid facing the complexities of the job. These are the tasks.

Build the team. A team is more than a group of people assigned to work together on a common task. Assigning people is only the first step. A real team has an intricate web of relationships among its members, relationships that must be established by the team members for themselves. Members must develop mutual trust and respect, agree on a set of common goals, and develop comfortable internal working processes for the team. Most people aren't very good at participating in teams, particularly if they have been in command-and-control organizations for a long time. You should plan to devote some time and money at the beginning to train your team members and to build the team. It will pay off handsomely.[9]

Bound the process. We discussed bounding the process as a task to be done before forming the design team. Why discuss it again? Because you have to do it again. The first bounding is done by senior executives concerned with strategic issues; their work is necessarily broad in scope and lacking in detail. It is also almost certainly wrong to some extent. As the team learns more about the process, the team must do the bounding again. And again. And again. This is not a waste of time and money. It is the price you pay for a truly insightful design, one that takes account of the intimate details of the business, broad strategic considerations, and the possibilities and limitations of technology.

Use the holistic flow analysis described above to reexamine the process as defined by senior management. Check scope (the amount of the value chain it encompasses), breadth (how it interacts with other processes), and size (how much work will be required to execute the design process). Exercise some judgment.

Is it too big or too broad? Does it cover too much of the value chain? The answer is probably yes to at least one of these questions.

If the process is too big, subdivide it into subprocesses along the lines suggested by the flow diagram. Remember that each subprocess must have an identifiable output. In the oversimplified case shown in Figure 6–1, you could split off activities G and H.

In general, each subprocess must terminate with an identifiable output delivered to a customer or an ultimate consumer. (The consumer is included, at least at the beginning of the analysis, to help identify bottlenecks and opportunities that may lie outside the boundaries of your company.) The easiest outputs to recognize are those that are delivered outside the company: widgets shipped to a distributor, a press release sent to the financial community, access to a telephone network provided to a customer.

There are internal customers as well as external customers. Suppose the overall process has been defined as "meeting customer demands for our products." You could subdivide this process into the subprocesses of soliciting the customer and taking the order (output is the order), shipping the order (output is the product on the truck), and so on.

You could specify a business process that ends with delivery of a production plan to the factory superintendent, who is the customer in this case. You could specify as a business process any set of activities that produces any identifiable output. In the end, you will do exactly that as part of the flow analyses described below.

Analyze process activities and flows.   This is a continuation of the flow analysis that was started to bound the process, in ever-increasing detail. Processes are divided into subprocesses, and the subprocesses are in turn divided until each reaches some kind of elemental state, where further subdivision makes no sense.

In a sales department, "check warehouse stock" might be an element. In a manufacturing activity, an element might be "paint the product." One could analyze the painting activity itself in the tradition of Frederick Winslow Taylor, but the details of the painting activity would seem to have little effect on the larger business process, so they probably can be omitted at this time. But be careful about early omissions. Maybe each part could be painted separately as it is fabricated; the "paint the product" activity might disappear.

Be sure all relevant flows are analyzed. Our example in Figure 6–1 showed flows of material, information, and people. Equipment also flows in some businesses. An airline is certainly interested in the flow of aircraft from airport to airport to maintenance to overhaul. A hauler of containerized freight must manage the flow of containers very carefully. Banks are interested in the flow of money; so are most other companies.

As the flows are analyzed, they should all be posted to the same holistic flow chart and careful attention given to how the various kinds of flows map to one another. A situation where a lot of material flows between two activities but no information is exchanged deserves careful thought.

Many tools are available to help in the process analysis.

- Computer-based graphics systems can be used to keep the flow diagrams up to date as new information is gathered.
- Critical path techniques or precedence diagrams can be used to understand the timing and interrelationships of various activities.
- A mathematical technique called network analysis may be useful if the business process under study is extremely large or extremely complex.
- Computer simulation of the process may be useful if capacity constraints are important. Some simulation programs present their results as animations that show how work flows and how queues build up in front of machines. These animations can show people outside of the design team how the new process will work, as well as provide new insights into the process itself.

Identify the critical success factors for the process. Critical success factors are those few things (perhaps three to five) on which the success of the process depends.[10] The idea is to focus efforts on improving those factors, rather than spending scarce resources on less important things. If the business process is manufacturing a high-volume price-sensitive product, say personal computers, low manufacturing costs will be a critical success factor. Another might be the ability to change the technology in the product quickly. In the automobile industry, cycle time for developing a new model is a critical success factor. So is low manufacturing cost. Within manufacturing, high quality is critical.

As you identify each critical success factor, define the metrics by which you will measure it. These should be objective where possible, subjective where necessary, but always quantitative. You will find that defining the metrics sharpens your view of the critical success factors by forcing you to be very specific about what you are trying to accomplish.

Once the flows are mapped and you have identified the critical success factors, design work can begin.

Eliminate what is unnecessary. If you find an activity that creates no useful outputs, eliminate it. This may sound cynical, and perhaps it is. But I know, and I suspect you know, that there are such activities in every organization that has been in existence for more than a few years. In most cases the activities were useful when they were instituted, but they have become obsolete as the business changed.

Sometimes a whole subprocess can be eliminated. If you look on the back of the title page of a paperback book, you may find a statement such as this:

> If you purchased this book without a cover you should be aware that this book is stolen property. It was reported as "unsold and destroyed" to the publisher and neither the author nor the publisher has received any payment for this "stripped book."[11]

It is the custom in the book publishing business for publishers to accept the return of unsold books from bookstores and to credit the stores with the full amount they paid. Apparently this publisher determined that the cost of receiving the book and returning it to stock was greater than the value of the restocked book. Rather than return the entire book for credit, the bookstore now returns only the cover, as evidence that the book has not been sold, and receives full credit. The entire book return process has been eliminated.

Simplify what is left.   One way to simplify is to minimize flows of all kinds: of materials, of information, of money, of everything. Flows do not create anything. They lengthen the cycle time of the process, they require management and supervision, and they cost money.

Decide how to organize to do the work.   You must consider several levels. In our example, activities A, B, and C are closely coupled for that business process. If they are also closely coupled for other business processes, perhaps they should be merged. If not, consider organizing a new unit to take over the parts of A, B, and C that serve this process.

Corporate strategy also plays a role. If your strategy is to have separate business units supported by a central research facility, you may find some redundancies in accounting that you cannot remove and some extra costs for travel and telecommunications between researchers and operating people.

You may want other companies to execute some of your business processes, if your corporate vision is of a high degree of excellence in a small number of business processes.

New airlines often contract with established carriers to provide maintenance service, handle baggage, and book reservations. Even some of the largest airlines use outside contractors for catering, having decided their core competencies did not include food preparation. The automobile manufacturers decided long ago not to invest their resources in retail sales, so they franchise others to sell the cars they manufacture.

Discover information needs and opportunities.   This is the topic of our next chapter.

SPECIAL DESIGN CRITERIA FOR A FEDERATED ORGANIZATION

Business processes are different in a federated organization than in a hierarchical one. They must support empowered workers and enhance local autonomy even as they provide mechanisms for central monitoring and ultimate control. The design team should pay special attention to these criteria:

- Reliance on individual skill and knowledge. Many activities can be carried out better by people than by machines; there should be no automation for automation's sake.
- Maximum local control of activities. The internal structure and work of a given unit should be determined largely by the workers in that unit, so long as they produce the required outputs.
- Maximum flexibility in operations of each unit. Each worker should be able to vary his work as conditions dictate or as his abilities permit, with minimum impact on the rest of the company.
- Widespread dissemination of crucial information. Each worker should have all available information about her task, and a lot of information about how her performance affects the business process as a whole.

THE END OF THE DESIGN PROCESS

When does the design process end? In a sense, it never ends. If we apply the ideas of total quality management to the holistic design process, we should continue to try to improve every process design forever. Practically, the process should be stopped when the team finds that it can meet the requirements of all critical success factors and when newly identified improvements seem to be not very important. The goal is excellence, not perfection.

TRAPS, WARNINGS, AND PITFALLS

The most dangerous trap is misjudging whether you need evolutionary change or revolutionary change in a particular business process. Revolution is fashionable (for the moment) but disruptive; evolution is less expensive but it may not give you the leverage you need to compete.

The worst pitfall in the process design itself is building the analysis around an organizational entity rather than around a business process. There may be cases where the organization structure reflects the business process quite well. If this is true, it will become evident as the process-based analysis proceeds, and nothing will be lost. On the other hand, an organization-based analysis will miss many opportunities where process and existing organizations do not correspond.

Supervisors tend to assign as team members the people who can be most easily spared from their regular jobs. Don't allow that to happen. The team needs your very best people.

There is an inherent contradiction between starting a process design with very large scope and breadth and finishing with detailed descriptions of every work element. You should start big and shrink very quickly. Once you understand the big picture, you can figure out where to subdivide the process without detailed analysis of each segment.

Long-term programs are difficult to sustain. Divide your processes into subprocesses, and design and install the new subprocesses as they are completed. That way you can achieve visible results sooner, and enhance your chances for success.

Whatever business process you are working with will change over time. That is another reason to work with small subprocesses. With a lot of skill and a modest amount of luck, you will be able to respond to changing needs by changing only a few subprocesses.

Don't seek change for the sake of change. Any change at all carries substantial hidden costs in addition to the visible ones. Prudence dictates that you make major changes only if you expect substantial gains.

Don't become enamored with the process design process itself. The final flowchart, with its neat lines and somewhat linear flows, will look like a fine blueprint for an automated assembly line or a comprehensive management information system. Don't be fooled. The 80/20 rule applies here as well as anywhere else. A 100 percent automation solution is always wrong. Ask anyone who has survived in the information systems profession. Exercise restraint.

Merely having a good design is not enough. After the new process is installed, begin a program of measuring its effectiveness and benchmarking it with other companies.

SUMMARY

What You Must Know

- In some cases, conventional design methods will give you the answers you need; in other cases, they will not.
- Good process design requires multifunctional teams with the authority and resources to cross both internal and external organizational boundaries.
- Holistic business process design is an effective method for designing business processes that take full advantage of all relevant technologies.

What You Must Do

- Be sure that your process design teams have members from every relevant discipline, and from both managerial and operational ranks.
- Put your best people on the process design teams.
- Give the design teams the authority and resources to do whatever they need to do to follow each process to its logical conclusion.
- Prepare for disruption and change as the design work progresses and as the new process is installed.

There is nothing more difficult to take in hand, more perilous to conduct, or more uncertain in its success, than to take the lead in the introduction of a new order of things.

—Niccolo Machiavelli, 1532

Chapter Seven

Discovering Information Needs and Opportunities

An organization can get the maximum benefit from the talents and energies of its workers only if each worker has the right information at the right time. Workers at every level need access to all the conventional kinds of information: transaction processing information, planning information, and performance monitoring information. They also need information to support actions that do not result in business transactions, such as responding to customer inquiries and ad hoc decision making.

Leaders and managers need new kinds of information—information oriented toward the external world and toward the future—in addition to the traditional information oriented internally and toward the past.

Each individual must determine his own information needs, in close cooperation with others in the enterprise. Managers, information systems professionals, and other individuals can help, of course, but each individual must take responsibility for specifying his needs and for judging whether they are being met.

In the end, efforts to disseminate information widely throughout the enterprise will succeed or fail depending on whether the need-to-know mind-set can be changed.

As we observed in the previous chapter, discovering information needs and opportunities is an integral part of business process design. We discuss it separately here so that we can explore information issues in detail without obscuring the importance of process design as a whole.

WHO NEEDS INFORMATION AND WHY

People commonly refer to this topic as "determining information needs." That sounds very straightforward: There are things called *needs* that you can identify if you just look for them. This is true as far as it goes, but we want to go much farther. We want not only to identify the information required to execute a business process, but also to discover opportunities for effective use of information that have never been known before.

When Bemis entered into its new relationship with its customer, described in Chapter 6, it found it did not have the information it needed to support that relationship. The customer's primary goal was to reduce the number of its vendors. Bemis is a very decentralized company: each of its five divisions is managed separately and has its own information systems, often incompatible with one another. If the customer would have had to deal with each division separately, the whole purpose of the relationship would have been lost.

Both Bemis and its customer wanted to monitor certain aspects of the overall relationship between the two companies, and there was no convenient way to do so. Simple questions such as, "How much business are we doing together?" could be answered only by calling each division and adding up the numbers. Bemis is now building a new information system to support this relationship.[1]

For now we are interested mostly in information, rather than in information systems. Information systems are a necessary evil, often required if we are to have the information we want, but usually of little value in and of themselves. There are two exceptions, which we'll discuss below. One is called *groupware:* information systems whose primary purpose is to support group activities, rather than merely to provide information to members of a group. The other consists of mathematical modeling systems, which are important because they create totally new kinds of information.

Traditionally (which is to say in hierarchical organizations), information was hoarded. It was controlled in much the same way that classified information is controlled by government intelligence agencies: on a need-to-know basis.

> Senior executives provided division managers with the minimum amount of information that they needed to run their divisions.

Division managers told factory managers only those things that were directly related to factory operations; and so on to first-line supervisors.

Line workers were given only the information they needed to do their jobs: specifications for parts to be fabricated, customer credit limits, and so on.

Administrators and middle managers had only the information they needed to monitor and control their operations and to report upward.

Staff support workers—production schedulers, engineers, quality control specialists—were given a somewhat broader view, but only as much as they needed to do their jobs.

In consequence, only the people at the very top had any overall view of the enterprise. They were the only ones with access to the information needed to understand enterprise successes and failures, to discover opportunities, and to plan and execute new initiatives.

In the world of empowered workers and federated organizations, this is no longer sufficient. The goal is to use information (and a lot of other things) to empower workers at all levels to manage their own tasks, to make them understand their roles in the enterprise, and to motivate them to use their power to enhance enterprise performance as well as their individual performance.

Everyone in a federated organization performs all kinds of tasks, and each person needs all kinds of information, tailored to her own context. Each worker—line, staff, and executive—not only needs information to perform her own tasks, but she also needs information to organize and control her work, to make decisions about how to do her work, and to monitor and control the resources at her command. In addition, each worker needs information about the effects of her activities on the larger groups of which she is a part: her work team, her department, the company as a whole, and the community.

Don't forget the other stakeholders: suppliers, customers, the community at large. They too need, and are entitled to, information about how the enterprise serves them.

POTENTIAL USES OF INFORMATION

Determining information needs, like other facets of business process analysis, requires a mixture of common sense, business understanding, and technical skills. Discovering new needs and opportunities requires creativity in addition to the other ingredients. There is not much we can do within the limitations of this book to help people learn to be creative, but we do offer some aids. One aid is the process flow diagram described in the previous chapter. It provides a different way of looking at a business process, which might stimulate a designer to structure the process in a new way.

This section contains another aid: a list of potential uses of information that you can employ to minimize the chance that something important will be overlooked. This classification scheme (or taxonomy) has the limitations of all such schemes. It is somewhat arbitrary, reflecting my view of the world; it is ambiguous, in that some individual items might logically be assigned to different places; and it is incomplete, because we can never know what lies beyond the horizon of knowledge. Nevertheless, it is useful as a way of classifying what we know and identifying what we don't know.

Our taxonomy is organized on the basis of the uses of information, not on the means of obtaining it. The same piece of data may be used for several purposes. The same information system may (and often should) generate information for a variety of uses. Several different systems may be needed to meet a single need. We suppress these differences to focus on use of information, however obtained.

Administrative Transaction Processing

Much of the early use of computers in business was to process the high-volume, routine administrative transactions necessary to operate the enterprise: entering orders, issuing shipping instructions, controlling inventory, accounting for sales and purchases. In most companies, administrative transaction processing remains the dominant use of computers, and most information for other purposes is derived from transaction processing systems.

This is the nub of much of the difficulty we have in using information for other business purposes. Systems designed for processing administrative transactions often aggregate or define data in ways that make it difficult or impossible to use for other purposes. A transnational company may find it essential to aggregate sales of all products by country for financial reporting, but these aggregates will not be very useful to managers trying to plan marketing strategies for a single product on a worldwide basis.

A classic example of problems with data definition is the sales forecast. The financial manager usually prefers a conservative number so as not to be embarrassed by lower than predicted profits. The sales manager wants an aggressive number to motivate the sales force. The manufacturing manager wants a slightly high number so that she never runs out of raw materials. Who is right? Everyone, and each should have the number he or she needs to do his or her job.

Information about past events is subject to the same kinds of ambiguities. Recording changes in inventory is an example. When do you remove an item from your inventory count? When it is allocated to a customer? When it is sold? When it is shipped? When it is delivered? When it is paid for? Again, different answers are needed for different business purposes.

About half of all information systems departments in American companies report to a financial officer, which tends to cause the information systems department to give priority to systems that process *financial* transactions. It is obviously necessary to process financial transactions, but it is not sufficient in the competitive world of the 1990s.

Operational Transaction Processing

Operational transactions are those things workers do to execute the company's production processes: make widgets, assemble parts into a product, process a credit card transaction, pack and ship a product, and so on.

This is an unconventional category. Logically, operational transactions should be grouped with administrative transactions. We consider them separately because in many companies, particularly manufacturing companies, operational transactions have not been given adequate attention by the information systems department. Spend an hour with a plant manager and that plant's controller and see whether you think there is a reasonable balance in the information available to each.

Routine Work Planning

In a factory, this would include machine scheduling, materials inventories, information on tools and fixtures, and production requirements. It would also include advanced computerized planning systems such as material requirements planning (MRP) and manufacturing requirements planning (MRP-2).

A service business has requirements that are similar in purpose but different in detail: allocating work, among workers rather than among machines; controlling perishable inventories such as airline seats; planning production levels in an environment where it is not possible to accumulate inventories either of work in process or of finished products.

Nonroutine Work Planning

Every business activity has nonroutine aspects. Some are generated by events outside of the enterprise, such as fire, flood, or power failure. Others are caused by things that happen within the company: receipt of an unexpected large order, machine failure, worker absence, changed sales estimates, product redesign, an extraordinary delivery promise. Any of these events might require information different from the information needed for planning regular work.

Action Support

Many business activities do not produce either administrative or operational transactions, yet are essential to the conduct of business. Examples include responding to customer inquiries and complaints and confirming inventory records for crucial production plans. Business process designers often overlook these activities because designers tend to focus on tangible outputs such as a product or a report, rather than the intangible outputs such as customer satisfaction. As a result, workers lack the information to perform these activities effectively, and supervisors do not have the information they need to monitor them. For lack of a better name, I call this kind of information *action support information*.

A large professional society has a telemarketing operation that sells books to its members. The systems that support the entry of orders work quite well: They allow the operators to check inventory, process credit card charges, issue shipping documents, and so on, all while the customer is on the phone. But if a customer calls to check the status of a back order more than 30 days old, the operator must disconnect his telephone headset, leave his workstation, walk 40 feet down the hall to the file room, find and retrieve a paper copy of the original order, return to his workstation, connect his telephone, and then try to answer the customer's question. This activity occupies about 20 percent of the time of the telemarketers, yet receives almost no information systems support.

The solution is obvious once the problem has been identified. The society is planning to revise its order processing system to keep back order information on line and available to service representatives for a year. The society expects to be able to handle a 25 percent increase in volume with no increase in staff. The focus on processing the operational and business transactions had obscured this problem from the analyst's view.

Consultant David Nigrelle reports that in his experience up to 70 percent of managerial time is spent doing things other than supervising work. One manager participated in a one-month study of his work time and found that he devoted 43 percent of his time to budgets and other financial work and 31 percent to customer complaints, leaving only 26 percent available for managing the operations for which he was responsible.

In addition, line workers spend much of their time on activities that are not tracked either by the workers or by their supervisors. Nigrelle tells about the claims department of an insurance company that had not supported or monitored activities that did not generate transactions. He built a PC-based information system that assisted claims agents in organizing their paperwork, reported status of incomplete files, and measured process times. After the system was installed, customer satisfaction and service timeliness increased by over 200 percent; output volume increased by 38 percent, and operating costs decreased.[2]

Performance Monitoring

The conventional idea of performance monitoring is to keep track of workers' activities and outputs, and report them to the workers' supervisors. In an organization of empowered workers, the emphasis is quite different. To be sure, there is reporting to supervisors, but it is minimal because "supervisors" do very little supervision. Workers supervise their own work, and most of the information that formerly went to supervisors now must go to the workers themselves.

First and foremost, workers need to know the direct results of their own work: quantity of output, quality of output, and measures of mistakes and waste.

Factory workers need to know how many widgets they produced, how many were defective, how much material was scrapped. Service workers need measures that look somewhat different but are in essence the same. At Mark Travel, weekly departmental reports of errors and other operational problems are posted on the bulletin board in the data-entry department. The workers decide which issues are most important and work on them, usually without management direction.[3]

Workers need to know the causes of problems, in addition to identifying the problems themselves. Is a shipment returned because the order taker did not record the correct part number or because the customer did not understand the specifications of the part he ordered? Was the widget defective because the raw material was of poor quality or because a cutting tool was not sharp?

You will recognize these kinds of questions as basic components of management of quality. Measures of quality are included in performance monitoring rather than being segregated in a class by themselves because high-quality operations can only be achieved when measurement and improvement of quality is an integral part of the work process, rather than being something attached as an afterthought.

Workers in a federated organization need information that even supervisors do not usually have in a hierarchy. If they are to conduct their own work in the interests of the enterprise as a whole, they must be able to track the performance of the enterprise as a whole. This means giving all workers information about costs, profitability of products and product lines, profits, finances, conformance to plans and budgets, and anything else bearing on the present health of the enterprise and its plans for the future.

Bill Ward of OTR Express, an over the road trucking company, has carried this idea to an extreme by organizing his company so that each individual truck is a profit center, with the driver as manager. He provides each driver-manager with a monthly profit and loss statement for his truck, and gives each driver wide latitude in how he manages his activities. Drivers decide whether to take or avoid toll roads, schedule maintenance, and buy fuel where it costs least. Each driver shares the profits generated by his truck. Its best drivers earn significantly more than the industry average, and the company benefits from lower expenses.[4]

Large companies can gain the same kinds of benefits by sharing information with line workers. Sam Walton said:

> Another important ingredient in the Wal-Mart partnership has been our very unusual willingness to share most of the numbers of our business with all the associates [employees]. It's the only way they can possibly do their jobs to the best of their abilities—to know what's going on in their business.[5]

The advantages of providing performance information to your line workers are enormous, and the costs are modest. Your largest expense may be educating the workers to understand the information, rather than the cost of delivering it to them.

Leadership Information

In a federated organization, leaders need both less information and more information than the managers of a hierarchical organization. They need less information about the past and less information about the internal operations of the organization because line workers are largely managing their own activities.

The leaders need enough information to be sure that results are in line with expectations, but not so much that they are tempted to micromanage the enterprise. They need to escape from administrivia, and the surest way to effect that escape is to not be deluged with information about issues other people can handle.

What leaders need most and get least is information about the external world. They need to know what is going on in the marketplace beyond their own sales, and how their markets are evolving. They must be able to monitor technology, legislation, regulation, and competition, both current and potential.

Leaders need to know as much as possible about the future. They need to understand the implications of their corporate visions and the potential consequences of their strategic decisions.

Cutting out unneeded information is largely a matter of self-discipline on the part of the leaders. Generating information about the external world, and creating useful views of the future are much more complex problems. We discuss some of the tools available to help with these difficult problems in the section below called *model generated information*.

External Stakeholder Information

There are several reasons for exchanging information with suppliers, customers, and the community. One is to become a preferred supplier, a preferred customer, or a preferred member of the community.

You may be able to become a preferred supplier by giving your customers direct access to your inventory information, so they can improve their production planning. Conversely, giving your suppliers information about your production plans may make it possible for them to decrease their costs, to your mutual benefit. Keeping the community apprised of the results of your normal pollution control efforts can help build the credibility you will need if things go wrong.

Another reason to give outsiders access to your information (and your information systems) is to get them to do some of "your" work for you.

We have been using dial telephones for so long that most of us have forgotten that we are doing work which historically had been done by telephone company employees: establishing connections within the telephone network.

Ameritech is testing a system whereby large customers can reconfigure their private networks from the customers' own computer terminals, without any intervention by company employees. Customers gain control and responsiveness to changing needs. The company saves the time of its network design experts.[6]

Group Task Support

We noted earlier that the important thing is usually information, rather than the system that delivers it. An important exception to this rule is a newly developing kind of information system called *groupware*. The basic idea of groupware is to use information technology to support the interactions that are central to group performance, in addition to supplying the needed information. These systems can be very important to organizations that use team-based work groups. The systems vary from simple to extremely complex.

Some uses of information technology to support work group activities are so common that we tend to lose sight of them. Electronic mail is ubiquitous in most large organizations. Fax machines are a kind of groupware. Videoconferencing is coming into wider use as costs decrease and equipment improves. These technologies are significant in the context of information systems because each can substitute for conventional information systems for some purposes, and each has the potential to create a substantial load on the same telecommunications facilities that are used to transmit telephone conversations and data.

One of the simpler examples of groupware is a document mark-up facility, now often included in standard word processing systems. A law firm without a mark-up facility might proceed to prepare a contract in this way. A contract specialist drafts an initial version. He sends separate photocopies for comments to a tax specialist, an environmental specialist, and a real estate specialist. Each marks up her copy and returns it to the originator, who incorporates the comments into a final document. With a document markup facility, the draft is made available to each of the other parties on her computer screen. Each appends her comments, and all the comments appear together on the screen of the originator, complete with the name of the person who made each comment. Each person can see all the other comments, as well as the final version. The groupware facilitates the interaction.

A much more complex kind of groupware is the group decision support system (GDSS). Its purpose is to make meetings shorter and more productive. A GDSS is often manifest as a computer-equipped conference room, with individual personal computers for the participants, a large-screen computer for the facilitator, with all computers connected to one another. In use, each member of a decision team has access to a variety of common data and mathematical models. He can generate cases for individual study on his own computer or pass them to the facilitator for display to the group. The group can brainstorm ideas, analyze business cases, and vote on proposals, all facilitated and mediated by the groupware system.

Group decision support systems can have large payoffs. IBM has reported that meetings conducted using its GDSS showed substantial benefits compared with pre-project estimates of time and effort using conventional meetings, based on historical data.[7]

- They consumed 55 percent fewer work hours than similar projects.
- Projects conducted through these meetings were completed in 92 percent less calendar time.
- Fewer meetings were required to complete most projects.
- Value of group time was 2.61 times greater using GDSS than group time in conventional meetings.

Group decision support systems are expensive to build and operate. A reasonable estimate is $300,000 to $500,000 to remodel a room, acquire and install computer hardware, and acquire and install the required software. One or two full-time support people are needed. But you don't necessarily have to build your own. Some companies and some universities have GDSS facilities available for rent as needed.

The important thing to remember about groupware is this: Information technology can be used in many ways to support the

activities and interactions that are essential to the effective operation of work groups and teams. Be aware of this as you design
your business processes.

Model Generated Information

Model-generated information does not fit neatly into our taxonomy. The taxonomy is based on the uses of information, and
model-generated information can be used for each of the purposes listed above. We consider it as a separate topic in this discussion because you may not appreciate how useful this kind of
information could be in your business.

Most of the information used to operate and manage a business is computed using elementary arithmetic. Annual production is the sum of daily production for a year. Inventory is initial
inventory plus purchases minus sales. And so on. An individual
could do the computations by hand if there were not so many of
them. Needs for this kind of information are relatively easy to detect because most people know what can be achieved with accounting and other arithmetic techniques.

Sometimes, very useful information can be developed using
complicated sets of formulas called mathematical models. There
are many different types of models, based on different kinds of
mathematics: linear programming models, statistical decision
theory models, and simulation models are just a few. All of them
use mathematical equations to describe a part of a business problem, allowing human decision makers to concentrate their efforts
on the parts too complex to be described by mathematics and
computed with computers. Here are a few examples.

Many banks and credit card companies decide whether to issue credit cards to new applicants based on computer "scoring"
of the applicant's credit history and answers to questions in the
credit application. Applicant characteristics (job tenure, salary,
home ownership, etc.) are compared statistically with similar
characteristics of people known to have good and bad credit his-
tories. Scores are computed that represent the likelihood that the
applicant is a good credit risk. High-scoring applicants are
granted credit, usually with no human intervention. The model
compares an individual applicant with statistical norms to deter-

mine credit risk; human decision makers decide how much credit risk they are willing to accept by setting a cutoff score for acceptance.

Another kind of model, particularly useful to senior managers, is the scenario generator. The basic idea is to construct a set of mathematical equations that mirror real world relationships, say among regulatory policies, education, and product usage. Managers can then vary the assumptions about regulatory policy and education to see the effects on product usage. (This is what econometricians do on a much grander scale when they predict the effects of tax policy on economic activity.) Predictions generated by these kinds of models usually aren't very accurate numerically, but they often correctly predict the direction of trends. For many business purposes, knowing the trend is far more important than numerical details. The computer model determines the mathematical consequences of changing assumptions; the human decision maker decides which assumptions are realistic and which consequences are important.

The city of New Haven, Connecticut, began a needle exchange program late in 1990 to combat the spread of AIDS among intravenous drug users. A monitoring system provided the basis for a mathematical model of AIDS transmission. The model showed that the program resulted in a 33 percent reduction in the infection rate for those who participated.[8]

Model-generated information can provide very large benefits in a wide variety of contexts, from securities trading to oil refinery operation to evaluation of corporate strategies. Building mathematical models is a specialized skill. Its practitioners are called management scientists, operations researchers, "rocket scientists" (in the financial community), quantitative analysts, and many other things. You should make it your business to find out what they do, and how they can help you.

Expert systems provide another kind of information, similar to model-generated information. The difference is that mathematical models of the type described above are representations of the business activities being modeled: The equations depict the chemical reactions in the oil refinery or the probability that a homeowner will pay her bills. Expert systems take a different approach: They model the thought processes of experts as they make decisions and record those thought processes so a nonexpert can emulate them later. Expert systems can be useful in situations where we don't understand a business problem well enough to build a mathematical model of it.

Expert systems are used by a number of banks to help make credit decisions for small commercial loans. Typically, a bank does not have enough data to build a statistical model similar to the ones used for credit card decisions, and the revenue potential of a small commercial loan does not justify the attention of a senior loan officer. The expert system guides a junior loan officer through the evaluation process in the way that a senior loan officer would carry it out.

There are undoubtedly uses of information not included in this list, some of which are specific to your business. There will certainly be new ones invented by the time you read these words. Watch for them, and incorporate them into your own list of important uses of information.

A CHECKLIST FOR FINDING INFORMATION OPPORTUNITIES

This checklist should be used as an integral part of business process design, whether the design is for evolutionary change or revolutionary change. As each business process and each activity is identified, ask these questions.

- What information do we need to operate and administer this activity, and where can we get it? What nonessential information would help?
- What information do we need to plan this activity, and where can we get it? What nonessential information would help?
- What information do we need to do the things necessary to support this activity, and where can we get it? What nonessential information would help?
- What information do we need to monitor and control the performance of this activity, and where can we get it? What nonessential information would help?

- What information do the business leaders need to monitor the enterprise and plan for its future, and where can we get it? What nonessential information would help?
- What information should we provide our outside stakeholders about this activity, and what information should they provide to us?
- What opportunities do we have to generate entirely new kinds of information to help us do business?
- How can information technology of any kind support our activities?

Each worker is the best judge of his own information needs. Start by having each worker ask these questions of himself. Then ask the people around him: team members, suppliers, customers, other stakeholders, and senior managers. Then have the individual correlate the results. This is not an easy task. Nearly everyone will need some training to learn to do it well.

The answers to these questions are input to the process design. You will find that the accumulated amount of information identified as "needed" will be staggering—far too much to use. That's fine. The design process will weed out the duplications and irrelevancies. Common sense can then be used to reduce the requirements to a reasonable size.

TRAPS, WARNINGS, AND PITFALLS

It will be very difficult to overcome the need-to-know mind-set. You must turn this completely around. The rule must be that the burden of proof is on the person who wants to limit the distribution of information.

There is some specific information which any company must restrict to a few employees: new product plans, plans for acquisitions and divestitures, and so on. But there is no sense in restricting access to corporate strategic goals such as increasing market share to 35 percent, or improving customer service. If your employees don't know your strategy, how can you expect them to support it in their daily work?

Many people will be asked to collect data on behalf of others, data for which they have no need in their own activities. They will resist collecting this data until they learn that it is in their own interests to do so.

Don't try to collect "all of the data". Because our process for determining information needs is so all encompassing, the people involved may have a tendency to want to collect all information about everything. Limit what you collect to items that have immediate use, or known future use. But be sure your new information systems can deal with additional information needs easily.

There will be claims that increased collection and distribution of information is too costly. This is usually a false issue, raised by those who do not want to collect data for others or those who want to keep it for themselves.

SUMMARY

What You Must Know

- Each individual must determine his own information needs.
- Both workers and leaders will need wider access to existing information systems.
- Needs for new kinds of information will lead to demands for new information systems.
- There will be profitable opportunities for you to supply information to outsiders and for you to receive information from outsiders.

What You Must Do

- As you design business processes, take the time to investigate all possible uses of information and information technology, rather than limit yourself to determining minimum information requirements.
- Provide the education, the training, and the time for each individual to analyze his or her own information needs.
- Develop a culture in which information is a corporate asset, rather than individual or departmental property.

III

GETTING THE INFORMATION YOU WANT

Most information is delivered to workers by means of information systems built by companies for their own use. The process of building an information system depends for its success on the joint efforts of the people who will use the system and the information technology professionals who build it. The process is elaborate, tedious, and slow. Many companies are trying to speed it up, with only modest success so far.

The overall needs of a company for information cannot be met by a collection of individual information systems, no matter how well designed each may be. The systems must be designed within a framework (an architecture) that facilitates exchange of data between systems and encourages multiple use of resources.

Despite the rapid advances in information technology, there are still significant limits to what is practical in a business setting. Some of the limits are technological, but many are human and organizational. It is essential that you validate your information technology strategy against all these limits before you try to implement it.

People and organizations must change to reflect their new roles and responsibilities. Information technology professionals will assume new roles in the corporation of the 1990s, and they will need new skills to play these roles effectively. So will users of the technology. Current information technology organizations will be split into two parts: the part that serves users directly will be moved near to or into user departments, while the part that serves the users indirectly, by supporting the IT professionals, will remain as a separate organizational unit.

The people who will have to change the most are two senior managers. In many companies, the senior information technology manager will have to become the chief information officer (CIO), a member of the senior management team with both general management skills and a deep understanding of the technology. The chief executive must learn to appreciate the potential of information technology to enhance the company, and must support and enable the CIO to do her job.

Chapter Eight

The Role of Users in Building Information Systems

Most information is delivered to users by means of custom-built information systems. Users must understand the process of developing new information systems because substantial user participation in the process is essential for the success of the development effort.

Most computer application systems are developed using one or another variation of a methodology called the systems development life cycle (SDLC). This methodology is based on the idea of a project organized in discrete segments. Each segment is bounded at the beginning by specific predecessor segments and bounded at the end by delivery of prespecified items such as computer code, test plans, documentation, and finally, a complete system. The SDLC is cumbersome and slow, but it has one advantage: It works.

In recent years, other ways of developing systems have been invented. Some, like computer-aided software engineering (CASE) seek to automate parts of the SDLC process. Others make major changes in how some SDLC tasks are accomplished, but in both cases the resultant systems are essentially the same as those developed using SDLC.

It is not necessary to build an information system to meet your information needs. You can purchase a standard system from a vendor or have one built to your own specifications by a contractor. But regardless of how you acquire a new system, substantial user involvement is required if the system is to be a success.

After a system is deployed, users have continuing responsibility for deciding when and how to modify it to meet changing business needs.

Information systems called *applications*, or application systems, are the next link in our chain from identifying business needs for information to supplying that information to those who use it to operate the enterprise. In this chapter, we examine the ways in which application systems are built or otherwise acquired, from the points of view of both the users of information systems and the senior managers who provide resources for them.

THE SYSTEM DEVELOPMENT LIFE CYCLE

Since the beginning of the use of computers in business, most application systems have been custom built for specific users by professional information technologists. This process, called *system development*, is lengthy and complex. We discuss it here in some detail so that you will know what is required of someone who commissions a custom-built system and have a sense of why IT professionals do things the way they do.

One method of building information systems has dominated the field for more than 20 years and will probably continue to do so for some years to come. It is called the system development life cycle (SDLC). As we shall see, SDLC has serious limitations, but no new methodology has emerged as a leading candidate to displace it. Rather, SDLC is undergoing a gradual metamorphosis into a more useful and flexible form. We will look first at traditional SDLC and then examine why and how it is changing.

The motivation for developing the SDLC methodology was simple: survival. Every information technology professional with more than a few years' experience is familiar with one or more major disasters in system development, either through personal experience or close contact with others who have had personal experience. I define a *major disaster* as the expenditure of millions of dollars and years of time trying to develop a system, followed either by total abandonment of the effort or by setbacks and delays causing project budget and duration to more than double. These disasters are less common today than in the past, but they still occur with appalling frequency.

The most recent example to receive wide publicity is the Taurus automated trading system project for the London Stock Exchange. It was abandoned in 1993 after 10 years and the expenditure of $645 million. The CEO of the exchange announced his resignation, 220 employees were declared redundant, and the contracts of 130 contractors were terminated. The failure has caused the exchange to rethink its entire business strategy.[1] These disasters are so common that one major consulting firm is marketing services specifically to control what it calls "runaway systems."[2]

Postfailure analysis has shown that many system development projects fail because specifications are changed during the course of the project, to meet changed business needs. The developers are forced to revise or discard work already completed; then, before they can complete the revisions, the specifications are changed again. The cycle never ends, and the project is never completed. SDLC was invented (or, more accurately, it evolved) as a method to help prevent this kind of disaster. It is elaborate and sometimes tedious. But it works.

SDLC is useful for building large information systems, systems that take a year or more to complete and require dozens or hundreds of people. Many small systems development jobs can be managed quite well without the burdens of using formal project management methods.

The basic premise of SDLC is that the development of a major information system is a project, rather than a process. A process, say in manufacturing or in accounting, is a set of activities that continue for an indefinite period of time, creating a sequence of similar outputs, such as automobiles or accounting records. A project is a set of activities with a definite beginning and a definite end. It is designed to create one specific result; the project is completed when the result is in hand.

The fundamental principle of project management is to partition the project into segments small enough to manage and small enough so that even very serious problems with any single segment will not jeopardize the success of the project as a whole. Here is how it's done.

- The project is divided into subprojects, each of which is defined by specific things that must be in place before the subproject can be started and specific outputs that the subproject must produce ("deliverables").
- The process of subdivision is continued until each subproject is a single task small enough to be completed in a week or so by one person or a small team.

- Each task is analyzed to determine what deliverables must be available from other tasks before it can be started and what deliverables it is to produce.
- A project plan is created that sequences and schedules the tasks so that each task is started only when all necessary prior tasks have been completed. The plan identifies those tasks that can be done simultaneously and those that must be performed in a particular sequence.
- The project is managed by controlling the initiation of tasks, and by monitoring task timetables and the quality of the deliverables.

SDLC is a particular way of applying standard project management techniques to the special characteristics and problems of building information systems. Table 8–1 shows how a typical system development project might be broken down into major sub-projects (phases) and smaller subprojects (activities). In a real project, there would be further breakdowns into tasks and subtasks.

Two standard project management techniques are particularly attractive to information system builders: (1) the discipline of never starting a task until all predecessor tasks have been finished and (2) the requirement for tangible deliverables as proof that a task has been completed. Use of these procedures goes a long way toward assuring successful completion of even the most complex information system development projects.

This assurance of completion comes at a very high price. A system is likely to be partially outdated the moment it is put into use because standard SDLC methodology requires that each phase be completed before the next phase is begun. A reasonable sized project might take two years to complete, with about one-third of that time being spent in each of the major phases. Thus, the statement of requirements would be completed 16 months before the system was finished, a virtual guarantee that the system would be at least partially obsolete on delivery, no matter how good the original analysis might have been.

There is another cost of using SDLC, less obvious but just as important in the long run: the cost of strained relations between the IT community and the community of users. Virtually all the

TABLE 8–1
Tasks and Roles in System Development

Activity	User Role	IT Role
Phase 1: Analysis		
Preliminary problem definition	Major	Minor
Feasibility analysis	Major	Major
Detailed problem definition	Major	Minor
Detailed problem analysis	Major	Major
Statement of requirements	Major	Minor
Phase 2: Design		
Input and output design	Major	Major
Data design	Minor	Major
Computational flow design	None	Major
Design of internal system interfaces	None	Major
Detailed system design	None	Major
Test plan design	Major	Major
Phase 3: Implementation		
Programming	None	Major
Program module tests	None	Major
System integration tests	None	Major
Computer operations training	None	Major
User training	Major	Minor
Documentation	Major	Major
System operation tests	Major	Major
Parallel operation	Major	Major
Transition to the new system	Major	Major

deliverables of the analysis phase and the design phase are documents—detailed written descriptions of *exactly* what is required of the system and even more detailed descriptions of how the system will meet the requirements. SDLC not only requires that these documents be created and delivered. It also requires that the users sign off on them—agree in writing that they are correct and complete. The theory is that this formal procedure will ensure that there are no misunderstandings between users and system developers. In practice, it often works the other way. Ray Dash, retired CIO of Benefit Trust Life Insurance Company, said:

By the time the approval meeting has gone on for 20 minutes or so, the users are so glassy-eyed that they will sign anything to get out of the room. The documents are so detailed and so hard to understand that the approval process is worthless. In fact, it generates more ill will than understanding.[3]

The ill will comes about because the users feel thrust into an adversarial position with respect to the information services department. They feel that these members of their own company are treating them like strangers who cannot be trusted to keep their promises, and they resent it.

THE NECESSITY OF USER INVOLVEMENT IN SYSTEM DEVELOPMENT

User involvement in the system development process is essential to assure that the system meets business needs, but users resent the requirement that they formally approve the multitude of documents that describe what the system is to do. This is not the contradiction it may seem to be. If the users are involved as they should be, the issues of correct functionality will have been understood and resolved long before they are formalized in any document and offered for approval.

The term *user* includes everyone who is involved with the authorization, design, or operation of the system. Someone must decide, specifically and in great detail, exactly what an information system is to do. The users of a system are the people best qualified to do this. If the users don't, the IT professionals will, and system effectiveness will suffer.

This doesn't mean that every salesperson or every warehouse worker who uses the sales processing system must be involved in its design. It means that the information needs of the salespeople and the warehouse workers must be taken into account, and at least one person who has personal experience with each of these activities should participate in the development process. To ensure continuity of thought and purpose, some of these users should be involved over the entire life of the project. In particular, the executives and managers who will rely on the outputs of the system cannot delegate their responsibility to see that the system does what needs to be done.

We addressed the same issue in our discussion of business process design. The difference is that here we must look at information needs from the point of view of the system that will provide them, as well as from the point of view of the business process that generates the needs. This means understanding the interrelationships between the information needs of different business processes, in addition to examining the information requirements of an individual process in great detail.

Users must do more than simply identify information needs. Table 8–1 shows the level of user involvement required for successful completion of each activity. "Major" user involvement means that the users have skills, knowledge, or organizational resources that are essential for that activity and that IT does not possess. In broad terms, users take major roles throughout the analysis phase and during implementation.

The table shows three important things about the roles of users. One is the number of activities in which users should be deeply involved. The second is the complexity and diversity of the activities. The third is that in many cases both users and IT have major roles. This means that effective communication and real cooperation between users and systems professionals are essential to development of a useful system.

We discussed the role of users in the analysis phase extensively in Chapter 6. In brief, it is the users who best understand the business and thus can best specify how information and information technology can contribute to business success.

There may be a surprise for you in the design phase. Users should work closely with IT professionals to design a plan to test the system. The reasons are these: no set of system specifications will ever be complete; and there is no way of testing any complex computer system to be certain that it is completely free of programming errors ("bugs"). The only protection against these kinds of problems is exhaustive testing of the system over a wide range of conditions, both technical and functional. The IT professionals can specify the technical situations that should be tested, such as high volumes of transactions or needs for many people to access the same data at the same time. However, only users can identify the range of business needs the system must satisfy. Some are obvious: the time it takes the system to respond to a request for information, in the context of customer satisfaction. Other needs are more subtle, such as whether the system will respond correctly to unusual combinations of events. Suppose an order is entered for millions of pieces at a price of fractions of a cent each; the system might not provide the correct total if it was designed for a minimum price of one cent, because of the way rounding is handled.

You may also be surprised by the amount of work required of users in the implementation phase, but remember our rule: users must do those things they are uniquely qualified to do. These include writing some documentation (for instance, the instructions that tell other users how to operate the system), testing the system, operating it in parallel with existing systems and executing procedures to be certain that the new system is producing correct results, and organizing and implementing the transition to the new system.

It may seem that I have prescribed a very large role for users in the process of developing an information system. I have, but it is essential that users do the things I have listed and do them well. No hard numbers are available about the correct level of user involvement, but preliminary research indicates that in a typical development project, users should allocate an average of one day of user time for each two days of IT time the project requires.[4]

As we have noted, the main complaint about SDLC methodology is that it takes too long to build a system, so long that many parts of a system are obsolete by the time the system has been completed.

The manager in charge of the development of a large information system is faced with a dilemma. Large systems take a long time to build, and the rapidly changing business environment means that information needs will inevitably change before the system is finished. If the manager does not accept changes in requirements after the completion of phase 1, the system will be obsolete the day it is completed. But if the manager does accept changes after phase 2 begins, there is a substantial probability the system will never be finished (although the manager may be).

In a standard SDLC operation, this conflict is resolved by finishing the system as originally specified, collecting a list of required changes, making them after the system is finished, and calling these changes "maintenance."

This is one reason most information systems departments spend from 50 to 90 percent of their application development efforts on "maintaining" systems that are supposedly complete.

IMPROVING THE SYSTEM DEVELOPMENT LIFE CYCLE

The shortcomings of the SDLC have been known for years, and many attempts have been made to overcome them or to design around them. These efforts have been of three general types:

- Automate all or part of the SDLC process.
- Relax some of the constraints of SDLC in an attempt to make it more responsive to changing conditions
- Design and organize systems so that each new system is small, and hence quick and easy to build.

Automate

Automation has been quite successful in improving some parts of the system development process. We have had computer programs for a long time that translate simple words such as print, store, and save into instructions computers can execute. More recently, programs have been developed which interpret much more complex commands and cause computers to execute them. The mathematical formulas in a spreadsheet are one example; the complex formatting commands in a word processor are another. Many of these individual pieces of automation have become essential parts of the way we build systems. They have helped speed the development of new systems, but not by enough.

Prototyping is a kind of automation worth special notice because it can help with one of the most intractable part of system development: determining user requirements. Prototyping is the construction of a simplified version of a system (or part of a system) with which users can experience the way the system will actually work, rather than relying on documents that describe how it ought to work. A good prototype will perform nearly all the functions of the final system that are visible to a single user, although it may lack the ability to support many simultaneous users or to perform behind-the-scenes functions such as sorting through large files or building audit trails.

Use of a prototype accomplishes several things. It helps the users understand their needs more clearly than paper documents, and it often provides a major improvement in communication between users and IT professionals. Once the user understands and approves the functions of the prototype, it becomes the statement of user needs, from which the system can be designed.

The most ambitious version of automating SDLC is called computer-aided software engineering (CASE). The ultimate CASE system would accept as input user descriptions of requirements in a language resembling English. Its output would be an information system, complete with computer programs, operating instructions, documentation, and all the other components of a complete system. The gains would be enormous. Once system functionality had been specified, a computer program would take over and create the system in a matter of hours or days, rather than months or years. The problem of changing specifications would disappear. Systems could be completed before needs changed very much. And later changes could be incorporated by changing the inputs to the CASE system and then running its programs again.

Unfortunately, CASE is still very much a developing technology. Some CASE tools work well; others do not. Not surprisingly, the CASE tools that work best are those that perform the detailed design and programming tasks; the least effective are those directed toward the analysis phase of SDLC. As things stand now, users of CASE tools must use a series of tools in succession and manage the sequence and the communication between them largely by manual methods. Vendors of CASE systems are working to solve this problem and are making good progress, but a complete solution, including robust tools for the analysis phase, seems to be some time away.

There is another problem with CASE. Even though the end product of CASE is a system that looks very much like a system developed by conventional SDLC, the CASE procedures are quite different from an IT point of view. The developers must learn new ways of looking at problems as well as new techniques to use CASE effectively. Reports about practical experience using CASE are mixed. Some companies are finding it very productive, others have yet to see any gains with it, and some have abandoned it. All report that CASE is difficult and expensive to implement.[5]

Even with CASE, users must still do most of the tasks listed in Table 8–1. They must do all the analysis tasks, although CASE can automate some of the associated record keeping and coordination. The CASE system may generate the technical portion of the test plan, but the users must generate the business portion. And the users must still conduct operations tests and parallel tests and manage the transition to the new system.

Ray Dash reflects on his experiences at Benefit Trust Life:

> The current SDLC methodology must change, and it is changing. It takes much too long to build a system. The real problem is that SDLC cannot respond to business changes because it takes from one to two years to respond to any significant change in the business.
>
> SDLC is too manually intensive. My solution is to automate it. If you have all of the models of the business in some computerized form, you should be able to change the models and have new code generated automatically. The goal is to be able to make changes in a matter of days or weeks, not in months or years.
>
> What I am suggesting goes far beyond CASE. I am proposing a system which permits business executives to change the process models and see the effects of possible automation.

Relax Constraints

One of the reasons SDLC is such a slow process is the requirement that each task be 100 percent complete before its successor tasks are started. An obvious way to speed up the process would be to relax this constraint. The trick is to do it without reintroducing the problem that generated the constraint in the first place: a constantly changing set of requirements that can never be satisfied.

Rapid application development (RAD) is the name applied to methodologies that permit some tasks that are required to be sequential in conventional SDLC to be performed concurrently, under very strict controls. We can see how RAD works by looking at the point where the analysis phase ends and the design phase begins (Table 8–1).

Standard SDLC requires all analysis to be completed before design is started. RAD begins with an overall analysis and design that specifies how the parts of the system relate to one another, without describing each part in detail. Then, as the requirements for each part are completed, design and coding begins on that part, even though specifications for other parts have not yet been completed.[6]

The basic idea behind RAD is this: after an overall framework has been established, knowledgeable users and IT professionals can make sound judgments about which parts of a system can be sufficiently isolated from one another so the overlap of phases or other activities will not cause large problems. RAD also includes procedures (and resources) to revisit previous decisions as the project proceeds, so that the process is responsive to changes even as the system moves toward completion.

RAD is working in companies today and is certainly worth considering. Success depends on highly skilled IT professionals working with users who understand and accept the fact that some specification and design work may have to be redone.

Build Small Systems

There is another way to get around the problems caused by the length of time it takes to build large systems. Don't build large systems; build small ones. One way to do this is simply to specify and design systems in smaller pieces. This may not sound very radical, but it is. Over the years we have been driven to think in terms of very large systems, largely to achieve economies of scale in use of computer hardware. The advent of inexpensive microcomputers makes large systems much less attractive.

These three ways of improving the SDLC have two characteristics in common. Each is designed to decrease the time required to develop a new system, either by automating part of the development process, by performing some operations simultaneously rather than sequentially, or by building smaller systems. Each of them may decrease the amount of work required of IT professionals. But none of them decreases significantly the amount of work required of users.

PURCHASING A CUSTOM BUILT SYSTEM

In the discussion above, we implicitly assumed that the users and the systems developers were members of the same organization. There is another way to get a custom system: have it built by an outside contractor. The process will be largely the same in both cases.

The outside contractor may be able to complete the system more quickly by assigning more people to the development project, but it is difficult to predict whether it will be cheaper or more expensive than in-house development. The contractor's people may be a bit better at the information technology in general, but they are likely to know less about the company's own technology base and they are certain to know less about the user's business problems. On the other hand, users may be less inclined to ask for changes when they are billed in real dollars rather than by interdepartmental charges.

More user participation is required with a contractor-built system than with a system built by an internal group. As with internally built systems, the users must specify their requirements in close consultation with the IT professionals. However, the buyer/seller relationship with the contractor requires that the specifications be more definite and more stable than with an internally developed system, if that it possible.

There are significant dangers in using an outside contractor to build a system that is central to your corporate strategy. If the contractor supplies all the project personnel, you will have no one within your company who understands the system in detail, and you may be unable to modify it as business needs change. You should always have a member of your own company participate in the development of an important system by an outside contractor.

Another danger is that the contractor will have learned in great detail about your business processes and how you support them with information technology. You can protect specific information from disclosure by means of confidentiality agreements, but the broad general principles will become part of the contractor's knowledge base and will be available to other clients.

USER-DEVELOPED SYSTEMS

There is one other way to acquire a custom-built system: have it built by those who will use it. This is almost always a bad idea for large or mission-critical systems.

The idea of a user building her own system is very attractive because it does away with all of the problems of communication between users and developers. Users are often quite successful in building small systems to solve local problems. But when a user builds her own mission-critical system—a system whose proper operation is essential to company success—she is assuming all the responsibilities of an information services department, without most of the resources required to fulfill those responsibilities.[7] Mission-critical systems have requirements of which most users are totally ignorant: system security, data security and integrity, software maintenance and updating to meet changed business needs, hardware and software maintenance and update to accommodate changes in information technology, change control, disaster recovery, documentation, and network and communications management, to name just a few.

PURCHASING A PACKAGE

There is another way to get some of the information systems you need. Purchase a standard system from a company that sells many copies of it (a "package"). Although we have listed it last, you should look at it first. This is by far the least expensive and most effective way to acquire an information system, if you can find a package that meets your needs. This is likely to happen with respect to universal business functions such as personnel, accounting, and so on. You can expect more and more standard packages to be available in the future.

There are many advantages in purchasing a package rather than having a system custom built for your organization.

- You can see the system actually at work, and in many cases you can get permission to test it in your own company with your own data. (This is the ultimate prototype.)
- You know the exact cost of the package in advance, although you may still misestimate the cost of implementing it in your company.
- The total cost will almost certainly be substantially less than the cost of a custom system.
- You can have the system in operation in a very short time.
- You can save your IT people to work on the strategic, mission-critical systems that you cannot purchase from others.
- Usually the vendor will provide maintenance and updates (for a fee), again allowing you to devote your internal efforts to things you cannot purchase from others.

One aspect of purchasing a package must receive very thoughtful attention. As we have seen throughout this book, the design of any information system is intimately related to the way the business operates. Our premise up to now has been that the information system is shaped to the business process it supports. When you buy a package, you must reverse the approach: You must shape your business process to the design of the information system.

There are both positive and negative aspects to this reversal. Any well-designed package will provide many facilities for customization to meet customer needs. Modern accounting packages, for example, allow users to design their own charts of accounts. Inventory management systems provide a variety of reordering schemes from which the user may select.

The most important benefit of shaping your business to the requirements of the package is that the designers of the package may know more about the business process in question than your own people. This won't be true about your core business processes, but it may well be true of common administrative support functions. A software vendor who has sold and supported hundreds or thousands of payroll packages may know more about payroll management than the payroll staff of even a large company.

Your users may not agree with this statement, and they may fight very hard for either a custom system or for major modifications in the package. You will have to decide whether to acquire a custom system based on the specifics of your own internal situation, but bear in mind that the economics favor purchase of a package by a very large margin.

Under no circumstances should you permit substantial modifications to any purchased package. You can safely add reports and analysis capabilities. Beyond that, if you are unwilling to use the package as intended by the developers, you are much better off building a custom system. Occasionally it makes sense to hire the vendor to modify its own package; it never makes sense for you to do it yourself. Here are a few of the reasons.

> Members of your technical staff will probably not have access to the basic documents that describe the system and will be unable to predict all the consequences of changes they may make.

> Your technical staff will find it extremely difficult to maintain and update the parts of the system you did not build.

> The seller will either refuse to maintain and update the modified package or will levy a very large charge to do so.

Here, for the first time, we find a way of acquiring an information system that requires less work of the users than the standard SDLC methodology. The trade-off is that the users may have to modify the way they operate their business.

USER ROLES IN INFORMATION SYSTEM OPERATIONS

When a new application system has been completed and installed, the user's next job begins: making the system work for the organization. One facet of this responsibility is the use of the system as a normal part of business operations. If the business process design and the information system are adequate for their tasks, this will happen as a matter of course. Operationally, the users can treat the information system just as they treat the other resources they use.

However, users must assume additional responsibilities with respect to information systems. A single user must "own" each system, and a single user must "own" each piece of data, in order to coordinate the constant demand for changes. There are two reasons for this:

- Most information systems serve more than one organizational unit, and most data is used by more than one information system.
- Changing business needs and changing information technology will require continual modification of systems, and continual changes in the data that is collected, the way it is stored, and the way it is used.

As a result, individual users will be constantly pressing for changes, and someone must serve as the focal point for coordinating those changes to assure that helping one user does not hurt others. A user must be in charge, rather than an information technologist, because most of these changes affect the functionality of the system, and system functionality must remain the responsibility of users.

Information system developers usually classify minor functional changes as "maintenance," along with fixing program errors and modifying the system to take advantage of changing technology. As we have noted, maintenance typically consumes from 50 to 80 percent of system development time. This represents a lot of money, and users should have a voice in how it is spent.

SUMMARY

What You Must Know

- As of this writing, SDLC is the only proven, reliable way to develop large-scale application systems, although it can be modified to make it more responsive to changing needs.

- Your applications systems will fail unless there is substantial user participation in the development process: user time equal to about 50 percent of information systems time is a reasonable estimate.
- Purchasing a package is the best way to acquire an information system, if you can find one that meets most of your needs and if you are willing to modify your business processes to conform to the requirements of the package.
- Users have a continuing responsibility to manage changes in systems that are in operation.

What You Must Do

- See that users of proposed new systems know enough about the system development process (whichever one is used) to participate in it intelligently.
- Allocate substantial time of users to the development process.
- Assign your best and brightest users to information system development.
- Have your IT department monitor the new technologies of application system development and be ready to change when the time comes.

Chapter Nine

Information Technology Architecture

Conventional, department-based information systems cannot adequately serve a federated organization, or any organization focused on business processes. A new kind of information system is needed, supported by a new set of design ideas that support cross-functional, business process-oriented information systems. This set of ideas is called application/infrastructure architecture.

Applications are the information systems that deliver information to users. The infrastructure is the base of technological capabilities on which applications are built. It typically consists of the organization's computer and telecommunications network, data that is useful for more than one purpose, the tools and standards for developing information systems to meet specific user needs, and the people who build and operate the systems. If the infrastructure is properly designed, it will enable applications to be built quickly and easily and will accommodate changes in business needs and information technology gracefully.

Difficult technical and managerial issues surround the infrastructure. These include the need to change the way systems are built and operated, managing data used by many systems, and the organizational and cultural barriers that develop around all efforts to achieve corporatewide uniformity in any significant activity. In addition, increasing the size and scope of the infrastructure will require that more resources be devoted to it, complicating problems of budgeting and cost allocation.

In the previous chapter, we discussed ways of building an information system to support an individual business process or a small group of related processes. We now address the problems of organizing and managing the entire set of information systems that support all the business processes in an enterprise.

THE NEED FOR INFORMATION TECHNOLOGY ARCHITECTURE

The ability (or inability) of information systems to interact with one another largely determines how effectively they can support cross-functional business processes and meet the needs of empowered workers. Information technology architecture is the key tool for organizing and managing information systems comprehensively over an enterprise.

An information technology architecture is the set of design criteria, implementation rules, and technical standards that governs the design, deployment, and operation of all information technology and systems in an organization. This is an unusually inclusive definition. We adopt it to emphasize the importance of proactively managing IT activities as a whole, in addition to managing the development, operation, and support of individual information systems.

All, of course, is an overstatement. There will always be a few systems and some technologies that do not conform to the architecture, for good reasons or bad. A well-designed architecture provides an orderly process for making exceptions and for monitoring them.

As we observed in Chapter 8, most information systems now in use were built to serve an individual business function or department. A manufacturing department might begin with an inventory control system and later build another system for production planning. Over time it might try to integrate these systems with one another, although even today it is rare to find a department (manufacturing or other) that meets all its information needs with a single integrated system.

In nearly every case, departmental systems stop at the bound aries of the department and typically have little interaction with the systems that serve other departments. These departmental systems have come to be called *vertical systems* or *smokestack systems* to emphasize the fact that each system is an isolated entity serving a single function in the enterprise, such as the accounting department.

Smokestack systems cannot support an organization structured around business processes. Recall our definition of business process: a set of activities that collectively produce an identifiable output. In our complex world, such an output is almost always the product of more than one business function (or department). Filling a customer's order involves sales, the warehouse, shipping, accounting, and perhaps manufacturing. In a world of smokestack systems, each department has its own information systems, and passing information between departments is difficult at best. At worst, data is created by one system, printed, and then entered manually into another system; the process is slow, expensive, and highly error prone.

We can envision a kind of "horizontal" information system designed to meet the needs of a business process, as distinguished from a vertical system designed to meet the needs of a single department. But the horizontal system would find the same kind of problems that vertical systems have, in reverse. A system designed to meet the needs of order processing would create data needed by the accounting system. So would an employee benefits system. Accounting data from these and other systems would have to be brought together somewhere; thus, horizontal systems would have the same data transfer and communications problems that plague vertical systems.

Even the business process view is too limited for a federated organization. Truly empowered employees not only control their own work within the scope of their jobs; they also plan and do their work in the interests of the organization as a whole. To accomplish this, they require information about the organization as a whole, information far beyond the business processes in which they participate directly. If production capacity is scarce, the production scheduler needs to know which customers are most important and what they have ordered. A salesperson should know which products are most profitable, as well as which ones are in short supply.

In theory, one way to get around the difficulties of communication and integration between systems would be to build a single, comprehensive information system meeting all the needs of the business. Unfortunately, this has thus far proven impossible to do.

The need to integrate information from all parts of a company has been recognized for at least 25 years. During the 1970s, it became fashionable to talk about a companywide management information system (MIS), an information system that would supply all the information needed to operate and manage an entire enterprise. After a decade of futile efforts by many companies, it became apparent that building a comprehensive MIS is simply not feasible. There was, and is, no theoretical reason why it cannot be done, but the practical obstacles have so far proven to be insurmountable. It costs too much, it takes too long, and constantly changing business needs prevent an overall MIS from ever being completed.

Smokestack systems cannot communicate adequately with one another; neither can horizontal systems; and we can't solve the problem by building a single, integrated companywide MIS.

We need some kind of structure for our information systems that will enable them to communicate with one another easily. We need to be able to build new systems and change old ones quickly, to meet changing business needs and to take advantage of new technology as it becomes useful. We need a new information technology architecture.

MAINFRAME ARCHITECTURE

We have had information technology architectures since the mid-1960s, although until quite recently the word *architecture* was not commonly used in this context. The need for some kind of coordinating mechanism arose when it first became practical to use a business computer to execute two or more programs simultaneously. The economies of scale in hardware made it very attractive to combine all enterprise computing on a single large machine, called a *mainframe*. Typically, a corporate policy would be promulgated that looked something like this: "All computing will be done on the mainframe computer(s) located at corporate headquarters. Remote terminals will be used only for data entry and local printing."

A direct consequence of this policy was the need for technical standards and administrative procedures specifying everything from arcane rules for using programming languages to such apparently simple things as rules for naming computer files to prevent duplicate names and other ambiguities. These standards grew increasingly complex over time as computers and information systems grew more elaborate. Although most of them are essential to good management of information systems activities, they constitute a major burden on the system development process and thus a major barrier to change.

Mainframe architecture does a reasonably good job of supporting the smokestack information systems that constitute the vast majority of business computing being done today. But, as we have noted above, events have overtaken it and made it obsolescent. Mainframe architecture (and mainframes themselves) will not be abandoned for a long time, because the costs of converting all applications to some new architecture would be prohibitive for most companies. Rather, new applications are likely to be done under new architectures, with bridges built to join new systems to old ones.

We will speak of the various IT architectures as though they are distinct entities, but keep in mind that at any point in time, your company is likely to be using more than one of them.

CLIENT/SERVER ARCHITECTURE

Client/server (C/S) architecture is a recent development. It is worth examining because it is likely to become the most important new architecture of this decade, and because its development illustrates some of the issues that arise as information technology evolves.

Client/server architecture is based on a very simple idea: do computations wherever they can be done best and at lowest cost, and store data and programs wherever they can be stored best and at lowest cost.

As the 1980s began, we didn't have much choice in where we did computations or where we stored data. The mainframe dominated the world of information systems. Large companies occasionally used minicomputers to support individual departments or remote locations, but this was rarely a major activity. The only real choice a big company had when it needed additional computer power was to expand an existing computer center or to add a new one in another location as a security precaution.

The personal computer (PC) changed all that. It presented an alternative to using the mainframe for computations, and many people embraced the opportunity with a vengeance. In the early 1990s, PCs began to appear that had speeds and data storage capacities comparable to those of mainframes. Data communications capabilities expanded greatly, and costs decreased. For the first time, it became practical to distribute data storage and computational activities over many machines separated by large distances.

Client/server architecture was developed to take advantage of this new opportunity in an orderly way. In general, the information systems community defines *client/server* in technical terms, probably because it is the new technologies listed above that made C/S practical and desirable. Usually, *clients* are desktop workstations that draw data from other parts of the enterprise, make computations with it, and interact with users; *servers* are computers that store data and make it available to clients who need it. A typical application might have programs and data in both the client and the server. In a C/S architecture, telecommunications facilities are generally considered part of the infrastructure, separate from both clients and servers.

A simple example of client/server (although it is not usually called by that name) is a customer using the Dow Jones stock quotation service to collect securities prices and using those prices in conjunction with a spreadsheet on his own PC. The Dow Jones computer system, accessible to many clients, is the server; the customer's PC is the client.

Many different kinds of commercial systems are being built using client/server architecture. Here is a scenario showing how an order-entry system might work under client/server. The server is a mainframe at corporate headquarters that contains inventory, price, and delivery information. The clients are PCs or other workstations located at regional order processing centers. The clients contain data about local customers and programs for collecting and recording information about a specific order. As an operator enters an order on a client machine, the system automatically obtains inventory availability and prices from the server (the mainframe), computes total cost of the order, and checks it against the customer's credit limit, which is stored in the client machine. If everything is approved, the client enters the order, decreases the customer's remaining credit availability recorded in the client machine, and sends a message to the mainframe telling it to decrement inventory, print shipping documents, and issue an invoice.

All these same functions would be performed in a conventional order-entry system; the difference is that all the data and all the programs would reside on one machine: the corporate mainframe.

When client/server architecture first came into prominence, many people felt that it would save money because computation and storage would be shifted from expensive mainframes to inexpensive microcomputers. More recently, we have come to understand that there are many hidden costs of implementing a system using C/S architecture. Client/server should make it easier to respond to changing business needs because it encourages systems builders to divide systems into smaller pieces, but it is unlikely to yield any cost savings, at least in the short term.

The technology needed to support a client/server architecture is not yet fully mature, particularly in the areas of system design, network management, security, and management of databases distributed over many locations. In addition, the people who design and implement client/server systems must learn new ways of working. For at least the next several years, these problems will constrain the implementation of client/server for many applications.

INFORMATION TECHNOLOGY ARCHITECTURE FOR A FEDERATED ORGANIZATION

It is clear that client/server architecture in its present form will not be adequate to meet the needs of a federated organization. C/S is fundamentally a way to build individual systems, rather than a way to interconnect systems. A federated organization requires all information from whatever source to be available to all workers. Thus, IT architecture for a federated organization must take an organizationwide view rather than a view focused on individual systems.

We need a new concept of IT architecture to get out of the individual system mind-set. One of the problems lies in the name itself and its connotations. *Architecture* evokes a vision of the detailed plans and specifications for the construction of a building. These include not only such things as room layouts, elevations, mechanical systems, and aesthetic and structural designs, but also exhaustive details of everything from the finishes on walls and floors to the locations of electrical outlets.

The purpose of architectural plans and specifications in construction is to constrain those doing the actual construction work to build the building exactly as the architect wants it, down to the last detail. This idea is based on the premise that the architect knows best and should be in total control. That is exactly the opposite of how a federated organization works. The goal of IT architecture in a federated organization must be to enable and empower workers, not to constrain them. (This comment applies both to IT professionals and to users of information.)

Nevertheless, the analogy with construction is rich and compelling; it just needs to be refocused. The need is not for architecture (conceptual and detailed design of one structure); it is for a framework within which architecture can be practiced. In construction, that framework is made up of building codes, zoning ordinances, and the public infrastructure of utilities, roads, and so on. We need the same kind of framework for building information systems.

The purpose of building codes is to protect us (and our successors in possession) from the consequences of our own follies: requirements for stair rails and grounded electrical outlets protect us from certain well-known hazards; structural standards prevent us from building a roof that might collapse under a normal snow load. Similarly, the information systems framework should protect us from such well-known (to IT professionals) hazards as loss of data in the event of system failure and the problems of improper operation and inappropriate modification associated with inadequate documentation.

Zoning ordinances are intended to protect us from actions of our neighbors, actions that may be in their own interests but are not in the interests of the community. A slaughterhouse in a high-fashion shopping district is not a community asset, no matter how profitable it may be for its owner. An information systems example is the promiscuous modification of data by one department to meet its own analytical requirements while destroying the reliability of the data for others who need it.

The public infrastructure is that set of facilities and services provided to the community as a whole from some central source, such as electrical service and sewage disposal. These may be items that in principle no single member of the community can provide (roads) or simply things that it is more economical to provide centrally. Infrastructure items in information systems include telecommunications facilities and programs and data used by many different parts of the company.

These are the natural monopolies so dear to the hearts of economists. As we noted about telephone service in Chapter 1, changes in technology can cause a natural monopoly to become a highly competitive business. One of the current traumas surrounding information technology is that computing power and programming skills are no longer the monopoly of the information technology professionals. Many organizations and many people are having a very difficult time adjusting to this.

If we apply these ideas to the information needs of a federated organization, we see that the key to meeting those needs is the infrastructure, and we are driven to an architecture that emphasizes its importance.

APPLICATION/INFRASTRUCTURE ARCHITECTURE

One architecture that addresses the needs of a federated organization is called application/infrastructure (A/I) architecture. It divides the components of information systems into two classes. The first class consists of only those elements unique to individual business activities and processes, called *applications*. The other class consists of all facilities and programs that can be used to support more than one activity or process, collectively called the *infrastructure*.

Applications (or application systems) are the systems that actually deliver the information we need to run the enterprise. A particular application may support a business process or a functional organization; most will serve both. Consider the example of the order-entry system we discussed in connection with client/server architecture. From the point of view of the system, the main difference between this system built using C/S architecture and a similar system using A/I architecture is that more elements would reside in the infrastructure. For example, customer data would be in the infrastructure rather than in the client. The main difference from a company point of view is that the data would be available for other corporate purposes, such as planning market strategies and assessing corporatewide credit risk.

The infrastructure in an A/I architecture encompasses all the resources used to build, connect, and support applications except those things unique to each individual application. It includes not only technology such as hardware, software, communications facilities, and programming tools; it also includes administrative procedures, standards, and people. The selection and integration of the elements of the infrastructure is a crucial part of information systems planning and design because the success of application systems depends in large measure on the capabilities and stability of the infrastructure.

Application/infrastructure architecture is another new buzzword, introduced here. I have coined it to denote the next evolutionary step after client/server architecture, which is the current approach to the problems described in the first paragraph of this section. As we shall see, A/I architecture is different technically because it requires a much clearer separation of applications from infrastructure. At least as important, A/I architecture is a managerial concept designed to meet needs of dynamic organizations in a changing world.

Client/server architecture is a way station on the road to A/I architecture. Much of the subdivision of programs and data that is required for client/server would survive intact in a migration to A/I architecture. The main difference would be that many more of the elements of each system would reside in the infrastructure.

The A/I infrastructure, by definition, includes facilities for communications between application systems. But there is much more to be gained from the infrastructure than ease of communicating between systems, provided we design it using the standard business criteria of efficiency and effectiveness and the new criteria of adaptability to business change and adaptability to changes in information technology.

Efficiency may mean gaining economies of scale by using the same resource to meet similar needs of a variety of systems. Or it may mean gaining economies of scope: using the same resource to provide a variety of different services.[1] Corporate telecommunications networks provide examples of both kinds of efficiencies.

Citicorp is gaining $60 million per year in economies of scale by consolidating more than 100 different networks into a single entity.[2] This experience is by no means unusual. Until quite recently, it was so difficult to build and manage networks to support more than one information system that many large companies found it most efficient to do exactly what Citicorp did: build a separate network as a part of each application.

Normal human speech contains large amounts of silence between words and sentences, which means that when you are having a telephone conversation, a lot of the telecommunications resources you are consuming are being wasted. Engineers have devised a number of ways to use those wasted fractions of seconds to transmit data, achieving economy of scope by simultaneously using the telecommunications resource for an entirely different purpose than voice transmission: the transmission of data.

Effectiveness means supporting the business needs of interconnectivity of applications and nearly universal access to data for the empowered workers and managers of the federated organization.

The division of IT functionality between the infrastructure and applications facilitates modification of applications, as well as providing efficient and effective systems. One goal is to make it possible to meet changes in business needs by changing the relevant applications without changing the infrastructure. Another is to be able to make a change in technology located in the infrastructure once on behalf of all applications that use the technology, with no effect on individual applications. You should be able to add a new product to an existing product line without affecting the infrastructure, although you might have to modify several applications. Similarly, you should be able to change to T-1 service (a wholesale telecommunications tariff offering) whenever increased traffic volume makes it economical to do so, without making any changes in the applications that use your network.

These, then, are the criteria by which we should judge whether a facility should be included in the infrastructure or left to the applications: efficient use of resources, effective use of resources, adaptability to changing business needs, and adaptability to changing information technology.

COMPONENTS OF THE INFRASTRUCTURE

We include in our concept of infrastructure both the technical facilities necessary to support applications and the managerial and administrative functions required to make the infrastructure effective. This unusually expansive definition is essential if we are to achieve the full economic and organizational benefits of using an application/infrastructure architecture.

The Computer and Communications Network

The computer and communications network is one of the four primary operational components of the infrastructure. We speak of computers and communications together because as time passes it is becoming increasingly difficult to determine where one ends and the other begins. Telephone central office switches are now computers, rather than the electromechanical devices they were in the past. More important is the fact that many functions that we used to think of as separate from the telephone network are becoming part of it.

Ameritech (as well as other Bell operating companies) is offering voice mail services to individual subscribers. The phone company's network switching computers take on the role of the home answering machine and augment it to provide advanced voice mail capabilities. Sophisticated users of electronic mail (E-mail) are incorporating E-mail address directories into their networks so that a user can send a message to a named recipient without knowing the recipient's physical location. In an earlier time, the directory would have resided in a computer outside the network.

Still earlier, the sender would have had to specify the physical location of the recipient, just as one has to specify a street address to have a letter delivered by the Postal Service.

From the communications network itself, we seek the capability for universal connectivity and the capability for universal functionality. Universal connectivity means that anyone can communicate with anyone else. Universal functionality means that communication can be in any medium: voice, data (at any volume and speed), images, computer-generated engineering drawings, full-motion video, multimedia, or whatever else is invented in the next 10 years.

Note that we have said the capability for universal connectivity and functionality. Providing 100 percent of everything to everyone does not make sense for any enterprise. Some people may be so remote and have such little need for communication that it will be more economical to serve them with the public telephone network than with access to the private corporate network. Needs for image transmission and full-motion video are not likely to be widespread for a while. The point is to have the ability to increase (or decrease) the connectivity and functionality of the network gracefully, with minimum disruption to the network and little or no effect on applications.

In terms of the technologies of the early 1990s, this means that a multilocation enterprise will probably have some combination of LANs, MANs, WANs, and internet connections.

- LANs are local area networks, networks that connect computers within about a thousand feet of one another, which generally means within a single building.
- The distance limitations of LANs have led to the development of a newer transmission technology called MAN, for metropolitan area network. MANs are intended for multibuilding campuses spread over several city blocks, such as research centers or hospital complexes.
- WAN stands for wide area network, which means a network connecting locations hundreds or thousands of miles apart. (Telephone companies call this long-distance service.)
- Internet connections are connections between networks. These constitute a separate and more complex technology

because they must allow for the special characteristics of each LAN, MAN, and WAN in order to operate them together.

The reason for this digression into technical jargon is to give you a sense of the complexity of the technical problems of managing an enterprisewide network. Each kind of network comes in a variety of flavors from a variety of vendors. While physical circuits and switches for WANs are usually provided by common carrier telephone companies, LANs and MANs are almost always owned and operated by their users, adding further to the network management task. Each of these transmission techniques is evolving because of technological advances and competitive pressures, and the boundaries between them are blurring. The whole world of networks is changing so rapidly that there is a severe lack of technical tools for managing and maintaining them.

The issues surrounding computers are also complex. Until about 10 years ago, the economies of scale in computers were so great that the best strategy was nearly always to concentrate as much computing as possible on a single large machine. More recently, the strategies of computer selection have become much more complicated. The advent of the inexpensive personal computer and its associated mass-produced application systems, together with decreasing costs and increasing capabilities of telecommunications, have drastically altered the economics of scale in computing.

Initially, changes in computer hardware strategy were called *downsizing* because in most cases companies were changing from large computers to smaller ones. As we have learned more about the problem (and as downsizing has developed unpleasant connotations of corporate reorganization and job loss) we have begun to call the design process *rightsizing*, which is in fact a more accurate description. But whatever we call it, it is a difficult problem, both technically and organizationally.

The most common strategy for large companies seems to be this: continue to use large computers (usually *mainframes*) to process the high-volume transactions central to business operations. These transactions may be sales in a marketing company, check clearings in a bank, or reservations in the airline industry. This may be changing. American Airlines recently announced that it is planning to move one of the functions of its famed SABRE reservation system from its mainframe computers to a network of microcomputer workstations. The application being moved is freight routing, the part of SABRE with the lowest transaction rate. However, American has said that if the new freight system works as well as expected, it may move other systems off the mainframe later. This is being done in the name of reducing costs.[3]

Many small- and medium-sized companies are abandoning their small mainframes and their minicomputers in favor of networks of microcomputers.

Effectiveness as well as efficiency (reduced costs) is driving us toward extensive use of microcomputers. Powerful computers on the desktop, easy-to-use software, and ready access to corporate data are providing end users with the ability to meet some of their own information needs without the intervention of information systems professionals. The result is often reduced technical efficiency but more effectiveness in meeting business needs.

As a consequence of near universal connectivity and inexpensive computers, the communications network will reach all parts of the enterprise, with computers of various sizes and types at whatever locations are required to meet both local and overall company needs.

Data

Data and the means of managing it constitute the second major operational component of the infrastructure. The primary reason for including data in the infrastructure rather than having it as part of individual applications is effectiveness: to make the data available to all applications and all individuals who need it.

In our earlier example, the order-entry system would retrieve data about the customer's credit status from the infrastructure (data that had been recorded previously by the credit department), and send data about the purchase to the infrastructure for the accounts receivable system, the warehouse management system, and the shipping system to use when there was need for it.

This is easy to say but hard to do well. Once data is in the infrastructure and widely available, new problems arise.

- Accuracy: We tend to think that data in a computer is accurate—the numbers are correct and that they apply to the item named. There must be computer programs and administrative procedures in place to assure this.
- Security: Who is entitled to look at the data? In a federated organization, the presumption is that all data is widely available, but there may be exceptions such as salaries, new product plans, and so on. Someone must decide what access to grant and what access to deny; someone else must implement the access decisions.
- Integrity: In the world of computers, access to data carries with it the power to change that data unless special restrictions are imposed. The process of changing existing data must be carefully managed. If crucial data is changed, there must be an audit trail showing who made the change, and when, and why.

These problems are much harder technically in an application/infrastructure architecture than they are with smokestack systems. The difficulties of maintaining data accuracy, security, and integrity increase dramatically with the number of people who have access to it and with the number of applications that use it. The managerial and organizational problems are even more severe than the technical ones. We will discuss some of them in the final section of this chapter and others in Chapter 11.

We have seen that including data in the infrastructure can increase the effectiveness of information in the organization. What it does to efficiency is less clear.

Substantial additional operating costs will be incurred when applications are separated from the data they need. Additional computer resources will be required to store the data in a form useful for more than one application. Storing and retrieving the data will be more expensive. Telecommunications facilities will be required to retrieve data stored at a distance from where it is used, which will often happen. However, there will be offsetting savings. Entering data once instead of many times and easy transfer of data from system to system will save both clerical time and the time of expensive programmers and analysts.

There is no general answer to the question of whether these savings will be greater than the additional costs associated with having the data in the infrastructure. Clearly the costs of handling data will be higher for the first applications built in this way; savings will accrue only later as other applications begin to use the same data.

The real savings will come as we achieve the goal of adaptability. There will be tangible savings as the work needed to modify systems decreases. In the long run, the benefits of providing the business with the new information it requires to respond to changing conditions will be more important than any savings in expenses.

Technical Tools and Administrative Procedures

Technical tools and administrative procedures are important but often overlooked parts the infrastructure. They are important because it would be impossible to build and operate a useful infrastructure without them. They are often overlooked by the end users (who ultimately pay the bills) because they are largely focused inward toward the information systems department, rather than outward toward the users.

The most important administrative procedure is the establishment and maintenance of standards for the tools and techniques used to build and manage information systems, both infrastructure and applications. The variety of tools and methods available to help information technologists do their work is staggering. They include:

- At least a half-dozen conventional computer languages such as COBOL and FORTRAN that are significant in the context of business. (These are commonly referred to as third-generation languages.)
- Over 30 advanced languages (called fourth-generation languages, or 4GLs). Fourth-generation languages are much more efficient for writing computer programs than third-generation languages; they also consume more computer resources when the programs are executed.
- Computer programs whose output is efficient third-generation code.

- A dozen or more variants of the system development life cycle methodology.
- Five or six different computer-aided software engineering (CASE) methodologies, each with its own set of computerized tools.
- Hundreds of prepackaged applications that require users to write no code and dozens of word processing programs and spreadsheet programs available for personal computers.
- Tools to manage the inventory of hardware, tools to manage the inventory of software (no easy task with the proliferation of PCs), tools to manage networks, and tools to manage the set of tools!

The strategy for tool selection is to use the same criteria that were used for inclusion of other elements of the infrastructure: efficiency, effectiveness, and adaptability.

Efficiency will bias us toward including the smallest possible number of different tools of each class. Many tools are expensive to acquire and maintain. All are expensive to learn and to support. As a starting point, try to get along with one or two tools of each class and expand the set only for very good cause.

Considerations of effectiveness may encourage you to add to the tool set, but be very cautious. Adding a little functionality may add a lot of indirect costs.

Adaptability to meet changing needs should also bias you toward a relatively small set of tools. The fewer tools you use, the fewer you must change.

On occasion, someone will object to a particular standard and make a compelling argument that a particular new tool is the best one for a specific purpose. That may be true, but it is essential to keep in mind the overall interests of the enterprise and weigh them against the gains of acquiring and using an additional nonstandard tool.

IT standards are made effective in the same way as any other administrative procedure. In a hierarchical organization, orders are issued, compliance is monitored, and those who do not comply are disciplined. Empowered workers will comply with standards without coercion, even at considerable personal inconvenience, when they understand how the standards serve a larger corporate purpose.

I have watched this scenario play out in two companies. Individual PC users had purchased their own word processing programs, and the company found itself with four (in the other case six) different systems. Initial efforts to reduce the number in the name of standardization were resisted, successfully. Then the information systems department publicized the costs of supporting a large number of different products and announced that it could afford to support only two. In one company, users selected two to receive support and those using the nonstandard products gradually migrated to the standard ones. The same things happened in the other company, except that it had a need for sophisticated desktop publishing capabilities, a need that standard word processors could not meet; the IS department acquired and supported an additional system for this purpose.

People and Organization

People and an organization for operating the infrastructure constitute the final major component of the infrastructure. Designing, managing, and operating a computer and communications network requires special technical skills and real dedication. We will address these issues at length in Chapter 11.

SOME CONSEQUENCES OF THE APPLICATION/INFRASTRUCTURE ARCHITECTURE

The adoption of an application/infrastructure architecture has major implications for the information technology department and for the people who work in it. Each smokestack system is the center of its own world. It collects, stores, and processes its own data in its own way and reports its results according to rules established by the department that owns it. Responsibility for designing, building, and maintaining the system lies with the group of analysts and programmers assigned to it, and responsibility for operations lies with the computer operations department.

The process of developing a system is intrinsically different under an A/I architecture. The designers must abandon the goal of building a "complete" system and learn to assemble a useful application from pieces they do not control. They must learn how to assign processing among diverse machines, how to coordinate the processing among machines, and how to store and retrieve data at scattered locations. As programmers have begun to use client/server architecture, they have found that they need a quite different mind-set, and many are finding this difficult to achieve. It will be even more difficult with A/I architecture because more components will be in the infrastructure, beyond the control of individual programmers.

Data management becomes much more complex when data is no longer the property of a single system. Someone must manage the data, someone whose responsibilities include data for all applications. The data manager is faced with a number of managerial and technical problems.

- Who should collect data needed by more than one system? In many situations, there is a choice. Which department should bear the burden and the costs?

- How should the data be stored so that it is reasonably accessible to all who need it? Efficient use of a customer name and address file for mailing requires Zip code sequence; efficient use of the file for order-entry requires access by name. Using the same file to meet both needs is a little more expensive for each user, but less expensive than providing the most efficient format to each. Who should pay the extra costs?

- How should each element of data be defined when different users need different definitions? Finished goods inventory means one thing to the warehouse manager who must store it, but means something quite different to the salesperson who wants to know what is available for sale (net of inventory sold but not shipped.)

- Who can authorize or restrict access to the data?

- Who can make changes to the data, and under what circumstances?

- Who is responsible for the accuracy and timeliness of the data? This may turn out to be the most vexing question of all. When data (or anything else) belongs to everyone, it belongs to no one, and no one will willingly undertake responsibility for it.

Every one of these questions arises in the design of vertical systems. What is different is that they must now be answered in the interests of the company as a whole instead of being answered in terms of a single system.

Much of the functionality of most systems will reside in the infrastructure, putting it out of the reach of the application developers. In some cases, users may not be able to get precisely what they want. There may be standards that prescribe how data is to be presented to all users. Methods of communicating with remote locations will certainly be specified by the designers of the network.

Troubleshooting will be much more complex. Instead of examining a single system and its own data (and perhaps its own telecommunications network), the troubleshooter must look at the application, at data that is also used by other applications, and at an infrastructure that may consist of many computers and multiple networks. As a practical matter, this means that cross-functional teams of specialists will be required to solve many problems.

In general, management of the infrastructure will become more difficult as more functionality is moved into it. Reliability of the network, availability of computer power and data, and security will all be more difficult to achieve.

Finally, as more functionality is moved into the infrastructure, more costs are sure to follow. This means that the financial managers of the company will see growth in expenses that cannot be logically associated with any single business process. These expenses are liable to be labeled overhead, with all the burdens and dangers that designation entails.

SUMMARY

What You Must Know

- Conventional systems cannot meet the business needs of a federated organization with empowered employees. A new kind of system is required, one based on a new information systems architecture called application/infrastructure architecture.

- The new architecture will move a great deal of functionality from applications to the infrastructure. Managing the infrastructure will be a major challenge.
- There will be constant pressure to violate the integrity of the infrastructure in order to achieve short-term gains for particular applications.
- Building and deploying a companywide infrastructure will generate a great deal of resistance from those who want to go their separate ways.
- As the infrastructure increases in size and scope, it will consume an increasing share of IT expenditures, and these expenditures will not be associated with any specific business process.

What You Must Do

- See that you have an infrastructure that will support all your foreseeable information needs.
- Support those who seek to maintain the integrity of the infrastructure.
- Retrain your information technology people to work in the application/infrastructure environment.
- Make sure your infrastructure is not starved for funds.

Chapter Ten

Validating Your Information Technology Strategy

Information technology strategy should be tested for feasibility first by analyzing each individual strategic initiative, then by examining the strategy as a whole. Feasibility may be limited by technical, organizational, or human constraints.

Today's information technology can meet current needs to reach everyone who requires information. Moving information into and out of old smokestack systems is difficult but not impossible; it should be much simpler with new systems. There are many possibilities for improving business processes and activities by bringing more information into them and by supporting group activities. The main area where current technology is lacking is the ability to respond quickly to changing business needs.

Organizational and societal effects must be considered in evaluating information technology strategy. They may constrain information technology strategy more than technical or financial limitations.

We have discussed the development of information technology strategy, how to meet information needs, business process design, and other topics in ways that imply that you can do anything you want to do and are willing to pay for. We now examine the practical limits to what you can do with today's technology and today's organizations. It is essential that you evaluate your IT strategy and plans in terms of these limits, to be sure you are not biting off more than you can chew.

TESTING YOUR INFORMATION TECHNOLOGY STRATEGY FOR FEASIBILITY

Evaluating your information technology strategy is not really different from evaluating any other strategy. First analyze each specific proposal, then see whether they make up a rational overall program both in terms of information technology and for the business as a whole.

Here is a brief checklist of tests you can apply to each strategic IT initiative. We will discuss each in detail in the sections which follow.

- How well does this strategy meet the overall information needs of the processes it will support?
- Does it use proven generic technologies, rather than new technologies, wherever practical?
- Are there serious constraints of people or other resources within your own organization?
- Are customers and business alliance partners willing to use the new information technology you propose?
- Are there societal constraints or governmental restrictions on what you are planning to do?
- Do the underlying information technologies impose any limitations?

Evaluate the risk of each individual strategic thrust and decide whether the potential gains are worth the risk. The goal is not to eliminate risk. It is often a good idea to take a risk, if success will give you a competitive edge. The goal is to understand the risks in advance so that you can prepare to deal with them.

For the entire strategy, or the portfolio of major initiatives:

- Determine the extent to which your IT strategy supports your corporate strategy.
- Determine the extent to which your IT strategy supports your organization's critical success factors.
- Evaluate the overall risk and the plans for dealing with it.
- Evaluate the overall organizational disruption that will be caused by the strategy and the plans for dealing with it.
- Evaluate how the strategy will affect your other constituencies and the plans for dealing with them

MEETING BUSINESS NEEDS WITH TODAY'S INFORMATION TECHNOLOGY

The capabilities and limitations of today's technology determine what we can and cannot do to meet our business needs. We can characterize these capabilities and limitations in terms of four attributes: reach, range, depth, and change.[1]

Reach is the combination of the geographic extent of an information system and the total number of people who have access to it.

Range is the extent to which information is shared across systems, across organizational boundaries, and across hierarchical levels.

Depth is the extent to which information penetrates individual business activities and processes.

Change is the ability of an information system to respond to changes in business and technology.

Reach

It is technically feasible to extend the reach of your information systems to any part of the developed world and much of the rest of the world, to as many individuals as you wish, both inside and outside your organization. There are two technical limitations.

1. You cannot transmit very large amounts of data by wireless.
2. Establishing and operating a large, geographically dispersed telecommunications network requires a high order of managerial and technical skills.

Information networks that cross national boundaries may be subjected to significant political and economic constraints; they may also pose technical problems associated with differing technical standards.

Range

The range of information available to you may be severely constrained by your old smokestack systems. It is possible to connect smokestack systems with one another and with new systems by building bridges designed for this purpose. (These are often called *front ends* by information technologists.) These front ends are difficult to build, and you may be unable to obtain all the functionality you need, particularly real time responses.

With systems built under an application/infrastructure architecture, all data will be available for all purposes. However, the total amount of data you have may be more than current technology can handle economically.

Depth

Information technology could probably be used in every business activity from the executive suite to the shop floor. Whether or not each use would be beneficial must be determined by careful analysis of each situation.

It is practical to supply every individual in the enterprise with whatever operational information is appropriate to his job.

It is practical to give every worker access to a personal computer and access to a corporatewide telecommunications network.

It is practical to give every worker access to any corporate data stored in devices attached to the network and to have her obtain information for her own use without the help of IT professionals.

Commercial systems are available that support work group activities, such as scheduling, annotating documents, and encouraging good work practices. The limitations on the use of these systems are no longer technological; they are human and organizational.

It is practical to build information systems to support those who make operational decisions, provided those systems deal with well-structured situations, such as production scheduling, inventory control, or physical distribution.

It is much more difficult to supply information system support to less structured work group activities, such as strategic planning. The best systems currently available, called group decision support systems, require specially equipped meeting rooms, extensive preparation of data and analytical computer programs, and experienced meeting facilitators.[2] As we noted above, these systems are very expensive to build and use.

Change

The ability of information systems to respond to changing business needs is one of the key determinants of how well information technology can support corporate strategy.

It is appropriate to rely on making minor changes to information systems (maintenance) to support minor business changes, provided sufficient people are allocated to this work. However, some systems are so old and have been modified so much that further changes tend to do more harm than good. These systems must be left alone or replaced.

Creating new systems when they are needed is a much more difficult problem. As a practical matter, with today's methods, the minimum time necessary to develop a new system is about one year after the need has been identified. Development time of two or three years is not unusual, much as we may wish it were. It is unrealistic to plan to deploy a new system in less than a year. If it is a particularly large system, count on two years or more.

One way to support changing business needs is to have the users of the system build it themselves, employing some of the new tools such as fourth-generation languages and database management systems. This procedure bypasses the queue for new work by the information systems department and may decrease actual development time. (This raises an interesting question. If users can save development time by using these advanced tools, why can't IT professionals use them and obtain similar results? We will deal with this issue in Chapter 12.)

It is practical for users to build an information system if it is solely for their own use, if it is relatively small, and if they accept technical guidance from IT professionals. This guidance is crucial: It is always a mistake for users to build systems in isolation from other IT activities in the company.

TODAY'S TECHNOLOGY BASE

The information systems we need to run our enterprises are made possible by the capabilities of some basic components. We examine these components in terms of the practicality of using them rather than in terms of costs because costs are dealt with as part of the value analysis described previously. In the next section, we discuss some ways these components can be used to provide generic IT capabilities—capabilities useful to many companies in a wide variety of situations.

Microprocessors

The microprocessors that are at the heart of all information technology continue to increase in capability and decrease in cost and physical size. Products are already available that can do all the things described in the following sections. The practical consequence is this: You can have as much raw computational power as you will need, whenever and wherever you need it, at reasonable cost.

Data Entry

Many new and useful devices have been developed for entering data and instructions into computer systems, in addition to the conventional keyboard.

Pointing devices allow the user to indicate a specific location on the screen to the system, say to select the name of a program from a menu of choices. A mouse does this by moving an arrow or similar indicator on the screen to the desired location; when the location is reached, the operator presses a button to select that location and transmit it to the system. The same functions can be performed by other devices in situations where a mouse is inconvenient. A touch screen performs the same functions as a mouse. It looks like an ordinary computer display tube, but it has special electrical circuits that detect the touch of a finger, calculate the location of the touch, and transmit the location to the system.

These are mature and reliable technologies. They are particularly useful in situations where only a limited amount of information need be supplied to the system by a user.

Another alternative to the keyboard is the pen-based computer. The user writes on a special pad with a stylus. The pad captures as an image of what is written and sends it to a processor, which analyzes the image and translates it into characters (letters and numbers) for further processing. The software for the translation process is not fully effective at this time.

Pen-based computing is still in the early stages of development. It may be useful in limited situations, but it would be risky to base a major information system development on pen-based computing at this time.

Data is often collected automatically as part of a business process and sent directly to a computer. The bar code scanners used in supermarkets are one example. The use of bar codes and scanners has moved far beyond supermarkets, to control inventory in warehouses, to route baggage in airline terminals, to record the locations of railcars, to track work in process in factories, and for a variety of other purposes.

Bar code technology is a reliable base on which to build an information system.

Scanners capture images of ordinary paper documents (text, numbers, photographs, etc.) and store them as images in computer memory. They are available with a wide range of capabilities, from those suitable for occasional use with a PC to sophisticated machines with automatic paper feeders that can scan documents at rates of hundreds per minute.

Scanners are reliable and effective means of capturing data in image form for applications involving almost any amount of data.

For many purposes, the best way to enter data into a computer would be by talking to it. The ideal system would be one where anyone could speak into a microphone and have accurate text appear on the screen, ready for further processing. Current systems seek this goal, but have not yet reached it.

Speech recognition systems can function adequately in limited situations. A quality inspector can use a vocabulary of up to several hundred words to route a part. A physician can record patient chart information, provided the system is "trained" to recognize the particular physician's voice, and provided she uses a preselected vocabulary of words and speaks with distinct pauses between words.

Speech recognition technology is currently in use in limited situations, and the limits are being stretched every day. Even so, it is unlikely that general purpose systems that recognize continuous speech will be commercially available soon.

Data Output

It is much easier to get information out of computers than to put it in. The capabilities of conventional printers and plotters are increasing rapidly. Direct printing of color is becoming more common and less expensive. Computer-generated voice output is in use in many situations, such as telephone company directory assistance activities and inquiries about credit card transactions generated by touch-tone telephone signals.

There are no important technical limitations that would interfere with your plans to use any kind of output from an information system.

Data Storage

As with microprocessors, data storage capacity has increased enormously over the past decade, while units costs have declined. On-line storage systems with gigabytes (billions of characters) of capacity are available for PCs and workstations. Terabyte (trillions of characters) storage devices are available for mainframes and large networks. These sizes are more than adequate for most numerical and text databases. Image storage is a different matter. Without data compression, document images require about 11,000 bytes per page, photographs require about 275,00 bytes each, and five seconds of full-motion video requires about 10 million bytes. Data compression can decrease storage requirements by 2 to 10 times, depending on the nature of the data.

You can plan to store on-line any amount of numerical and text data you are likely to need for new applications.

Large image-based systems using documents that contain mostly numbers and text are practical. As the proportion of photographs increases, capacity may be strained.

Systems requiring on-line storage of large amounts of full-motion video are impractical at this time for ordinary business use.

You can store an unlimited amount of data off-line on magnetic tape, provided you maintain a directory to help you find the data when you need it.

Telecommunications

Telecommunications relies heavily on two technologies: microprocessors and optical fiber. Fiber is following the same path of increasing capability and decreasing costs as microprocessors, and so is telecommunications as a whole.

The combination of satellites and *wirelines* (the term includes both fiber and conventional copper wire) has made telecommunications access ubiquitous in the developed world, and it is rapidly becoming so elsewhere. The transmission capacities of fiber are almost incomprehensibly large: One fiber cable of 26 strands can transmit 150,000 simultaneous conversations or 6,000 video channels, or any combination of the two. Improved electronics will soon increase the capacity of that same fiber cable to 32 million conversations or 320,000 video channels. Intelligent electronics and innovative software are also increasing the capacity of conventional copper wires, although not to the same degree.

It is practical to connect any set of locations (up to tens of thousands) with any amount of telecommunications capacity that is required for an information system.

Wireless communication is limited in principle by the size of the electromagnetic spectrum, although this limitation is not as severe as we had thought in the past. Engineers have developed many innovative ways to transmit more information through the electromagnetic spectrum. One way is to use the "spaces" that exist within most transmissions to shorten transmission time, as with the compression of the white spaces in a fax transmission. Another way is to mix two or more simultaneous transmissions, with each using the spaces left by the others. This process, called *multiplexing*, can be used for voice, data, video, or any other digital transmission. A third way is to confine a transmission to a small geographic area so that the same portion of the electromagnetic spectrum (the same frequency) can be used simultaneously by people in different geographic areas.

Cellular telephone systems are based on these ideas, combined with some others. (A *cell* is the limited geographic area over which a transmission is carried by wireless before it is transferred to a wireline circuit.) The current cellular frequencies are beginning to become congested in major metropolitan areas. An advanced version of cellular technology, called personal communication systems (PCS), is being developed using much smaller cells. This allows more users to talk simultaneously and lowers power requirements for individual portable phones, resulting in smaller instruments. The shirt pocket phone will become a reality with PCS in three to five years.

> You can build information systems that involve large numbers of portable phones and portable computers, provided you limit wireless transmissions to small amounts of data (say data at rates generated by a keyboard). Reliable transmission of data at rates 10 to 50 times greater is difficult but possible.
>
> You may not have to build your own network; several public carriers provide wireless data transmission on demand.
>
> Private wireless transmission (as opposed to public broadcasting) of large amounts of data or video images can be done from an engineering point of view, but it is impractical politically: it is unlikely that scarce spectrum would be allocated for this purpose.

Portable Computers

Portable computers with capabilities equal to high-end desktop machines are now available from a number of manufacturers. Many have built-in fax boards and modems for communicating with other computers; some have built-in cellular phones. The only practical limit on their use is battery life, which varies from two to eight hours, depending on use and on whether the display is monochrome or full color.

It is practical to build large information systems that depend on portable computers if data transmission is limited to low speeds and if operation between battery charges is not more than a few hours.

Special Purpose Computers

Over the past few years we have seen a wide variety of special purpose computers developed for particular applications in specific companies. One of the most visible is the "clipboard" on which the Federal Express driver records pickups and deliveries. At pickup, she scans the bar code on the waybill that represents the waybill number and enters the Zip code of the recipient using the keypad on the clipboard. This information is transmitted by radio to Fed Ex's central computer, where it is used to route and track the package. Fed Ex knows the exact location of the package at all times until it is delivered, when the driver asks you to acknowledge receipt by signing your name on another clipboard. The signature is recorded digitally and transmitted to the central computer to complete the record of the transaction.

McKesson Corporation supplies special purpose computers to its drugstore customers, which they use for taking inventory and automatically reordering. When the order reaches McKesson's warehouse, it is transmitted by radio to another special purpose computer that the order picker wears on his arm. The order is displayed on a screen, the items are picked, and a laser scanner checks bar codes on the products against the order as entered.[3]

It is practical to build systems based on special purpose computers, provided the number you need is large enough to justify the development costs. A few thousand units is probably the minimum quantity that makes sense.

General Purpose Software

Another very powerful element of today's information technology base is the ability to design and build truly general purpose software (packages). Some of this software is used as it comes from the vendor to meet a generic need; word processors and presentation graphics programs are examples. Other packages are designed to permit extensive customization. General purpose database management packages are regularly used at the heart of major operational systems. Effective accounting systems can be built from packages that allow each company to design its own chart of accounts. There are dozens of other examples.

> You can use general purpose software packages to meet a variety of company needs, often with substantial savings of money and time to implementation.

GENERIC USES OF TODAY'S TECHNOLOGIES

Some uses of information technology are generic: Either they are useful in many different organizations without modification, or they can be used as parts of larger information systems, or both. As a result, commercial products are available that offer many of these capabilities. These products are always less expensive than building a similar system in-house and they usually have more capabilities.

The various forms of telecommunications are generic uses. Voice communication systems (telephone systems) are so common that we often don't even think of them as information systems, even though they are the most ubiquitous and most used information systems we have.

Voice mail with its related automatic receptionist functions—recording verbal messages and directing them to specified recipients—has become so inexpensive and easy to install that the technology has outrun our ability to use it effectively.

> Voice mail systems are practical so long as they do not alienate their users (many of whom are your customers) by locking them into endless chains of choices and preventing them from talking to human beings.

Electronic mail (E-mail) is the occasional transmission of information from computer to computer. E-mail is usually text and sometimes files of data. This is different from the routine transmission of data that is part of a business information system, such as financial data from a sales entry computer to an accounting department computer.

E-mail is a mature technology, usable in companies of any size. There are a number of private E-mail networks with tens of thousands of users. Public E-mail services are offered by many vendors.

Transmission of moderate amounts of text and small data files is practical in any E-mail system.

Transmission of large amounts of text or large data files (such as computer-aided design drawings) is practical provided the network has sufficient capacity.

Rapid transmission of images is practical if the network has sufficient capacity. Even a low-capacity network can transmit a high-quality image if given enough time.

There are important behavioral and organizational issues of which you should be aware if you plan to install E-mail. Northwestern University researcher Linda Brennan has studied and worked with E-mail in a number of companies. She says:

There is an aura of informality which surrounds E-mail; people seem willing to express themselves in E-mail in ways which would otherwise be uncomfortable. This can have many positive effects, such as mitigating group dynamics and encouraging member participation or flattening the organizational hierarchy and making executives more accessible. However, this same informality can encourage people to express themselves in ways which would otherwise be inappropriate, leading to hostile and emotionally charged electronic exchanges.

E-mail can also exacerbate the general information overload faced by most professionals, with the proliferation of electronic "junk mail" and the undiscriminating use of distribution lists. The timeliness and convenience of E-mail may be lost because of others' ineffective use of the tool.[4]

Full-motion video teleconferencing is commercially available. Costs are decreasing drastically as less expensive terminals come onto the market and as the communications engineers invent ways to minimize needed transmission capacity.

Videoconferencing can be an effective substitute for face-to-face meetings, provided the proper groundwork is laid. A videoconference is intrinsically different from a face-to-face meeting. All participants are not visible at all times, and much body language is lost. It takes time and effort to learn to participate effectively in a videoconference. Best results are obtained when the conference group also meets in person from time to time.

Image-based applications are being developed to serve many different business needs, from processing insurance claims[5] to managing legal documents.[6] Scanners can collect images of documents rapidly and efficiently, but the utility of these images depends on the application.

If the system uses the images *as images*, scanners can be reliable, effective tools. The success of an image-based application depends on redesigning the business process it supports. Experience has shown that simply using images without changing the process is more likely to increase costs than to decrease them.

High-speed scanners can be used to capture text and numbers from images for further processing. The software for this task (called optical character recognition, or OCR) works well with clean printed or typed documents. It has problems with torn or dirty documents and uncommon type faces, and it cannot recognize handwriting. In consequence, any system that uses OCR needs provisions for human interpretation and editing. A scanner-based system can recognize that a character is a "d" or a "g," and it can construct the word "dog." But there is as yet no software that understands the meaning of the sentence, "Man bites dog."

Multimedia computer systems—systems that simultaneously employ video, audio, and text output (and perhaps input)—are receiving a great deal of attention in the press. There are commercial products that make it possible to build very sophisticated multimedia applications using high-powered PCs.

Although multimedia systems are beginning to become technically practical, the only significant business use so far is in training programs, and even that use is quite new. Furthermore, it is likely that as multimedia is extended into new application areas, unexpected technical and operational problems will arise.

At this time, any use of multimedia systems beyond training must be viewed as experimental and risky.

ORGANIZATIONAL CONSTRAINTS

Organizational factors may constrain the development and deployment of information technology even more than the limitations of the technology itself.

Money and People

The most obvious constraints are the limits of money and people available to pursue IT opportunities. Investments in information technology must compete for the pool of corporate capital against other potential uses, in a climate where IT is already consuming substantial amounts of money. IT expenditures commonly range from 2 to 3 percent of revenues in manufacturing companies and from 10 to 12 percent of revenues in banks and financial services companies. Deciding how to allocate capital between IT and other activities is a major strategic decision.

Expenditures for information technology must be sufficient to support corporate vision, strategy, and operations; if not enough money is available for IT to support important business initiatives, it may be necessary to modify corporate strategy.

In many cases, the availability of people is a more serious constraint than the availability of money. The need for information technology specialists is obvious; the need for substantial user participation is less well understood.

Each major IT initiative should be tested not only against the availability of IT professionals, but also against the availability of the users who will be needed to work with them.

The time and attention of senior management is usually the scarcest resource of all. Major changes in the direction of IT use or major new initiatives within existing IT strategy will require some participation by senior management.

A major IT initiative is practical only if senior management will devote significant time and attention to it.

Resistance to Change

New uses of information technology require people to change the ways in which they do their jobs, and most people resist change. They resist change because they are comfortable with their current ways of doing things, because they know that the change process itself will be painful, and because they are unsure about how the new situation will work out. This is particularly true of changes that add information technology to jobs that did not previously use it. Many people are uncomfortable with computers, some to the point of fear. People who perceive themselves to be successful in their jobs are particularly prone to resist changing the ways of working that helped them achieve their success.

> An IT strategy will fail unless it includes *specific* provisions for encouraging workers to change, by easing the process of change itself, and by helping them understand that the new ways of doing things will be better for them.

> There is an organizational resistance to change similar to individual resistance to change. It too is caused by comfort with current procedures, recognition of the costs of change, and fear of how the new situation will work out. This resistance is enhanced by issues of bureaucratic politics and power. Will my job or my budget be diminished in the new organization? Who will control the information that I have relied on to do my job? Who will control the operation of the new system, with its attendant budget and people and power? The bureaucratic uncertainty created by a major IT initiative is enormous.

> Bureaucratic issues should be settled as early in the process of change as possible, to minimize uncertainties and the consequent losses of commitment and productivity.

Organizational Disruption

Change in information technology disrupts an organization far beyond the business process that is the object of the change. Interpersonal relationships, organizational procedures, and many other things are inevitably changed. A review of IT strategy should consider the total amount of disruption it will create and the amount of disruption that the organization can endure. The totality of individual IT initiatives—each tolerable in itself—might simply be too much for the organization as a whole.

Professor Rubenstein of Northwestern University offers his views about organizational disruption:

> Based on observed industrial experience over many decades, some organizations can survive continuous and massive changes across the board. Others cannot. It is not clear whether good indicators are available for predicting which firms fall into which categories.
>
> In highly decentralized organizations where the center of operations and decision are in units that are fairly distinct. . . . and operate independently of each other (no transfer pricing, no joint product development or production or marketing), "complete" changes may be possible in a short time period. For more integrated firms, "small changes" tend to generate large waves and destabilize organizational units which are not (apparently) directly affected by the changes.
>
> Actual "piece by piece changes" can and do succeed when related functions (other than the target function) are brought into the picture early and "participate" in the change, even if only vicariously.[7]

Don Frey, retired CEO of Bell & Howell, suggests that at most about 10 percent of all employees be involved in major job changes at any one time. He is a strong advocate of systems that can be installed in six months or so, meaning that at most 20 percent of all jobs might be affected in a single year.[8]

An IT strategy that causes major changes in more than 20 percent of the jobs in the company at the same time should be viewed with extreme skepticism, unless the units affected are quite independent of one another. For any major new system, there should be detailed plans to deal with the disruptions to operations, to organizations, and to people.

Risk

Building any new information system is risky; it might not be completed on time, within budget, or with the required functionality. The degree of risk can be characterized in three dimensions. Building a system that employs unfamiliar information technology is inherently riskier than building one that uses known technology. It is more risky to automate a function that has never been automated than to work with one that has previously been automated. It is riskier to build a large system than a small one.

Each system proposed in an IT strategy should be analyzed in terms of these dimensions of risk, and then total risk should be reviewed. The safest strategy from an IT point of view is one in which no new systems are risky in all three dimensions and only one or two new systems are risky in two of the dimensions. Whether this is the ideal IT strategy for the company depends on the imperatives of business strategy and vision.

System Size

One other issue must be considered as IT strategy is reviewed. It is extremely difficult to manage either the construction of a very large information system or its operation. This is particularly true of telecommunications systems.

Before you approve any very large information system, identify the members of the management team that will build and operate it. (As a rule of thumb, consider a system to be very large if it requires more than twice as much effort or money as any other recent system.)

WORKING WITH OTHER STAKEHOLDERS

Many important IT initiatives involve working closely with other stakeholders: customers, business alliance partners, and the community at large.

Your customers may not like your new IT offering. There have been dozens of attempts to sell home banking systems to consumers. Nearly every one has failed; none has been a real financial success.[9]

Conduct market tests if you are planning to introduce a new product category with significant customer exposure to information technology. Monitor market acceptance carefully, and be prepared to withdraw if the product does not meet expectations.

Business alliance partners—other companies with which you work closely to deliver goods and services to consumers—may be unwilling to participate in your IT strategy. Each of them may have all the internal problems we described above. They may be concerned with the costs they incur in doing some of "your" work for you (for instance, when a customer uses your information system to place orders rather than working with your order clerk). They may not want to disclose their confidential data to you. They may be unwilling to participate because they analyze the business situation differently than you do and do not see the benefits to them of your IT strategy.

> Bring your alliance partners into your business process design and the related information system design activities, both to get their ideas and to gain their commitment.

Information systems are increasingly subject to government regulations and societal pressures. Credit reporting companies are required to meet federal and state standards for accuracy and rebuttal.[10] Airlines have been forced to modify their reservation systems to provide "unbiased displays" of all carriers' flights, even though the systems are owned and operated by individual airlines for their own competitive purposes.[11]

> Evaluate the impacts your new IT initiatives might have on society and whether it will be acceptable to the communities in which you do business.

New information systems are particularly likely to cause problems if they cross international borders. Laws regulating the transmission and use of personal data (from salaries to credit card purchases) differ from country to country, making it very difficult to design and operate international systems.

> Determine whether your new IT initiatives are subject to governmental regulations or are likely to generate new regulations.

SUMMARY

What You Must Know

- You can meet any requirement for geographic reach with today's technology and most requirements for range and depth that you can specify.

- Current information technology cannot support rapid changes in information systems.
- User-developed systems will continue to play a major role in meeting organizational needs.
- Organizational constraints may be a bigger roadblock to your IT strategy than technological limitations.

What You Must Do

- Use generic information technology wherever feasible.
- Be sure your strategic plans include provisions for dealing with change and disruption.
- Use this chapter as a checklist to test the feasibility of your information technology strategy.

Chapter Eleven

People and Organization

As information technology becomes more oriented toward customer service, information technology professionals must take on new roles, for which they will need new business skills and new technical skills. People with both business and technical skills will be hard to find. The best strategy is to recruit new graduates for their technical skills and build their business skills through experience in your company.

Just as technologists will require business skills, users of the technology will require technical skills to participate in systems development activities, either as members of development teams or as developers of small systems for their own use.

Application/infrastructure architecture allows you to organize your IT activities so that application development is located close to the functional units it serves, while the infrastructure and IT strategy remain located near the center of the enterprise.

Information technology may or may not be of strategic importance in a particular company. If it is, there should be a chief information officer reporting to the chief executive. If not, the IT infrastructure and strategy units should be part of some central administrative organization, preferably not finance.

It is not a good idea to manage the information technology function as a business within a business, charging for and profiting from its services. This kind of arrangement is usually not really driven by market considerations, and the idea of an internal department earning a profit by selling to its sister departments is very unpopular.

The attitudes and activities of the CEO have a great deal to do with the success or failure of information technology to contribute to the bottom line. The CEO must learn enough about information technology to make informed judgments about it and must demonstrate his or her concern to everyone in the enterprise.

Our general approach is to identify business needs first and then discuss ways of satisfying those needs. Thus, we move now to the last links in the chain of requirements for supplying information to an enterprise: the people who build and operate information systems and the organizational structures that support them.

As you read this chapter, you may get the impression that IT professionals are somehow different from other people in the organization and that they should get special treatment. That statement is both true and misleading. We know that salespeople tend to be different from research scientists or factory workers; each group works in its own unique context and each context tends to attract a particular type of individual. Good managers understand this and treat each group accordingly. The same thing is true of IT professionals: They work in their unique context, and many of them share certain personal characteristics, which we will discuss. The point of this chapter is to explore the context in which information technologists work, so we can understand their unique problems and develop ways to deal with them.

NEW ROLES AND SKILLS FOR INFORMATION TECHNOLOGY PROFESSIONALS

In this section, we discuss the changing roles and skills of IT professionals from an overall company point of view: the set of roles IT professionals as a group must play to support the company and the skills they as a group will require. The next section deals with what these requirements mean to individuals, their jobs, and their careers. As we shall see, some of the new skills are quite different from current ones. You will have to provide the time and resources for your IT professionals to learn these new things.

Changes in the business world demand that IT professionals assume new and changed roles in their relationships with their customers—the users of their services. This change in nomenclature is deliberate and important. IT professionals must provide *service* to *customers*, rather than providing *systems or information* to *users*. *Service* means being responsive to needs; *customers* are people who can choose their suppliers. Information technologists no longer have a monopoly of the technology or a monopoly of the ability to use it, and their customers know it.

The primary requirement is that information technologists become more directly involved in business issues than ever before. This means providing high-quality systems to run the enterprise and high-quality support for those systems. It means working with customers as their business processes change, both by continuous improvement and by the radical process redesign we discussed in Chapter 6. It means working with more customers and different customers. In common with the rest of the enterprise, IT now has a much larger set of constituencies than before: information technologists must look beyond the bounds of the enterprise to consumers, suppliers, and the community at large.

The old responsibilities remain, with a new twist. IT professionals must still design, build, and operate information systems to support the enterprise, traditionally their most important and prestigious role. But the users' priorities have changed. A study by Curt Hartog and Rose Brower, of Washington University in St. Louis, found that users think the most important single role of IT is to provide technical support services, rather than to build new systems.[1]

There are two dimensions to this support, equally important. One is to help IT's customers use the systems built by IT. This means having people available who can identify and solve users' problems with information systems, whether the problems are caused by operational difficulties, computer failure, network outages, software defects, user misunderstanding, or anything else. The other dimension of user support is helping users who build their own information systems. This may take the form of giving advice about system design or operation, providing access to networks, or making data available from mainframe databases.

That's not all. Information technologists must be more than designers and builders of systems. If information technology is to achieve its full potential to contribute to corporate performance, the information technologists must be consultants on the effects of information and information technology on business processes, as well as consultants on information technology itself. They must be teachers of IT-related skills and trainers of the users of information systems. They must be marketers who understand business well enough to design useful IT solutions to business problems and salespeople who can convince users that these solutions are worthwhile.

To fulfill these varied roles, IT professionals, as a group, must augment their business skills and knowledge in these areas.

General business skills: planning, project management, organization design, work flow analysis and design, business economics, consulting, marketing, and teaching. In addition, each individual will need substantial understanding of one or more functional areas of the business (manufacturing, marketing, etc.)

Company-specific knowledge: corporate vision, goals and strategies, competitive situation, company markets, business environment, company culture, and so on.

Interpersonal skills: team building, team participation, communications skills, and political skills in the best sense of that term: the ability to reconcile competing interests in support of overall enterprise goals.

In addition to their new roles with their customers, information technologists find themselves in a new relationship to their own jobs. The underlying premises of information technology and its application have changed drastically in the last decade.

• People, rather than computing and telecommunications capacity, are the scarcest and most expensive resource in an information system. The old goal of a system that makes the most efficient use of hardware is being supplanted by a new goal: a system that makes the most efficient use of people, both as system builders and as system users. There are still parts of many systems that require the most efficient possible use of hardware, but they constitute only a small fraction of any given system.

• The economies of scale, which drove information systems toward the largest and fastest computers, have reversed for many kinds of systems.

• The old monopoly of the internal information services department has been eroded to the point of extinction by personal computers, packaged software, and outsourcers.

Changes in business needs and practices have reverberated into the technical work of information technologists. As elsewhere in the enterprise, the standard business processes of IT are no longer adequate to meet business needs. Rapid deployment of new systems has become more important than efficient use of resources in the system development process.

Add-on automation, the straightforward automation of existing business activities, was the mainstay of information system development. It has become less attractive in recent years as the base of existing automation has increased. And, as we have noted repeatedly, business process design involves IT in new and deeper ways than add-on automation.

Changes in the technological base of IT requires that information technologists take a new view of their jobs and themselves. The application/infrastructure architecture has changed the definition of an application system. An application system used to be conceived of as the complete set of components needed to accomplish a business purpose: computer programs, data, communication systems, work procedures, people, and so on. Now an individual application is much less. All of the same things are needed, but some of them are no longer part of the application. The data may be part of the infrastructure; telecommunications surely is. Some work processes that would have been part of an application may be part of several applications, restricting the options available to the system designer.

Some of the technical skills the new IT professional must have are old, some are new. Most of the old skills must be preserved, even as these new ones are being developed:

- The ability to work within the new technical environment of infrastructure separated from applications, particularly the current version: client/server architecture. This in turn will require expertise in the design of systems in which processing is distributed over more than one computer and data may be distributed over large areas. Telecommunications expertise will be essential.
- High-level professional IT expertise in personal computers, workstations, and networks, both for use in IT-developed systems and to support user-developed systems so they can operate effectively over long periods.
- The ability to deploy new information systems substantially more quickly and less expensively than is now the norm.

Skills alone are not enough. The new IT professionals will need a set of attitudes that are not as common in the IT community as they should be:

- Recognition that business needs take priority over technological considerations.
- Willingness to work as equals in teams made up of both IT professionals and users.
- Willingness to change in response to changes in business and in technology.

CHANGING CAREERS OF INFORMATION TECHNOLOGY PROFESSIONALS

In the past, we have expected some IT professionals—the systems analysts—to be both business experts and information technology experts. This is no longer a reasonable expectation, given the increasing involvement of IT people in business process design and the increasing complexity of information technology.

We are moving in the direction of two different kinds of IT professionals, paralleling the application/infrastructure architecture described in Chapter 9. One kind is the business analyst. He has the business skills necessary to understand business processes and needs and enough technical skills to build applications, provided the infrastructure is in place.

The other IT professional is the technical analyst, who designs, builds, and operates the infrastructure. She has enough business skills to direct the infrastructure toward business needs, without the detailed business process knowledge of the business analyst.

The distinction between the two is not clear cut, and in practice there is considerable overlap of skills and roles. Peter Keen suggests four categories, with changing proportions of business and technical skills: business/organizational specialists, business/ organizational hybrids (business and technological skills, with the emphasis on business), technical hybrids (emphasis on technology), and technical specialists.[2] The important thing is to recognize that every information technology professional must have a mix of business and technical skills, even though any one individual will spend most of his or her career on one side of the business/technology boundary.

STAFFING THE NEW INFORMATION TECHNOLOGY FUNCTION

The best place to look for the new information technology professionals you will need is among the people already on your staff. But don't expect to name them, anoint them, and have them change. It's not easy for anyone to make radical changes in behavior, particularly behavior that has produced success in the past. It is particularly difficult for IT professionals to change their professional practices.

Changes in the processes by which information systems are designed, built, and operated are more risky than similar changes in other business processes. Building and operating information systems is (or should be) an engineering discipline, analogous to electrical or chemical engineering. But unlike the older branches of engineering, information systems does not yet have a substantial scientific base on which to build its practices. Very little in computer science directly supports the practice of information systems, in the sense that physics supports the practice of mechanical engineering. And IT professionals are only beginning to learn to use some of the other relevant disciplines, such as organization development. In consequence, IT professionals have only their own collective experience on which to base their evaluation of new ideas, and that experience is limited to about 25 years.

This experience has shown IT professionals how easy it is to be led astray. We have discussed the failures of ideas such as the corporatewide management information system. It is understandable and appropriate that today's attractive new ideas, such as computer-aided systems engineering and object oriented design and programming, are viewed with skepticism.

IT professionals often have no one to help them work through the process of change. In many organizations, information technology is the driver of business change, and the information technologists become the experts in understanding and managing it. When the time comes for IT processes to be changed, information technologists often must be their own experts and consultants, a notoriously difficult task.

As you look at the individuals in your IT function, you will find that they tend to fall into three groups. One group will consist of the people who are primarily interested in the business aspects of information systems. They read *The Wall Street Journal* and spend as much time as they can in the field with users. These will be your new business analysts, after they learn how.

The second group will consist of people whose primary interest is in information technology. They are the ones who are constantly pressing to acquire the latest hardware and use the latest programming techniques. They read *Byte* magazine and *Dr. Dobbs' Journal* and spend most of their time at their terminals, programming. With proper training, these can be your new technical analysts.

Unfortunately, you will find a third group—those who are not very interested in either the business or the technology. In many cases, this is not their fault. Information technology is very dynamic as seen from the outside, but like most other business activities, it has its share of dull, routine jobs on the inside. The people who have had those jobs are just as likely to become time servers as people with dull jobs in any other function. With caring, motivation, and training, some of these people can be made productive in the new world; others will have to go.

These are some of the crucial points to remember as you change the processes with which IT carries out its mission.

> Information technologists are likely to need more assistance from outside change agents than others in the company. It may appear that they will need less, particularly if they are acting as change agents for others in the company, because they understand the change process. But understanding is not enough; working through changes is best accomplished with outside help.

> There will be substantial costs of training for both business analysts and technical analysts.

> Each IT employee must have a basic set of both business skills and technical skills, whatever her job assignment, to earn the respect of peers and clients.

> Training for IT professionals never ends. David Moon of Mark Travel allocates 10 percent of work time for training for every worker.[3] Peter Keen recommends 10 percent of work time for training for all IT professionals.[4]

> No amount of training is a substitute for experience, particularly for the business analysts. Plan a program of temporary

assignments to line functions for business analysts and another program of temporary assignments where business analysts and technical analysts switch jobs. You will lose a little efficiency in the short term, but you will gain a lot of effectiveness over the long haul.

Motivation is more important than training. Technical analysts can be motivated by giving them opportunities to work with leading edge technology and by encouraging them to interact with their technical peers at professional societies and trade shows.[5] Business analysts, at least the good ones, will be motivated by the opportunity to work on projects with significant bottom line effects.

If you cannot find all the people you need within your IT function, look elsewhere in your company, particularly at those people who have become departmental PC experts. You may find some people with useful functional and business experience who are interested in doing IT work. With the right training, they make ideal business analysts.

Experienced recruits from outside your company are likely to need the same kinds of business training your own IT people need. If you can't find outside people with most of the technical skills you need, you will be better off training members of your own staff.

Entry-level IT recruits offer you the maximum flexibility and the best chance for ultimate success, if you can wait for them to mature. You should hire based on two criteria.

- Seek graduates with good technical skills (which can be taught in school) rather than business skills (which must be gained largely by experience).
- Seek people who want to be business analysts rather than those who want to be technical analysts. Experience shows that many of those who think they want to be business analysts ultimately change their minds and take the technical path, but very few with an initial technological bent switch to the business side.

Rotating entry-level recruits through different IT jobs and through assignments outside of IT can give both you and them important insights about their talents and goals. Keen suggests that they are very adaptable for the first four to six years and can take either path. After that, career directions become fairly well fixed.[6]

OTHER PEOPLE WITH INFORMATION TECHNOLOGY RESPONSIBILITIES

When we think about the impact of IT on people in the workplace, we must not lose sight of the many people whose primary jobs are not in information technology, yet who have significant responsibility for IT work. These people need IT training appropriate to their jobs, and they need to know how to incorporate IT productively into their work.

Part of this is getting easier as time passes. Virtually all new graduates come into the work force with basic personal computer skills. They can use word processing programs and spreadsheets; many have experience with simple databases and presentation graphics. Most important, they are comfortable with computers.

But familiarity with PCs and their elementary applications is only the first step to the professional skills many will need as their careers advance. Users of information systems must know enough to participate effectively in business process design (Chapter 6) and information system development (Chapter 8). They also need to know how to access data and construct reports from corporate databases, a task that is quite different from using a private PC database and somewhat harder.

Users need IT training and guidance as they build their own systems. They will be encouraged to build and operate systems to meet their own local or departmental needs because the IT professionals will be busy with major interdepartmental and cross-functional systems. This task is much more complex than it seems. As we observed in Chapter 8, when a user undertakes to build an information system that serves more than one person, however simple that system may be, the user becomes an IT manager with all the choices and responsibilities that position entails.

ORGANIZING INFORMATION TECHNOLOGY TO MEET BUSINESS NEEDS

The organization required to support the people and activities we have been discussing should be structured according to our fundamental rule: Business needs determine the scope and shape of support activities.

In our discussion of the sources of value of information (in Chapter 5), we divided IT activities into three classes: those that support current operations, those that support improvements in current operations, and those that support the future of the enterprise—its vision and its strategy. This classification, in conjunction with application/infrastructure architecture, suggests that we group IT activities into three major organizational units: information infrastructure, application system development, and information technology strategy.

The role of the information infrastructure unit is to support the current operations of the enterprise. Its major tasks are:

- Operating the corporate computer and telecommunications network, supporting the users of the network, network maintenance, and short-range network planning.
- Making minor technical changes in existing systems, changes that have no effect on system functionality.
- Managing databases used by more than one application, including technical design, access control, and possibly administration of data codes (a bigger task than you may imagine).

Application system development supports changes in current business operations, at three levels:

- Making minor modifications of existing application systems to enhance their functionality.
- Designing and building new application systems to improve existing operations.
- Supporting major business process redesign, both by participating in the design process and by building the new information systems that new business processes require.

The information technology strategy unit supports the future of the business, in a variety of ways:

- Establishing information technology vision and strategies to support corporate vision and strategies.
- Seeking new opportunities to use information technology to reach corporate goals.
- Monitoring advances in information technology and encouraging the timely introduction of useful new technologies into the company.
- Developing long-range information technology plans.
- Planning and administering personal and professional development programs for everyone in the IT function; this includes training, rotating assignments, and planning career paths.
- Establishing IT standards to promote interconnectivity of systems throughout the enterprise and to gain economies of scale in purchasing and in operations.
- Providing a locus of responsibility for all corporate IT activities.

Notice that we are characterizing these units in terms of the tasks they are to perform rather than by the technical specialties required to perform the tasks. Each of these units may be organized by technical specialty internally, but that internal organization should be totally invisible to users and to senior managers.

Grouping IT activities into these three separate units allows us to place each of them where it can be most effective.

Information technology and strategy is an enterprise-wide function, and should be a part of the corporate headquarters group. Its specific place depends on how important information technology is to the company. If corporate strategy is heavily dependent on IT or if IT is central to current operations, then information technology and strategy should report directly to the CEO.

Every senior executive wants to report directly to the CEO, but the CEO just doesn't have time for all of them. The real question is whether IT is important enough to displace some other function from the CEO's direct view, and if so, what should be displaced. If IT is not sufficiently important to report directly to the CEO, it should be placed in a headquarters administrative services department with other staff support groups, such as human resources and law.

The least desirable option is to have IT strategy report to a major user of IT services, for example, the operations department of a bank. The problem with this arrangement is that the other users of IT may not get the attention they deserve.

There is ample historical precedent for this concern. Financial systems were the first applications of computers in most businesses, so many information systems departments began as units of finance departments. To this day, about half of all information systems departments in the United States report within a financial function. And to this day there is less computerization of nonfinancial functions than there should be in many of these companies. The general inadequacy of information system support for manufacturing activities is documented in a recent article in *Information Week* titled "Modern Times?"[7]

To see if this true in your company, look at the contents of your system development backlog, say for the last two years, and see whose needs are not being met.

Infrastructure, like IT strategy, is an enterprisewide activity, with most of the same reporting options: reporting as part of an information services department at a headquarters location or reporting to a major user of its services. The advantages and disadvantages are similar to those listed above for IT strategy. Headquarters reporting allows evenhanded treatment of all users. On the other hand, it may be a burden on headquarters administration, particularly in a company with a tradition of small staff operations. Location within a user group may result in degraded service to other users.

The most important thing is to keep the Infrastructure unit intact. There is sometimes a tendency to break it up—for instance to have telecommunications report to a central administrative department and computer operations report to an operating division. This is always a bad idea.

Application development is a very different matter. Its work must be attuned to the needs of the business processes it serves. The best way to accomplish this is to have a large number of relatively small application development units, each assigned to serve a particular business process or set of users. Each unit can be assigned organizationally to the business unit it serves, or it can report in a headquarters department, provided each unit remains dedicated to its own user group.

The minimum workable size of an application development unit is about 4 to 10 people, depending on the nature of the systems they must build and maintain. A typical unit may have from 4 to 5 people up to about 25; only rarely should a single application development unit have more than 25 people. Resolve any doubts in favor of having a larger number of smaller units.

THE CHIEF INFORMATION OFFICER

The growing importance of information technology, particularly as it interacts with corporate strategy, has caused many companies to reexamine the leadership of their IT activities. As we noted above, in a company where information technology is an integral component of corporate strategy, it is logical to have the senior information technology executive report directly to the CEO as a full-fledged member of the senior executive team.

It has become common to refer to this person as the chief information officer (CIO), although often that is not the person's official job title. The job of CIO is a different job from being the head of data processing or information systems. The essence of the CIO's job is to be a member of senior management, looking outward toward the corporation as a whole. The primary task of the head of information systems is to look inward to manage the information systems function. One individual often fills both roles, but many large companies are now separating them.

The CIO's job is to ensure that information technology is used as effectively as possible in the interests of the enterprise. The specific tasks are those we listed above as the tasks of the information technology strategy unit. To carry out these tasks, the CIO needs a rare combination of skills and abilities. The CIO must:

- Be a businessperson of talent and perception, in order to participate in business strategy and policy development.
- Be a technologist who understands the information technologies currently in use well enough to manage them or to supervise their management.

- Have the insight into the direction and practicality of new information technologies to decide whether and when to introduce them into the company.
- Be able to communicate the possibilities and limitations of information technology to other senior managers.
- Be able to communicate business issues to IT professionals to help them focus on the things important to business success.
- Have the leadership qualities necessary to function effectively in a world where a significant portion of the IT resources in the enterprise are under the administrative control of others.[8]

You could use the same words, with appropriate changes, to describe the qualities required for a chief manufacturing officer or a chief marketing officer who reports to the CEO and serves as a member of senior management.

There are well-worn paths to the jobs of vice president of manufacturing and vice president of marketing. Typical candidates have had experience in several diverse functions, both line and staff, and perhaps have had profit and loss responsibility for a business unit. Other senior managers usually know enough about the candidates' prior assignments to make informed assessments of their past performance and their potential in senior assignments.

None of this is true for the CIO job. Most senior IT executives have spent their entire careers in the IT function. Other senior managers have little or no IT experience, and thus have no basis either for judging past performance or estimating future potential. Furthermore, the senior IT executive is often seen as someone with few general management skills and little perspective on the business as a whole. This is much less likely to be true today than it was a few years ago, but the perception remains.

If you are looking for a CIO and have no obvious candidate, you have three options, none of them particularly attractive.

- You can recruit a CIO from another company, who will not have experience with your own company or perhaps even in your own industry.

- You can give the job to one of your own line executives, and hope that he can learn the technology quickly enough to be productive.
- You can promote your senior IT executive and hope that she can learn enough about the business to be productive as quickly as required.

Each of these options has been tried by many companies. Each has succeeded in some cases and failed in others. The failures seem to have outnumbered the successes. Different surveys indicate that the average tenure in office of a CIO is either two years or four years, but the surveys agree that a significant amount of turnover (one says 35 percent) is a result of failure of the CIO to perform.[9]

Other things being equal, your best bet is probably to work with your senior IT executive to give her the business experience and senior management exposure she will need to become an effective member of your management team.

INFORMATION TECHNOLOGY AS A "BUSINESS WITHIN A BUSINESS"

Two closely related ideas often surface when we discuss ways to focus the use of information technology on the bottom line. One is charging users for IT services. The other is organizing the IT function as a "business within a business."

Charging Users

The motivation for charging users for IT services is the same as the motivation for any transfer pricing of goods or services within an enterprise: to help the manager of each business unit understand the costs of the resources his unit consumes and to give him control of his discretionary costs. Charging users for IT services has all the advantages and disadvantages of other transfer pricing.

It is very difficult to determine appropriate prices. If you tie transfer prices to market prices, you may suppress the advantages of corporate economies of scale. In addition, spot market prices often reflect marginal costs rather than total costs, unfairly penalizing the internal supplier.

For these reasons, determining transfer prices is often a political process, generating more heat than light.

Transfer charges for IT are often adjusted at year end so that IT department costs are recovered exactly. Because so much of the IT budget is for fixed costs, if one manager cuts IT expenditures below budgeted amounts, overall expenses may not change much, and other managers will be punished with higher unit costs.

Cross charges within the company are often regarded as funny money, of no real importance.

The overriding consideration is corporate practice. If other staff departments charge for services, charge for IT services; if not, don't. Treating IT as a special case will generate nothing but ill will on everyone's part.

Operating IT as a Business within a Business

Operating IT as a business within a business (BWB) sounds attractive on the surface. After all, if you can outsource to an independent third party, why not outsource to your own wholly owned subsidiary? You can capture the outsourcer's profit and gain the efficiencies associated with an independent, profit-seeking IT business.

You should address several issues before you start your business within a business.

- Will your users become captive customers of your BWB, or will they be permitted to purchase IT services from others? If your users are captive customers, the BWB is a sham. It has no more incentive to cut prices or to innovate than if it were an internal department charging out all its costs.

- Will your BWB be permitted to sell its services outside your corporate family? If not, there will be no marketplace benchmarks against which to measure the BWB's performance. If you do serve outside customers, how do you determine who is served first in times of scarcity of, say, network management professionals? If you serve your outside customers first, internal customers will be enraged. If you give your internal customers preference, your outside business will disappear.

- Will you permit your BWB to earn a profit and keep it? Experience shows that internal customers tend to resent a related company earning a profit from their business. Yet you must permit the BWB to earn and retain profits if it is to be a real business. The IT business is risky, and you need profits to cushion that risk. Suppose the BWB enters into a fixed-price contract to develop a new application system for the marketing department. The consequences should be the same to the marketing department as entering into a fixed-price contract with any outside supplier. The supplier should perform for the fee specified. If the supplier misestimates the costs, he should bear the losses out of his accumulated surplus. If you do not allow your BWB to earn and retain profits, there will be no surplus to pay for losses. Misestimates will have to be renegotiated with the customers, and you will be right back where you were: IT services supplied on a cost plus basis by a captive supplier.

Few companies have the corporate will or the corporate culture to allow their IT departments and their users to operate freely in the marketplace for IT services, and fewer still are willing to allow a BWB to earn and keep profits.

Even if you do all these things, operating your IT department as a business within a business is probably a bad idea. As IT becomes more important to corporate strategies and corporate vision, outsourcing of any kind becomes less attractive, and outsourcing to a wholly owned business within a business is no exception.

THE ROLE OF THE CEO IN INFORMATION TECHNOLOGY SUCCESS

The attitudes and actions of the CEO are crucial to the success of every component of an enterprise, but more so for information technology than for most others. IT is the newest major function in most organizations, and many people do not understand it very well. IT consumes a growing share of corporate resources, and it causes disruptions wherever it goes. Without the understanding and active support of the CEO, the potential for IT to improve corporate performance will never be realized.

The first task of the CEO is to evaluate the importance of IT to the organization. This means learning what benefits IT can provide to your organization and what costs it entails. It means getting involved with the technology enough to begin to develop an intuition about what makes sense and what does not:

- Start by looking at some of the IT activities in your company at the operational level. Spend an hour in the telemarketing center and watch how computer support helps (or doesn't help) your frontline workers.
- Take a careful look at your monthly financial reports. Identify some things you would like changed, and then go to the systems development department and watch the analysts make those changes. (Plan several trips; it won't happen quickly.)
- Sit in the back of the room at a business process design team meeting and see how difficult it is simply to agree on what a business process is, much less what it should be.
- Spend an hour at the IT help desk to see what concerns users and what it takes to satisfy them.
- Finally, if you insist, get a PC and make a few spreadsheets. But don't let this mislead you. The world of corporate information technology is far more complex than anything you could possibly do with your PC.

As you develop your intuition, think about this question: How important is IT to your organization, now and in the future? If the answer is "not very important," put IT aside and move on to more significant things. But if you reach this conclusion, make it your business to revisit IT every year or so; your business may change and you may change your mind.

If you conclude that IT is important to your company, you must take the same kind of leadership role with respect to IT that you take with respect to any other important function. Learn about it, let your workers know you care, allocate some of your time to it, and encourage your other executives to do the same.

In any event, see that IT is organized so that it is as close as possible to the business processes it serves, and develop a comprehensive IT training and development program: for IT professionals, for users, and for executives and managers. After you develop it, insist that it be followed. It is all too easy to cut back training in order to complete some urgent project and to resist rotational assignments because they reduce productivity.

A comprehensive training and development program will cost more than you expect, but the benefits will be well worth it. In studying the introduction of new technology into US manufacturing firms, Professor Martin Starr of Columbia University has found that the more successful companies spend more money on training than less successful ones.[10] The more successful companies he studied spent an average of $2 on training for each $1 spent on the technology itself. I asked him whether he thought this ratio would apply to information technology, as well as to manufacturing technology in general. Here is his response:

> We did not track information technology as a separate item. There were many instances where it was a major part of new manufacturing technology, and I have the impression that training expenses in those cases were even higher. For information technology in general, the number might be $3 of training costs for each dollar of technology costs.[11]

We have no comparable numbers for IT training, but the few numbers we do have imply that we are spending much less proportionately on training as we introduce new information technology.

Finally, let everyone in the company know you have decided that information technology is important to your company's future.

SUMMARY

What You Must Know

- The roles of IT professionals are changing, and they will require new skills, primarily business skills, to fulfill them.
- It is practical, indeed desirable, to keep the infrastructure organizationally separate from the applications development activity.

- The application development function should be organized to be very close to the users of its services.
- The support and understanding of the CEO is crucial to IT success.

What You Must Do

- Allocate resources—money and worker time—for educating and training IT professionals in business skills and for training non-IT professionals in information technology.
- Establish a program to rotate people into and out of information system activities as a regular part of career progression.
- Appoint someone to take on the responsibilities of chief information officer, whether or not you use that title.
- Find out what you need to know about information technology and learn it; make sure everyone in the company knows of your interest.

IV

INTO THE 21ST CENTURY

The business climate will continue to be highly competitive at the beginning of the 21st century. Companies will be struggling to please increasingly demanding customers even as they seek to serve their other constituencies: workers, suppliers, and the community at large. Organizations will be flat and flexible. They will be continually changing both their internal structures and their external alliances to meet market demands.

Information will penetrate more deeply into every organization, affecting every worker. Empowered workers and effective teams will be the keys to success.

The information technology explosion will be felt throughout society. The nature of everyday life will change as human interactions give way to transactions between people and machines. Important issues of public policy must be addressed, including the meaning and ownership of intellectual property, and ways of maintaining individual privacy while not depriving individuals or society of the benefits of the information age.

The United States is well positioned to be a world leader as the 21st century begins. Our people are particularly well suited to the new structure of business and the climate of increased competition. Our national history of individual freedom, our racial and ethnic diversity, and our propensity to form voluntary organizations to accomplish special goals mirror exactly the characteristics necessary for the success of the federated organization of the future: empowered workers of diverse backgrounds working in teams toward common goals.

Chapter Twelve

Information for the Organization of 2004

Business in the year 2004, a decade from now, will be more competitive and more global than it is today. The MTV and Nintendo generations are accustomed to receiving much of their information from sources other than the printed page, and businesses will have to accommodate them both as customers and as workers.

By 2004, information technology will have substantially increased its reach, its range, and its depth in most organizations. The application/infrastructure architecture, together with powerful new tools, will improve the ability of IT to respond to business changes. Multimedia and video-based systems will be coming into general use.

The best IT strategy for the next 10 years is an evolutionary strategy, moving toward the new architecture to enable broader use of information. The success of this strategy will depend heavily on the ability and willingness of people to change the ways they approach information technology. This in turn will depend on the organization providing guidance and support as changes are made.

Meeting today's challenges in business and technology is not enough; tomorrow's demands must be taken into account as well. Our organizations must be able to respond to those demands if they are to survive, much less prosper. It takes so long to make significant changes both in business processes and in information systems that we should look ahead at least a decade to develop a vision of our future and plan strategies to realize that vision.

Most of the important drivers of change are already visible to those who look for them. It remains only to bring them together and interpret them in business terms. To be sure, some new and important phenomena—commercial and technological—will arise unexpectedly. This makes it all the more important to plan now for what we know will happen and to plan to have some resources available to deal with the inevitable surprises.

BUSINESS IN 2004

Competition will intensify dramatically as information about products and prices becomes more widely available.

Mail order catalogs and toll-free telephone services will continue to expand consumer choices.

New electronic marketplaces for securities and other financial instruments will allow buyers and sellers to come together in much larger numbers than before, substantially reducing the spread between bid and offer.

Electronic marketplaces for other goods and services will expand dramatically as two-way video capabilities allow buyers and sellers to communicate more effectively.

Globalization of most businesses will become an established fact, noteworthy only when it is disrupted. Distance and national boundaries will gradually become irrelevant as barriers to commercial transactions. There are many examples of this phenomenon even today.

- Managers at JC Penney stores all over the country evaluate new products by private television network, rather than traveling to showrooms.[1]
- Texas Instruments maintains a major computer programming group in Bangalore, India, using satellite transmission for data and programs, as well as to conduct meetings.[2]

As competition increases, so will the focus on customer satisfaction, which we are only now beginning to understand. But it will take new and different kinds of products and services to satisfy the consumers of 2004, because they will be different people.

They will be comfortable with computers and information technology because many of them will have been using computers since grammar school or before. As a result, many past restraints on use of information technology will gradually erode. Services that have failed in the past, such as home banking, may succeed.

- They will demand information in many forms. Text and numbers will not be enough. The most effective way to convey some kinds information to the MTV generation is with sound and video. Videocassette instruction tapes already accompany many new products, from home exercise equipment to power tools to computer programs. The Nintendo generation may demand interactive video.
- They will expect to have more information than ever before about their business transactions. Federal Express has offered its customers information about the location of packages in transit since 1980. By 2004, consumers will want real time tracking of all business transactions that take more than a few minutes to complete.
- They will expect information technology to make products easier to use, rather than more difficult. Many manufacturers of PC hardware and software are doing an excellent job of making their products simple to install. Products that are difficult to install or awkward to use will be unacceptable.
- They will demand to be treated as individuals. Five hundred TV channels, the capacity of the next generation of cable TV systems, may not be enough to supply every consumer with whatever program he wants whenever he wants it.

The workers of 2004 will be the same people as the customers of 2004. They will be comfortable using information technology in their jobs. They will know that it can help them, and they will demand that it be available. We already have a generation of college graduates who look on the availability of information technology as an important factor in choosing a job. In a few years, high school graduates will be doing the same.

Access to current information systems will not be enough. The new worker of 2004 will come to the workplace having received much of his store of information from television. To be most effective, the information systems that he uses in his work will have to supply information in the video formats familiar to him, as well as in the conventional business formats of words, numbers, and graphs.

The worker of 2004 will be the same as the worker of 1994 in important ways. She will still be eager to do a good job, proud of work well done, caring about the success of her organization, and concerned about the world beyond self and company. Corporate success will still depend on her knowledge, skills, and dedication.

The future of organizational structures is less clear. Many American businesses have gone through cycles of centralization, decentralization, recentralization, and so on, driven as much by management fads and internal bureaucratic imperatives as by business needs. The old tendencies of bureaucracies to seek size, power, and control will always be present. In some companies, they will probably prevail over the ideas of flat organizations, low overhead, and focus on core competencies.

The current management trend is toward flat, decentralized, federated organizations. Some organizations will treat this trend as the road to future success. For others, it will be a fad that will be replaced in its turn by another. As with most trends, this one will probably take many organizations too far. When they discover this, they will recentralize, but they will probably never restore most of the middle managers and support personnel who have been eliminated.

Important business considerations drive companies toward centralizing certain functions. One is the need to comply with laws and other governmental regulations. Equal employment opportunity laws virtually mandate some central bureaucracy for human resource management. Another consideration is the major savings a large company can make by combining the buying power of its units and negotiating corporate contracts for everything from airline tickets to janitorial supplies to computers. A decentralized company needs at least two corporatewide activities to take advantage of these opportunities. One is an information system to provide a basis for negotiations and the means of monitoring results; the other is a purchasing department to negotiate the deals.

In our target year of 2004, there will be many centralized companies. Some will have never decentralized; others will have recentralized, for good reasons or bad.

The most successful organizations will be either federated organizations or niche businesses which are so small that there is no question of decentralization. The dominant organizational feature of both will be that the organization structure itself will be dynamic. The niche business will have an ever-changing set of alliances with suppliers and customers. The federated organization will have the same kind changing alliances and will also be constantly changing its internal structure, building new units and rearranging old ones. The marketplace will accept no less.

INFORMATION TECHNOLOGY IN 2004

Current trends in the development of information technology will continue largely unchanged in the next decade. Unit costs of most of the elements of information technology (computing power, memory, storage devices, telecommunications capacity, etc.) will continue to decrease at about current rates, which is to say 20 to 30 percent per year, compounded. However, total IT expenses will increase in most companies as the demand for information rises faster than the cost of supplying it falls.

Software will become increasingly useful and increasingly complex, but not increasingly expensive.

Teleconferencing with full-motion video will become an accepted way to conduct meetings, as costs decrease and workers learn to use it effectively.

Multimedia computing will have come of age. Commercial systems that integrate conventional computer display screens with sound and full-motion video will be available to meet generic needs such as training. Development tools will be available that will make it practical for individual companies to build custom multimedia systems for their own use.

Some of the experimental efforts to build completely different kinds of computers to solve special problems will begin to have practical applications in the next decade. One new type of computer, called the massively parallel computer, is made up of hundreds or thousands of the same processors that power advanced PCs. It can perform computations that are impractical even with today's fastest conventional computers, such as detailed weather forecasting. These computers require specially written programs;

so far, they are useful only for a limited set of problems. They will become increasingly important in the next decade.

Another new technology is the neural network computer. It is fundamentally different in structure from existing digital computers and requires different programming tools and techniques. Neural network computers are already being used for speech recognition. By 2004, your company may be using a neural network computer for some specific applications purchased turnkey from a vendor. It is unlikely that your own staff will be writing custom applications for your company or that you will be using a neural network computer for general business purposes.

For most companies, the right strategy is thoughtful monitoring of these new technologies, rather than planning now for their use.

With this background of business and technological trends, let's look at the use of information technology in the organization of 2004 in terms of the four characteristics we used in Chapter 10: reach (geographic coverage), range (extent of data and information sharing across functions), depth (extent of penetration into business processes), and change (the ability of information technology to respond to changes in business and technology).

Reach

It is technically possible today to extend the reach of an information system to virtually any fixed point in the developed world and to as many such points as any company may need. The limitations are cost, the availability of high-capacity transmission channels (video) in some parts of the world, and the ability to manage very large networks. In the next decade, costs will decrease substantially and high-capacity channels will be extended into many new areas. Network management will remain a difficult task, but new tools are being developed that will make it practical for any company that needs a network to manage it internally. A reasonable planning premise is that you will be able to communicate to any place with voice or data, and to most places with video.

You may not have to manage the network yourself. Several large telecommunications carriers offer total network management services for private networks, including negotiating with local telephone companies, system integration, and network operation.

The reach of wireless communication is actually broader at this time than the reach of wireline systems because it is easier to install wireless systems in remote or hostile environments. Current limitations on data transfer rates for wireless communication will probably be relaxed somewhat. You can plan to maintain wireless contact with as many people as you need to, as long as data transmission requirements remain moderate.

The most important change in reach will be that many private corporate networks (and information systems) will be connected with other private and public networks. You will be able to be connected not only with all of your own employees, but also to the employees of your customers, your suppliers, and the consumers of your products.

The most important unknown is political, not technical. Countries all over the world are increasing their scrutiny of transborder data transmission, and some are beginning to place controls on it. It is reasonable to assume that over time it will be possible to operate most transborder networks with only modest inconvenience; it is also reasonable to assume that there will be major political impediments in some areas.

Range

Exchanging data and information among systems will be much easier 10 years from now than it is today. New tools will make it easier technically, but it will still require skilled professionals.

The most important factor in increasing range will be that many of your current smokestack systems will have been replaced with new systems designed with the need to exchange data firmly in view.

Depth

The depth of information technology—the extent to which it penetrates individual business processes and activities—will increase dramatically by 2004, driven by the forces of competition as other companies use IT, and as customers, suppliers, and workers demand more information. Holistic business process design, with its integration of information requirements with other business needs, will enable and encourage increased IT depth in every process it touches.

In the next 10 years, we will see greatly expanded use of decision support systems. These systems, based on the mathematical models of operations research and management science, automatically compute either the optimal solution to a problem or the results of possible decisions. Most of this technology is mature and has been used extensively. Its use has been limited by the costs and complexity of building the mathematical models, the difficulty and expense of obtaining the data necessary to use them, and the difficulty of training workers to use them. Each of these constraints is being eased as better software is developed and workers become more familiar with computing on the job.

By 2004, it will be practical to build large-scale information systems using some technologies that are now of only marginal utility.

- Speech recognition will be a reality in a variety of settings, including many office applications.
- E-mail and voice mail will work together and be able to include graphics, animation, and video with voice annotation. Engineers already use animated three-dimensional models of parts; adding voice annotation and transmitting via E-mail is possible today. The only barrier is cost. By 2004, that barrier will be substantially reduced.
- Multimedia information systems will be used in a variety of ways beyond training. Possibilities include monitoring operations, alarm systems for complex industrial facilities, and sales systems that allow customers to design and fabricate custom products on the spot. This is not as farfetched as it may seem. Hallmark Cards has installed a system in retail stores that enables a customer to generate a personal message and have it become an integral part of a printed greeting card, which is delivered instantly. The New Car Showroom, a database on the CompuServe system, describes every automobile, van, light truck, and multipurpose vehicle sold in the United States. It contains specifica-

tions, features, options, prices, and everything else you need to order a car. It would not be difficult technically to modify the system so that a consumer could enter an order.[3] (This would, of course, require certain modifications of the current retail distribution system.)

- Image-based systems will become a common way to deal with large volumes of documents, particularly when those documents are generated outside your organization.
- Groupware—information systems that support work groups—will be common in many organizations. It will advance from simple E-mail and automated document markup systems to systems that facilitate engineering design and encourage generation of new ideas and scenarios of possible futures.

As we move into the information age, it will become increasingly important to provide IT support for knowledge workers—physicians, lawyers, architects, and so on—beyond word processors and spreadsheets. Companies that can improve the productivity of their knowledge workers will have a substantial competitive advantage over those that cannot. This will be one of the leading edge application areas of IT in 2004.[4] We are just beginning to understand the problems of providing IT support to professionals and to discern the outlines of solutions. At least some of these systems will be available by 2004.

- Systems that not only retrieve text from a variety of databases, but also analyze its content and extract important ideas.
- Systems that help resolve conflicts, say in contract negotiations. These systems would analyze proposals, identify areas of conflict and areas of agreement, and compute the costs to each party of giving up some of its demands.
- Systems that identify trends in text documents, analogous to the ways in which statisticians analyze trends in numbers. Successive news articles about pending legislation might contain the words *possible, pending, unpopular,* and *unlikely.* The system would analyze this sequence and suggest that the legislation in question would not be enacted.

Overall, the most important challenge for IT professionals in the next decade will be learning to deal with the masses of data being generated throughout our society. This includes not only the means to generate the data, store it, and retrieve it, but it also means the ability to analyze the data in any form (numbers, text, images, video), the ability to correlate data from different sources and in different modes, and the ability to synthesize data into a form suitable for further analysis by people.

NEW KINDS OF INFORMATION SYSTEMS TO MEET CHANGING BUSINESS NEEDS

Current information technology can barely support current rates of change. It is totally inadequate to meet the needs for ever more rapid change that will characterize the next decade of business. Yet these needs must be met. Companies that cannot do so will fall behind in the race to serve their customers and fulfill the expectations of their workers.

Historically, IT professionals have favored the evolutionary approach, and with good reason. Most organizations have a lot of information technology already in place: computers, telecommunications networks, application systems, development methodologies, and so on. They have a substantial investment in this technology and should not lightly cast it aside. Indeed, in most cases they cannot abandon existing systems wholesale without jeopardizing current business operations.

We discussed various ways in which IT professionals are attempting to improve the standard system development life cycle (SDLC) methodology in Chapter 8. These include supporting evolutionary business change as long as possible by information system maintenance; building new systems around existing business processes; automating the standard SDLC methodology; and building new systems to support redesigned business processes. Note that the end product of all these tactics is a conventional information system, essentially the same as if it had been built using conventional SDLC methods.

Information without Information Systems

If we apply the principles of holistic business process design to the process of providing additional information to support changing business needs, a new goal emerges. As we shall see, the means of reaching that new goal is the application/infrastructure architecture we are already approaching by evolution.

When we look at the *business process* of meeting changing needs for information, we find ourselves faced with the same strategic issue that confronts every process design team. Should we plan evolutionary changes in the existing SDLC process, or should we revolutionize the process by redesigning it from the ground up?

Nearly all the ideas we discussed above are attempts to meet the needs for change by providing new or modified information systems more rapidly. But perhaps this is the wrong approach. Perhaps we can meet the needs for dynamic information support without using conventional information systems. Perhaps we can have information without information systems (IWIS).[5]

As in all process design, we begin by defining the output required of the process. In this case the output is timely *information support* for a new or changed business activity, rather than an *information system* to support a current activity. The meaning of timely is clear: information must be provided as soon as the business needs it, which will often be in a matter of days or weeks after the need is recognized, rather than months or years.

The goal of IWIS is to provide the information necessary to support a new or changed business process in about the same amount of time and with about the same amount of effort as it now takes to design and create a complex spreadsheet. If we can achieve this, there will be no need for the kind of long-lived information system applications we now have. It will be easier to build an entirely new "system" than to modify an old one.

The design philosophy of IWIS is based on two things: (1) the goal of flexibility to meet changing business needs and (2) the recognition that many elements in every organization do not change or change very slowly compared with changes in business needs. We call these unchanging elements *business primitives*. Business primitives are analogous to the invariants of physical science. I don't presume to use that term because our understanding of business processes is not sufficiently clear to assert that any of these things is unchanging throughout time. However, it is sufficient for our purposes that they change slowly relative to other business changes.

Some business primitives are the same in all companies: all companies have employees, all companies have books of account, all companies have customers. Other primitives are company-specific, discernible in current operations, or apparent in corporate strategies and visions of the future. A corporate vision to remain exclusively in the copper mining business defines copper as a business primitive; a vision of expanding into mining other minerals might require metals as a primitive.

Each business primitive has certain information always associated with it (invariant information). Workers have names, addresses, Social Security numbers, current assignment, job skills, and so on. A worker may change residence or be transferred to a new assignment but will always have an address and an assignment.

Invariant processes may be associated with each business primitive and its invariant information. A worker's salary may change, but net paycheck will always be computed as gross salary minus deductions. A piece of capital equipment will always have a book value determined by original cost and subsequent depreciation.

To bring the IWIS idea to fruition, we will need to take advantage of the fact that many things do not change and to develop powerful methods to deal with those that do.

- The invariant information and processes must be stored in a safe place, readily accessible to all who need them.
- There must be tools to retrieve the invariant information and processes.
- There must be tools to collect variable information generated by business processes and external events.
- There must be tools to create automated procedures which bring together invariant information and processes with variable information and processes to provide the information needed to support business processes.
- All tools must be easy to learn and easy to use.
- There should be a means of storing automated procedures for future use. Although IWIS is designed to support unexpected changes in business processes, many processes actually remain unchanged for long periods. No matter how easy it is to construct, say, a payroll procedure, it will always be easier to construct it once and continue to use it than to construct it from scratch each month.

The facilities necessary to support IWIS can be summarized in terms we have already used: an infrastructure containing invariant information and processes, tools to manipulate the information and create automated procedures that meet business needs, and a set of procedures stored ready for use—a set of applications.

Revolutionary business process design has brought us to the same design toward which evolutionary changes are taking us: an application/infrastructure architecture. The main difference is that the revolutionary process design is explicitly motivated by the business need to accommodate change, whereas the evolutionary process is focused more on technical considerations.

Barriers to Change

Human and organizational barriers to changing your organization's information technology may prove more difficult to overcome than the technical problems. In the decade just past, our relationships to information technology have been turned upside down, and in the decade ahead they will again change radically.

Information systems used to be associated with organizational entities; the movement toward reengineering demands that they be associated with business processes. Computers and data used to be isolated organizationally in information services departments. Now they are scattered organizationally, and users often have the option of building and/or operating their own systems, without the intervention of IT professionals.

The application/infrastructure architecture toward which we are moving will require another major shift in how information technology is distributed and managed. Users will be less able to build isolated systems because they will need the infrastructure, both as a source of data and as a supplier of communications facilities. This in turn will lead to increased influence on the uses of IT by the managers of the infrastructure—the IT professionals. Perhaps most distressing of all, the focus on business process as the basic unit of information system design will change to a focus on business primitives.

The IT activities of the organization of 2004 will be built around an application/infrastructure architecture

- An information services department (ISD) will design, maintain, and operate the infrastructure.
- Most small and medium-sized applications will be built by users, with substantial consulting and technical support from ISD.
- ISD will build all large systems, typically the transaction systems that support daily operations.
- Outside vendors will supply a significant proportion of information technology, including generic applications, tools, network services, and so on.

The organizational changes that will accompany these operational changes will be resisted for the same reasons that organizations always resist change: the old ways are familiar and therefore safe, the new ways are unfamiliar and therefore risky, and the transition will be difficult. Power will be redistributed, individuals must learn to do new things or learn new ways of doing old things, and they must reestablish the informal networks that lubricate the flow of work. The organizational resistance to change will be prolonged and tenacious.

In the end, we can probably achieve the information technology capabilities we will need in 2004 more quickly than we can mold our people and our organizations to take advantage of it.

AN INFORMATION TECHNOLOGY VISION FOR 2004 AND A STRATEGY TO REALIZE IT

Information technology vision and strategy for any company must be driven by that company's corporate vision and strategy. In Chapter 2, we defined corporate vision as the description of what the corporation aspires to be for a long period of time, and corporate strategy as the means to achieve the vision. Thus, it is appropriate to use our 1994 corporate vision for a federated organization as our vision for 2004.

The generic business vision, abbreviated and grossly simplified, is to be able to respond in a timely way to changes in markets, technology, and other aspects of the business environment. We take the part of the vision specific to federated organizations from Chapter 4.

- Our company serves the needs of all its stakeholders.
- Our company performs its core business processes extremely well.
- Our company provides excellent products and services to its customers.
- Our company gives workers at every level the maximum possible responsibility for their own work lives.

The information technology vision resulting from this corporate vision can be described in terms of range, reach, depth, and change.

Range

We will have the ability to extend our current uses of information technology to any part of the world in which we choose to operate.

We will be able to expand or contract our telecommunications capabilities quickly and easily, without disrupting operations.

Reach

We will have the ability to exchange data and information among systems at will, to meet changing business needs or changing organizational structures.

Depth

We will have the ability to provide additional information technology support to businesses whenever that support is in the interests of the company. This includes support for both line and staff activities, particularly support for managers and other knowledge workers.

Users of information will be able to acquire much of the information they need without the intervention of IT professionals.

Change

We will have the capability to meet all new needs for information quickly enough so that lack of information or information technology never impedes the progress of our business.

We will monitor advances in information technology and be prepared to deploy new technology whenever it is advantageous for the company to do so.

The information technology strategy to realize this vision has four components: technology, people, money, and organization. Remember that this is a strategy to fulfill a vision of 2004, which means you should start executing it almost immediately.

Technology

The best technical strategy for most companies is to promote aggressively the evolution from conventional information systems architecture through client/server architecture to the more general application/infrastructure architecture. The focus should be on meeting new needs, rather than on polishing old systems. Most existing systems should be allowed to survive until they fail from the effects of changing technology and too much modification.

People

An active program to help workers make the transition to their new responsibilities should be planned and started very soon. Both users and IT professionals will be asked to make profound changes in the ways they view their jobs and themselves. They must be shown how these changes will benefit them as individuals, as well as how they will benefit the company.

Users must be told what information is available, how to retrieve it, and how to use it.

Users must be shown how to recognize opportunities for new uses of information and information technology.

IT professionals must increase their understanding of business operations and business strategy.

Money

You must provide financial support for this strategy by allocating money to build and operate the infrastructure on the basis of its strategic importance, without requiring tangible short-term benefits. You must support the infrastructure when money is scarce because you cannot maintain it with sporadic expenditures.

Organization

Organizational changes must reflect the changes in roles required by the new information technology architecture. Everyone must understand that expanded information-related activities are an integral part of every job. And in addition to changing the structure itself, staffing levels and budgets must be adjusted to allow for the expanded IT responsibilities in business units.

Finally, the strategy should reflect the fact that many barriers will be erected to slow or stop the changes it mandates. An active program of change management should be instituted to demolish those barriers whenever and wherever they arise.

A NOTE OF CAUTION

Of course, it won't happen this way. The world is much too messy a place. Any number of events could occur that would upset the neat pictures I have drawn.

Some powerful new information technology might be developed that would finally make corporatewide management information systems practical. It might be an advance in software for massively parallel computers.

Companies might find it attractive to recentralize if they could really have a single information system to meet all their needs.

Neural network computers might take over many of the managerial decision tasks that now take so much effort to automate on conventional machines.

The trend toward business alliances might be cut short by social pressures or governmental regulations.

Small companies might be driven to the wall, unable to survive increasingly onerous regulation of business or information technology.

Large companies might drown in their rivers of data or choke on their own bureaucracies.

The technical ferment will surely continue. By 2004, there will be several new IT architectures and a cornucopia of new hardware and software. Your company will have competing and incompatible systems, no matter how hard you try to prevent it. The management of these systems will remain a major challenge.

Your defense is to be flexible, plan for change, and embrace it when it makes sense for your company. You can draw comfort from the knowledge that you will have ample notice of new things such as these, if you keep alert for them.

SUMMARY

What You Must Know

- Major changes in business will continue through the next decade, and many of them will cause an increase in the demand for information.
- An application/infrastructure architecture will enable you to change information systems in response to business changes much more rapidly than current architectures.
- As you attempt to meet the information needs of the next 10 years, people and organizations may be greater barriers than technology.

What You Must Do

- Incorporate information technology into all your business planning processes.
- Organize and implement a program to educate all workers about the relationships between information and business.
- Develop a proactive change management process that recognizes the needs of individuals as well as the needs of the enterprise.
- Devote some resources to tracking and testing new technologies.

Chapter Thirteen

Reverberations into Society

As information technology permeates business processes, echoes of it resound through our society. No one can predict all the effects, but some general directions are becoming clear. Recognizing these trends can help us prepare to face the problems and seize the opportunities the technology will bring.

Most facets of daily life will be affected. Customers will increasingly interact with sellers solely or largely through technology rather than through people. As the amount of human contact decreases, its nature may change from mostly routine transactions to mostly problem transactions, which may mean from pleasant to unpleasant. Individuals will have no choice but to become comfortable using information technology if they are to function effectively, outside of the workplace as well as within it.

We must address the societal issues that are beginning to appear. We have no general agreement or effective policies concerning personal privacy, ownership of intellectual property, and ethical use of information. The reality of constant change means that our educational system must improve dramatically. It is not sufficient to train our young people in the use of information technology, although training is essential. We must also educate them about it, so they can be effective lifelong participants in the information age. Those who cannot or will not learn to use information technology will be outsiders, perhaps members of a permanent underclass.

Information technology and the changes it is enabling in business and society present an historic opportunity for the United States to maintain and improve its position as the world's preeminent economic power. Our national culture of personal freedom, individual initiative, and diversity has given our people precisely the characteristics that make for success in the age of information. The question for the United States is whether we have the wit and the will to seize the opportunities before us.

We have been discussing the use of information technology to support organizational goals such as profits, service to customers, and compliance with governmental regulations. We now examine the other face of information technology: its effects on individuals and on society. The law of unintended consequences applies to information technology, with a vengeance.

Many of these issues are not unique to IT, but rather are parts of larger trends in business and society. They are important to our discussion of the interactions between information technology and society because information technology is often the most obvious manifestation of them, and because the rapid changes in IT have made them more disruptive than they otherwise might have been. Each of these issues is a problem for those who do not understand it and an opportunity for those who do.

IMPACTS OF INFORMATION TECHNOLOGY ON DAILY LIFE

The proliferation of information technology is making daily life easier for individuals in some ways, more difficult in others, but certainly different. We can presume that these new uses of IT are good for the companies that create them, but what about their customers?

Improved Consumer Services

On one hand, IT offers opportunities for vastly improved consumer services, from communications to health care.

- A new generation of portable wireless telephones, called personal communication systems (PCS), will connect people anywhere to the worldwide telephone network, both to initiate and to receive calls.

- A service is being deployed in Europe that will enable travelers to be reached automatically by anyone calling the traveler's home phone number. The traveler carries a SIM ("subscriber information module") card, which she inserts into a special telephone, say in a taxicab. (The SIM card is a kind of smart card, a card the size of an ordinary credit card that contains microprocessors and computer memory chips.) The telephone in the taxi becomes, in effect, the traveler's home telephone. She can receive calls and originate them. Calls she originates will be routed to the long distance carrier of her choice and charged directly to her home phone. She removes the card when she leaves the taxi and inserts it into the phone in her hotel room, whereupon the hotel telephone becomes her home phone.

- Smart cards are also being used for many other purposes, including as a substitute for cash in parking meters, toll booths, and college cafeterias.[1]
- Another kind of card shows promise of both improving health care and decreasing its cost. Cards are now available that contain enough computer memory to store a complete record of an individual's health and medical history, including images of X-rays, electrocardiograms, and so on. The availability of an up-to-date health record can help physicians make correct diagnoses and treatment decisions and eliminate redundant medical tests. No one is yet offering these cards in the marketplace, but several vendors are considering doing so.

On the other hand, these same technologies create difficulties for their users, as we shall see.

Changing Distribution of Work

Information technology is changing the distribution of work, often from sellers to buyers.

- The public telephone system requires customers to establish their connection to the network and route their calls to the recipient, rather than make a request of a human operator.
- Voice mail systems substitute customer input from a touch-tone telephone for work formerly done by a telephone receptionist.
- Some securities firms allow customers to transmit buy and sell orders from the customers' personal computers to the company's computers, without intervention by any company employee.

There is nothing intrinsically wrong about this redistribution of work. The question is, Does the customer get sufficient benefits to justify his increased efforts? In the case of the telephone network, the answer is clearly yes. In the case of voice mail systems, which typically require callers to act as telephone

switchboard operators for the company being called, the answer
is probably no.

Reduced Person-to-Person Contact

There is less person-to-person contact in many commercial transactions. In the examples above, customer-to-machine communication replaces person-to-person communication. Much of the
remaining human contact is problem oriented; for instance, handling a discrepancy in a credit card bill. In catalog marketing,
telephone communication substitutes for the face-to-face encoun-
ters between customer and salesperson in a retail store. Some
people like the quick, impersonal telephone contact. Others prefer the more leisurely, more social interaction in a store.

Less Privacy

Despite having less direct contact with other people in everyday
commercial transactions, we have less control over who has access to information about our personal lives—less privacy. More
people and more companies know about each individual transaction. Sometimes this is good for the consumer, sometimes not.

- If I make a plane reservation and a rental car reservation at
  the same time through my travel agent, the car rental company knows which flight I have booked. This is fine if the
  flight is late, because the car will be held for me. But if I
  choose to change my airline to arrive on time when my
  original flight is late, my car may not be available.
- If you subscribe to a special interest magazine, you probably receive catalogs of related products. You may be interested in them, or you may view them as more junk mail to
  throw away.

We are reaching the point where a person's entire life history
can be reconstructed in detail from computer-based records. Suppose someone had access to the records of your accounts in these
computer systems: American Express, Visa, MasterCard, your
bank, your telephone company, and one of the major airline reservation systems. Your life would be an open book, and you
might not want other people to read that book.

The SIM system we described above signals your exact location to the network whenever you insert your card into a telephone. (It must, or it would not be able to forward calls placed to your home telephone number.) Combine this location information with real time access to the systems listed in the previous paragraph, and someone could monitor your life as you live it.

No one has all these capabilities yet, so far as we know. But that doesn't mean someone won't try to get them. The technology is available; the question is, How do we manage it?

Most of us like to keep our financial transactions private. But sometimes it is in our own interests to have others know a great deal about them, for instance when applying for credit. How do we keep this information private for some purposes and make it available for others? Who decides?

Less Information

Ironically, information technology sometimes restricts the information you receive from others, rather than adding to it.

- Some magazines have special editions for business subscribers; these editions have both news and advertisements that do not appear in the consumer versions. Other publications have regional editions, each containing some content presumed to be of only local interest.

- Direct mail companies often make targeted offers to customers. They analyze past purchases and send special catalogs only to those *the company thinks* are likely to buy. The company's goal is simple: to save money by sending catalogs only to good prospects. But the consumer loses the opportunity to learn about and purchase goods of which he may not have been aware.

The consumer may or may not benefit from this segmentation.

Automated Transactions

It is now possible to make many commercial transactions completely automatic. One consequence of this is that the consumer has less control over each individual transaction, although she still has overall control in most cases.

The federal government will deposit Social Security payments and some other regular payments directly into the recipient's bank account by electronic means, saving time and costs for both parties. Many banks offer automatic bill paying services. The depositor preauthorizes certain regular payments, and the bank makes them on the specified date without further contact with the depositor. Another automatic transaction consumers never see is the transaction whereby the credit card issuer pays the merchant for goods purchased by the consumer.

Automatic transactions are clearly easier for the depositor when things are going smoothly. But what if the depositor's paycheck is late? Or what if the depositor has a dispute with her insurance company and wants to withhold payment, but payment has already been made by the bank? Some companies have procedures for dealing with this problem; some do not.

IMPACTS ON SOCIETY

Ownership of Information

The question of ownership and control of distribution of personal data is as much a societal question as a personal one. In the best interests of society, who should own personal data about an individual's purchase transactions, or reading preferences, or medical history? Who should control its distribution? And who should profit from its distribution? We in the United States have not yet decided.

On a broader level, our individual freedom is at risk. The availability of comprehensive personal information, as we described above, will invite analysis, and then control.

We see it in our political process today. In 1992, one aspirant to high office in our government admitted that he had once smoked marijuana as a young man. Another acknowledged a similar act at a similar age, but said he did not inhale. One achieved the office he sought; the other did not. But that is beside the point. The point is that in both cases, the act in question was irrelevant to the issue of qualification for office, but the information was there, so it was used. If comprehensive life information is available, it too will be used, relevant or not.

We have privacy laws. Are they too strong, too weak, badly focused? Do they deal adequately with the specific problems associated with information technology?

Maintaining the accuracy of data about individuals is becoming more important daily as society depends more and more on computerized records. Individuals can be seriously damaged economically when credit records are inaccurate. Recent reports of widespread inaccuracies have led to legislation regulating the operations of credit reporting companies.

Information is power in society, just as it is within an enterprise. We must learn to curb that power in the interests of individual freedom, just as we curb all other societal power.

Telecommuting

Information technology is modifying one of our fundamental assumptions about work: the idea that business is conducted in an office or a factory.

Telecommuting is the name given to working at home, using computers and teleprocessing facilities to provide the same tools at home as are available at a conventional office. Various studies suggest that there are between 5 million and 27 million telecommuters in the United States.[2] Some are full time and some are part time, which may account for the variations in the estimates. Some are clerical workers, doing internal clerical tasks. Some are customer service representatives, talking by phone to customers (who think they are talking to people in offices). Others are computer programmers, engineering designers, and financial analysts. Telecommuting is a reasonable approach to any job that does not require face-to-face contact with customers or co-workers and does not require close supervision.

There are many excellent reasons for telecommuting.

- Parents of young children can combine work and child care, to the benefit of all concerned.
- Telecommuters save time and transportation costs.
- Companies save office space and related expenses.
- Telecommuting decreases highway congestion, air pollution, and energy use

There are some disadvantages.

- Telecommuters forgo the informal personal contacts that support work processes and are an important part of social life for many workers.
- Telecommuting can strain family relationships, particularly if both parties work at home.

Telemarketing is a kind of reverse telecommuting, in which the customer stays at home. There is no longer a store or a showroom as a place where the customer meets the salesperson, although there may be a "telemarketing office" where the salespeople work.

Once we abandon the idea that business is conducted in preselected places outside of the home, many secondary effects come into play. The construction and real estate industries will see decreasing demand for commercial space. Big six accounting firm Ernst & Young expects to cut its office space requirements by 40 percent by having its junior staff telecommute except when they are required to be in the office for a specific purpose[3]. Energy companies, and later highway builders and automobile manufacturers, may see related decreases in demand for their products.

International Currency Trading

The law of unintended consequences has come into play in at least one important segment of our economy, international currency trading.

Nearly $1 *trillion* worth of currency is traded each day in the international currency market, a market that exists only as a computer and telecommunications network connecting banks, brokers, and other traders. Not only does the market not exist in any tangible form, the money itself does not exist, except as computer records and telecommunications messages. Yet the volume of transactions (and hence the volume of money) dwarfs the combined reserves of all the central banks in the world. This unregulated, almost unfindable international market determines the relative values of the world's currencies, despite any efforts of central banks. Individual nations have lost the one of the pillars of national sovereignty.[4]

Money is power, just as information is power. What, if anything, can society do about the international currency market? What, if anything, should it do?

Ownership of Intellectual Property

Information technology is modifying some of our notions about property, just as it is modifying our ideas about the workplace. Two concepts demand our attention: the concept of ownership and the concept of possession.

In the case of tangible property—a machine or building—ownership carries with it the right of possession unless that right has been bargained away. The owner of a building can "sell" the right of possession in exchange for rent. Or the owner can sell the building and retain the right of possession, if the buyer is willing. In either case, when one party gains possession, the other loses it. This is not true of information. Many people can possess and use a given piece of information at the same time, without depriving the owner of possession and use.

In the United States, we have developed some fairly clear ideas of the meaning and ownership of some kinds of intellectual property, such as inventions and computer programs. The rules concerning data, particularly collections of data and information, are less clear.

Another dimension of the question of possession and ownership arises in connection with electronic data transmission. In the international currency market, when is a deal consummated? When the buy order is transmitted, or when it is received? There may only be milliseconds between the two events, but much can happen in milliseconds these days.

Public Policy

Information technology affects public policy in a myriad of ways, direct and indirect.

For the past decade or more, there has been substantial public concern about the safety of the users of various pieces of computer equipment. The longest lasting bone of contention has been video display terminals (VDT), the screens through which most people communicate with computers. The first concern was that electromagnetic radiation from the screens could cause cancer or birth defects in the children of pregnant women who worked with VDTs full time. A definitive review of the scientific literature has shown that there is no such effect, but the argument rages on.[5] Despite scientific proof that radiation is not a problem, at least one country has passed legislation mandating extra shielding on VDTs. Several companies are marketing VDTs that meet these requirements, at extra cost and with no discernible benefits.

Health problems are associated with VDTs, even though radiation is not among them. Extended work with VDTs can cause various orthopedic problems including carpal tunnel syndrome and back problems. Eyestrain and other visual problems are not uncommon. Companies must deal with the health concerns of VDT workers voluntarily, or society will force them to do so.

Information technology can affect public policy indirectly when it is used to create "junk science"—opinions and biases masquerading as science. (A lot of junk is science created without benefit of computers, but that's another story.) Two examples come to mind.

In 1970, a self-appointed group of people interested in "the predicament of man" commissioned a study of trends in population, energy production, food production, and related topics. The study was carried out using a large, complex computer model, and the results were published under the title "The Limits to Growth."[6]

The authors studied the effects of a number of different assumptions *about the data used to drive the model:* rate of population growth, supply of natural resources, rate of generation of pollution, and so on. The model predicted widespread starvation and other calamities over the next century unless constraints are placed on resource utilization, population growth, and related things.

In presenting their results, the authors of the study assert: "We can thus say with some confidence that, under the assumption of no major change in the present system, population and industrial growth will certainly stop within the next century, at the latest."[7] The report ends with a call for immediate action to limit population growth, natural resource utilization, and economic activity.[8]

I do not share their confidence. A review of the model I made at the time the book was published revealed that the results were heavily dependent on an *assumption embedded in the structure of the model* concerning rates of innovation. Reasonable changes in that one assumption would have completely changed the results and the predictions.

The point is not whether my assumption is correct and theirs is incorrect. The point is that a large and complex computer model was used in an attempt to influence public policy without a full discussion of the assumptions built into the model.

Data mining is another kind of junk science using information technology, particularly dangerous in health care. Here is a hypothetical example of how it works.

A "researcher" acquires a database about all deaths in the state of Illinois for a 10-year period. The database shows the cause of death of each person and data about other factors such as age at death, number and gender of siblings, color of hair, color of eyes, height, weight at death, weight at birth, and so on. The researcher uses a computer to calculate the correlations of each of the other factors with cause of death. (Correlations themselves are simple. Two factors are said to be positively correlated with one another when they tend to occur together. For example, body weight is correlated with height: tall people tend to weigh more than short people.)

Given enough different factors, some positive correlations are almost certain to be found. A researcher might find a positive correlation between having red hair and dying in an automobile accident. A correct statement of this result would be: there is a 95 percent probability that people with red hair are more likely to die in automobile accidents than people with hair of other colors. Unfortunately, this quickly gets transformed into a newspaper headline that says, "Red Hair Linked to Auto Deaths," with the implication that red hair causes auto deaths.

The problem is confusing correlation with causality. Just because two factors are correlated does not mean one causes the other. To justify the statement that red hair causes death in automobile accidents, one would need to postulate a mechanism, and then prove that the mechanism exists and has the predicted effect.

I have deliberately chosen a silly example to make the problem obvious. But there are recurring instances when exactly this kind of "analysis" has caused unjustified public concern. A few years ago someone found a "link" between alcohol consumption and breast cancer in women. Further research found no causal mechanism, but many women were upset by the original report.

Data mining would occur only rarely without high-powered computers and extensive computerized databases. Doing correlation studies without a computer is so time consuming and so tedious that most researchers would prefer to find a causal mechanism first and test it statistically later, rather than blindly seeking correlations.

Direct Democracy

Information technology has made it possible to govern a major nation by direct democracy for the first time since the decline of the city-states of classical Greece. The contemporary equivalent of the debates in the Athenian agora is the electronic town meetings Bill Clinton conducted during the 1992 presidential campaign and during his efforts to influence Congress to pass his economic program in the spring of 1993. In 1992, a political party in Canada demonstrated the feasibility of electronic voting for public office when it used an 800 telephone system to record votes for party officials.

It is possible to govern with a direct democracy, each person voting on each law, but is it wise? Our founding fathers thought that a representative democracy would be superior, in part because of the built-in delays between public clamor for action and completion of the legislative process would help prevent hasty and ill-considered laws.

That viewpoint was right for its day and for a long time after. Is it right for our time? We will have electronic town meetings; they cannot be stopped. Should we carry it the last step, to electronic voting?

Changes in Individuals

Information technology is affecting individuals in ways that may well affect society as a whole. Will students use information technology as a crutch and never learn basic skills such as arithmetic and spelling? If so, does it matter? Yes, but not only for the sake of the skills as such. These skills are important because learning them builds self-discipline and self-confidence and because having them contributes to precision of thought and expression.

The information explosion, as manifest in the proliferation of books and other publications, is nearly incomprehensible in magnitude. Over 50,000 titles were published in hard-cover books in the United States in 1992, in addition to newspapers, magazines, newsletters, and professional journals. Individuals defend themselves against this onslaught by scanning, by reading abstracts, but mostly by reading special purpose publications rather than general interest publications. One effect of this is that the knowledge each individual has is likely to be deep within a few topics rather than wide over many. IT makes further specialization possible by enabling special purpose search services, which will send a subscriber stories about only those topics selected in advance by the subscriber.

Will this selective acquisition of information create a society of narrow specialists who cannot communicate with one another and have little knowledge about or interest in the world as a whole?

Multimedia information systems at their best enhance communications and learning by adding the information contained in sound and images to the precision of thought and expression inherent in words. At their worst, multimedia systems substitute sound and images for words, degrading emotion and destroying thought.

A Permanent Underclass

The biggest societal problem of the information age, the age of the knowledge worker, is that we are in danger of creating a permanent underclass of people who are unable to participate in the mainstream of life because they lack the necessary education and training in information technology. There are signs that information technology can be used to help alleviate this problem, which it helped create. We are seeing some successes in using computers in the classroom. Our challenge in the 1990s is to extend the scope of these activities to all students. We must meet this challenge. If we do not make it possible for everyone to participate in our society, we will have failed, no matter what our other accomplishments.

OPPORTUNITIES FOR BUSINESS

We have been focusing on the impacts of information technology on society, particularly information technology used by businesses for their own purposes or provided to the public for public use. The effects of this technology on society and public reactions to it can provide important guidance to business executives.

Use this checklist to test each of your planned new products or new uses of information technology against the impacts on daily life and on society that we listed above.

Work shifting: Does this product (or service) shift work from your company to your customer? If so, does the customer benefit enough to make it worth his while to do "your" work? Can the customer choose whether or not to do this extra work?

Personal contact: Does this product diminish personal contact between your workers and your customers? If so, does it matter to the customer? Can the customer choose between a personal channel of communication and an impersonal one?

Privacy: Does this product or service give information about your customer to a third party? Is it useful to your customer for the third party to have this information? Does the customer have a choice as to whether or not the information is given to the third party?

Information transmitted to the customer: Does this product or service give the customer more or less information than she was previously receiving? Is that desirable, from the customer's point of view? Does the customer have a choice?

Automatic transactions: Does this product or service provide automatic execution of a transaction, without customer intervention? Are there circumstances when the customer might not want automatic execution? Can the customer easily stop an automatic transaction? Can the customer easily reverse a transaction once it has occurred?

Telecommuting: Do your plans for implementing a telecommuting program include ways to replace lost social interactions? Do they include support for potential family stress?

Telemarketing: Is your telemarketing operation structured so that it will be as personal as possible to each customer? Will your telemarketing representatives be trained to provide personal contact and personal service?

This list is by no means complete. As you look at specific products, more questions will occur to you, but they will always fall into one of three categories:

- Is this product "right" for my customer?
- Does this product offer my customer the choice of using information technology or not using it?
- Is this product acceptable to society?

This last question is worth a bit of elaboration because it is so easy for information technology to carry an idea from an individual to a company and then to society at large.

In 1991, Lotus Development Corporation announced a new product called MarketPlace: Households. It contained the name, address, and certain demographic information about 80 million households in the United States, and it stored the information on compact disks that could be accessed by a personal computer. Lotus offered the product for sale on terms that made it extremely attractive to small businesses.

Consumers were outraged. They made such an outcry that Lotus withdrew the product before any were sold. In one sense, the objections were irrational. None of the information was secret. All of it was already available in computerized form to companies with mainframe computers. The only thing new was that the information would be available to a large number of small businesses in addition to a few large ones.[9] Societal perception of an attack on personal privacy, whether or not it was well founded, destroyed this product.

We all know we should test our new product ideas with potential customers. Many of us neglect to test them against the expectations and concerns of society at large.

INFORMATION TECHNOLOGY AND THE UNITED STATES IN THE 21ST CENTURY

The United States is especially well situated for competitive success as we stand at the threshold of the 21st century and the information age. Our history, our people, and our national character contain all the necessary elements. Our national task is to create an environment in which these elements can coalesce into the organizations we need to build our prosperity and retain our leadership in the world.

We have seen the shape of the business environment in the 1990s and beyond. Competition will be intense as companies from around the globe compete in every market. Organizations of every kind will be driven by the demands of their customers as well as by the needs of their owners. Success will be measured at the bottom line and beyond, as companies are compelled to recognize the needs of other stakeholders: workers, suppliers, and the communities in which they live. The response of successful businesses to this environment will be to give each customer individual attention at every stage of every business transaction, from product design to sale and entry of the order through production, delivery, and aftersale service.

Three things will characterize the organizations that succeed in providing this level of customer service: competent, dedicated workers; an organization that enables them to function effectively; and information technology to support them throughout the business process.

As the hierarchical organizational structure has been made obsolete by the changes in business environment, many alternate forms, and names, have been proposed: the networked organization, the flat organization, the virtual corporation, and others. Each of these new organizational forms is based on the ideas of fewer levels of management, decision making at lower levels, and less central bureaucracy. We have called our form the federated organization, as suggested by Charles Handy. He chose this name because it evoked the image of the structure of the government of the United States: a group of largely independent states, brought together under the broad guidance and control of a central authority. This is an excellent description of the kind of organization structure that will be successful in the 21st century.

But structure alone is not enough. In the end, people are the key to success. As we saw in our discussion of holistic process design, the best results come from a team of people of diverse backgrounds working together on a common problem.

The United States has an enormous competitive advantage in its tradition of personal freedom and the racial, ethnic, and cultural diversity of our people. We have a long national history of diverse people coming together to pursue a common interest. Alexis de Tocqueville observed in 1831 the tendency of Americans to form organizations devoted to specific purposes, from bird-watching to public service, from religion to politics. He was particularly intrigued by the fact individuals met their needs by joining a large number of groups, each representing one particular interest. A Protestant Democrat and a Catholic Tory might both be members of the same bird-watching club[10].

This willingness to join special purpose groups and work with others from different backgrounds in pursuit of a common goal is exactly the habit of mind necessary to function as an empowered worker on a team in a federated organization. We had it in 1831, and we have it in 1994. And this is precisely what is needed for success in the competitive world of the 21st century.

We have the people. We have the resources. Our national task is to bring them to bear on the problems of the global information age without losing our freedom along the way.

SUMMARY

What You Must Know

- Society as a whole is in a state of continual change similar to that of business, and for the same reasons.
- The pace and nature of change means that everyone must engage in lifelong learning.

- Each new intrusion of information technology into our lives brings problems along with opportunities. Some of these problems reach to the core of our lives and our beliefs.
- The United States is uniquely suited to take advantage of the opportunities of the information age.

What You Must Do

- Force our educational institutions both to educate their students and to train them for life in the information age.
- Influence all the organizations of which you are a part—economic, social, and political—to encourage individual initiative rather than to stifle it.
- Think beyond the business consequences of your information technology decisions and try to understand the personal and social consequences as well.

Endnotes

Chapter 1

[1]"AT&T and Microsoft Posts Stock Market Milestones," *The Wall Street Journal*, January 22, 1993, p. C2.

[2]Corporate annual reports.

[3]"Nucor and Oregon Steel Agree to Build Sheet-Steel Minimill in Western US," *The Wall Street Journal*, December 30, 1992, p.1.

[4]Corporate annual reports.

[5]Steven Burke, "Business," *PC Week*, August 6, 1990, p. 132.

[6]Michael Schroeder, "The Recasting of Alcoa," *Business Week*, September 9, 1991, p. 62.

[7]Clinton Wilder, "Kodak Hands Processing over to IBM," *Computerworld*, July 31, 1989, p. 1.

[8]E J Muller, "The Top Guns of Third Party Logistics," *Distribution* 92, no. 3 (March 1993), p. 30.

[9]"Four Big Regional Banks to Consolidate Operations," *The Wall Street Journal*, July 22, 1992, p. 4.

[10]Adam Smith, "An Inquiry into the Nature and Causes of the Wealth of Nations," originally published in 1776. Reprinted as Volume 10 in *The Harvard Classics* (New York: P.F. Collier & Son, 1909).

[11]Kathleen Morris, "Prodigal Son," *Financial World*, September 15, 1993, p. 60.

[12]Teleport Communications Group press release dated September 16, 1992.

[13]*The Wall Street Journal*, June 24, 1993.

[14]"AT&T Will Purchase New Shares of McCaw for about $400 Million," *The Wall Street Journal*, November 6, 1992, p. A8.

[15]Robert O Metzger, "The Ominous Exporting of U. S. Clerical Jobs," *USA Today (magazine)*, March 16, 1989.

[16]Joanne Cummings, "Another Bright Idea," *Network World*, November 23, 1992, p. 31.

[17]Joan O'C Hamilton, "How Levi Strauss Is Getting the Lead Out of Its Pipeline," *Business Week*, December 17, 1987, p. 92.

[18]James W Michaels, "They Thought It Was Just for Propellor Heads," *Forbes*, October 12, 1992, p. 10.

[19]Gregory A Patterson, "Demise of Sears's Big Book Sparks Race by Catalog Retailers to Win Its Customers," *The Wall Street Journal*, May 26, 1993, p. B2.

[20]Emily Leinfuss, "USAA's Image of Success," *Datamation*, May 15, 1990, p. 77.

[21]Christopher Barr, "The Evolution of Pentium," *PC Magazine*, April 27, 1993, p. 117.

For a fascinating history of the development of microcomputer technology, see George Gilder, *Microcosm, The Quantum Revolution in Economics and Technology* (New York: Simon & Schuster, 1989).

Chapter 2

[1]Hal F Rosenbluth, *The Customer Comes Second* (New York: William Morrow and Company, 1992).

[2]Lawrie Thomas, *Amoco Torch*, March 8, 1993.

[3]Interview with William La Macchia, president of The Mark Travel Corporation, and David Moon, vice president and chief information officer, March 31, 1993.

[4]Richard L Huber, "How Continental Bank Outsourced Its 'Crown Jewels,' " *Harvard Business Review*, January–February 1993, p. 121.

[5]Michael Totty, "As Big Firms Farm Out, MaxServ Scoops Up New Pacts," *The Wall Street Journal*, July 30, 1993.

[6]Robert Howard, "The CEO as Organizational Architect: An Interview with Xerox's Paul Allaire," *Harvard Business Review*, September–October 1992, p. 106.

[7]Robert N Ford, *Motivation Through the Work Itself* (New York: American Management Association, 1969).

Chapter 3

[1]Gregory A Patterson, "Demise of Sears's Big Book Sparks Race by Catalog Retailers to Win Its Customers," *The Wall Street Journal*, May 26, 1993, p. B2.

[2]John A Byrne, "Business Fads, What's in—and Out," *Business Week*, January 20, 1986, p. 52.

[3]Robert Howard, "The CEO as Organizational Architect: An Interview with Xerox's Paul Allaire," *Harvard Business Review*, September–October 1992, p. 106.

[4]John A Byrne, "Management's New Gurus," *Business Week*, August 31, 1992, pp. 44–52.

[5]William H Davidow and Michael S Malone, *The Virtual Corporation: Structuring and Revitalizing the Corporation of the 21st Century* (New York: HarperCollins, 1992).

[6]Charles Handy, *The Age of Unreason* (Boston: Harvard Business School Press, 1989).

Chapter 4

[1]Interview with Professor Albert H Rubenstein of Northwestern University, July 27, 1993.

[2]There are many instances of this in the business press. See Simon Brady, "How to Avoid an Upgrade," *Euromoney*, December 1992, for one example.

[3]Linda Wilson, "Stand and Deliver," *Information Week*, November 23, 1992, p. 33.

[4]Marilyn M Parker and Robert J Benson with H E Trainor, *Information Economics: Linking Business Performance to Information Technology* (Englewood Cliffs, N.J.: Prentice Hall, 1988), p. 59.

[5]Bruce Caldwell, "A Banner IS Shop Loses Altitude: Turbulence at AMR," *Information Week*, July 19, 1993.

Chapter 5

[1]John P McPartlin, "Not the Best of Times," *Information Week*, June 21, 1992, p. 74.

[2]Paul A Strassman, *Information Payoff* (New York: Free Press, 1985), pp. 151–64.

[3]Stephen S Roach, "America's Technology Dilemma: A Profile of the Information Economy," Special Economic Study for Morgan Stanley & Co., April 22, 1987, p. 1.

[4]This topic has been widely discussed recently. For some examples of the dubious basis for many productivity figures, see Alfred L Malabre Jr. and Lindley H Clark Jr., "Productivity Statistics for the Service Sector May Understate Gains," *The Wall Street Journal*, August 12, 1992. For more recent information and viewpoints, see Myron Magnet, "Good News for the Service Economy," *Fortune*, May 3, 1993, pp. 46–52, and "The Redemption of the 'Inept,' " *Information Week*, April 19, 1993.

[5] Raymond R Panko, "Is Office Productivity Stagnant?" *MIS Quarterly*, June 1991, pp. 191–203.

[6]*Unlocking the Computer's Profit Potential* (New York: McKinsey & Company, Inc., 1968).

[7]David Woodruff, "High Tech Keeps a Retailer from Wilting," *Business Week*, June 14, 1993, p. 64.

[8]Edward Cone, "Parts Smarts," *Information Week*, August 2, 1993, p. 36.

[9]*Standard Federal Tax Reports* (1993), Commerce Clearing House, paragraph 27,119.

[10]Mark Hulbert, "State of the Letters," *Forbes*, May 10, 1993, p. 195.

[11]"Survey Gauges CIOs' Outsourcing Acumen," *ABA Banking Journal*, May 1992, p. 84.

[12]Clinton Wilder, "Kodak Hands Processing Over to IBM," *Computerworld*, July 31, 1989, p. 1.

[13]Clinton Wilder, "Kodak Focuses on Next Outsourcing Frontier," *Computerworld*, August 28, 1989, p. 3.

[14]Richard L Huber, "How Continental Bank Outsourced Its 'Crown Jewels,' " *Harvard Business Review*, January–February 1993, p. 121.

[15]Joseph Maglitta, "Squeeze Play," *Computerworld*, April 19, 1993, p. 86.

[16]Interview with William La Macchia, president of The Mark Travel Corporation, and David Moon, vice president and chief information officer, March 31, 1993, and August 4, 1993.

Chapter 6

[1]Interview with William La Macchia, president of The Mark Travel Corporation, and David Moon, vice president and chief information officer, March 31, 1993.

[2]Thomas H Davenport, *Process Innovation: Reengineering Work Through Information Technology* (Boston: Harvard Business School Press, 1993), p. 140.

[3]Mohan Kharbanda, "Back From the Brink," *CMA Magazine*, July–August 1991, p. 9.

[4]Ken Freeman, "Business Process Redesign: A Corning Perspective," *SIM Executive Brief*, Summer 1993.

[5]Martin K Starr, *Operations Management* (Englewood Cliffs, N.J.: Prentice Hall, 1978), pp. 591–98.

[6]Shawn Tully, "Can Boeing Reinvent Itself?" *Fortune*, March 8, 1993, p. 66.

[7]Interview with Thomas Barrett, director of the Information Services Division of Bemis Company, March 30, 1993.

[8]Ibid.

[9]Jon R Katzenbach and Douglas K Smith provide an excellent introduction to the essentials of teams and team building in their article "The Discipline of Teams," *Harvard Business Review*, March–April 1993, p. 111.

[10]John F Rockart, "Chief Executives Define Their Own Data Needs," *Harvard Business Review*, March–April 1979, pp. 81–93.

[11]This particular wording is from Robert B. Parker, *Early Autumn* (New York: Dell, 1981).

Chapter 7

[1]Interview with Thomas Barrett, director of the Information Services Division of Bemis Company, March 30, 1993.

[2]David J Nigrelle, "First Hand Information for Front Line Management," *Information Management Forum*, May and June 1991.

[3]Interview with William La Macchia, president of The Mark Travel Corporation, and David Moon, vice president and chief information officer, March 31, 1993.

[4]Edward O Welles, "Riding the High-Tech Highway," *INC.*, March 1993, p. 72.

[5]"Sam Walton in His Own Words," *Fortune*, June 29, 1992, p. 98.

[6]Ellis Booker, "Centralization Is His Calling Card," *Compterworld*, April 30, 1990, p. 66.

[7]Ron Grohowski, Chris McGoff, Doug Vogel, Ben Martz, and Jay Nunamaker, "Implementing Electronic Meeting Systems at IBM: Lessons Learned and Success Factors," *MIS Quarterly* 14, no. 4 (December 1990), pp. 368–83.

[8] Edward H Kaplan and Elaine O'Keefe, "Let the Needles Do the Talking! Evaluating the New Haven Needle Exchange," *Interfaces*, January–February 1993, p. 7. This issue of *Interfaces* contains six other examples of model-generated information that provided significant benefits to the organizations that used the models.

Chapter 8

[1]Glenn Whitney, "Stock Exchange in London Drops Trading Project," *The Wall Street Journal*, March 12, 1993, p. A8; and Glenn Whitney, "Giant London Bourse Seeks New Identity and Focus after Costly Project Fails," *The Wall Street Journal*, April 22, 1993, p. A8.

[2]Sharon Kindel, "The Computer That Ate the Company," *Financial World*, March 31, 1992, p. 96.

³Interview with Raymond Dash, March 1993.

⁴Preliminary results of research in progress at Northwestern University's Center for Information and Telecommunications Technology.

⁵For contrasting views on the merits of CASE, see these two articles: William M Smith, "CASE Works, But Not Alone," *Computerworld*, April 13, 1992, p. 74; and Ned Snell, "Users Rethink Life Cycle Case," *Datamation*, May 15, 1993, p. 102.

⁶W Burry Foss, "Fast, Faster, Fastest Development," *Computerworld*, May 31, 1993, p. 81.

⁷Gerald M Hoffman "Every Manager is an Information Systems Manager Now, or, Managing User-Controlled Information Systems," *Information & Management*, December 1986, p. 229.

Chapter 9

¹Joel D Goldhar and Mariann Jelinek, "Planning for Economies of Scope," *Harvard Business Review*, November–December 1983, p. 141.

²Stephanie Stahl, "A Less Sprawling Citi," *Information Week*, March 15, 1993, p. 15.

³Mark Halper, "SABRE Eyes Downsizing," *Computerworld*, March 29, 1993, p. 1.

Chapter 10

¹The concepts of reach and range are taken from the work of Peter G W Keen, *Shaping the Future: Business Design Through Information Technology* (Boston: Harvard Business School Press, 1991).

²Ron Grohowski, Chris McGoff, Doug Vogel, Ben Martz, and Jay Nunamaker, "Implementing Electronic Meeting Systems at IBM: Lessons Learned and Success Factors," *MIS Quarterly* 14, no. 4 (December 1990), p. 368.

³Myron Magnet, "Who's Winning the Information Revolution," *Fortune*, November 30, 1992, pp. 110–17.

⁴Interview with Linda L. Brennan, August 2, 1993.

⁵Yvette DeBow, "A Marriage of Convenience," *Insurance & Technology*, June 1993, p. 36.

⁶Thomas Hoffman, "Law Firm Makes a Strong Case," *Computerworld*, December 7, 1992, p. 20.

⁷Interview with Professor Albert H Rubenstein of Northwestern University, July 27, 1993.

⁸Interview with Donald N Frey, August 3, 1993.

⁹Jan Jaben, "Can Home Banking Rise from the Ashes?" *Bankers Monthly*, May 1989, p. 55.

¹⁰John Stewart, "The Credit-Reporting Mess," *Credit Card Management*, July 1991, p. 54.

¹¹Bob Brown and Paul Desmond, "American, SABRE Pan Plan to Level CRS Field," *Network World*, April 1, 1991.

Chapter 11

[1]Curt Hartog and Rose Brower, "The New IS Professional: Prospects for the '90s," *Working Paper Series* (St. Louis: Center for the Study of Data Processing, Washington University, 1990).

[2]Peter G W Keen, *Shaping the Future: Business Design Through Information Technology* (Boston: Harvard Business School Press, 1991), chap. 5.

[3]Interview with William La Macchia, president of The Mark Travel Corporation, and David Moon, vice president and chief information officer, March 31, 1993, and August 4, 1993.

[4]Keen, *Shaping the Future.*

[5]J Daniel Couger and Robert A Zawacki, *Motivating and Managing Computer Personnel* (New York: John Wiley & Sons, 1980).

[6]Keen, *Shaping the Future.*

[7]David Bartholomew, "Modern Times?" *Information Week*, July 26, 1993, p. 34.

[8] Various studies show that in many companies, from 20 to 50 percent of IS resources are under the direct budgetary and managerial control of operating managers, rather than IT managers.

[9]Alan Alter, "A New Twist on Turnover," *CIO Magazine*, October 1990, p. 48; and Cheryl Currid, "Congratulations on Your Promotion to CIO—Now Dance!" *InfoWorld*, June 29, 1992, p. 55.

[10]Martin K Starr, "Comparative Investment Strategies in Training and Technology," to be published in *International Journal of Technology Management*, January 1994.

[11]Interview with Professor Martin K Starr of Columbia University, August 4, 1993.

Chapter 12

[1]Grace Leone, "Business TV is Growing Up," *Satellite Communications*, November 1989, p. 9A.

[2]Elizabeth U Harding, "U. S. Companies are Finding that CASE Travels Well in India," *Software Magazine*, November 1991, p. 24.

[3]Mick O'Leary, "Database Review: New Car Showroom Selects Right Car," *Information Today*, October 1991, p. 13.

[4]A H Rubenstein and H Schwärtzel, eds., *Intelligent Workstations for Professionals* (Berlin/New York: Springer-Verlag, 1992).

[5]I am indebted to Mark Hauf and Gerald Tang of Ameritech for formulating the issue in these terms and for many discussions that have added to my understanding and helped me elaborate it.

Chapter 13

[1]William L Bulkeley, "Someday, Cards May Make Coins Obsolete," *The Wall Street Journal*, May 10, 1993, p. B6.

[2]Bob Filipozak, "Telecommuting: A Better Way to Work?" *Training*, May 1992, p. 53; Jill Kirschenbaum, "Home Base: Workplace for the 90s," *Incentive*, May 1989, p. 78; and Lloyd Gite, "The Home-Based Executive," *Black Enterprise*, January 1991.

[3]Mitchell Pacelle, "To Trim Their Costs, Some Companies Cut Space for Employees," *The Wall Street Journal*, June 4, 1993, p. 1.

[4]Walter B Wriston, former chairman of Citicorp, has described this in detail in his book *The Twilight of Sovereignty* (New York: Charles Scribner's Sons, 1992).

[5] Kavet R Tell, "VDTs: Field Levels, Epidemiology, and Laboratory Studies," *Health Physics* 61, no. 1 (July 1991), p. 47.

[6]Donella H Meadows, Dennis L Meadows, Jorgen Randers, and William W Beherns III, *The Limits to Growth* (New York: Universe Books, 1972).

[7]*Ibid.*, p. 126.

[8]*Ibid.*, p. 183.

[9]Cyndee Miller, "Lotus Forced to Cancel New Software Program," *Marketing News*, February 18, 1991, p. 11.

[10] Alexis de Tocqueville, *Democracy in America* (New York: Alfred A. Knopf, 1951).

Index of Organizations

General Index

Other books of interest to you from Irwin Professional Publishing . . .

SELF-DIRECTED WORK TEAMS

The New American Challenge

Jack D. Orsburn, Linda Moran, Ed Musselwhite, and John H. Zenger

This is the definitive guide to self-directed work teams, which are increasingly a key component of effective total quality improvement efforts. The book details each step of the team-building process, demonstrating what needs to be done, who should do it, and how. (354 pages)
ISBN: 1-55623-841-8

LEADING TEAMS

Mastering the New Role

John H. Zenger, Ed Musselwhite, Kathleen Hurson, and Craig Perrin

Shows how managers can successfully adjust to today's changing team-based work environment. Includes several self-tests and quotes, stories, and advice from successful team leaders. (275 pages)
ISBN: 1-55623-894-0

WHY TQM FAILS AND WHAT TO DO ABOUT IT

Mark Graham Brown, Darcy E. Hitchcock, and Marsha L. Willard
Co-published with the Association for Quality and Participation

Offers a way out of the frustration, wasted energy, and endless waiting that has lately stigmatized the quality movement! Readers will uncover the root causes for the collapse and failure of total quality and find practical advice for correcting and preventing them. (285 pages)
ISBN: 0-7863-0140-6

MANAGING MICROCOMPUTER SECURITY

Edited by Dr. Robert S. Snoyer and Glenn A. Fischer
Co-published with Chantico Publishing Co., Inc.

Essential for any organization serious about protecting its computer system investment! You'll find strategies for increasing security awareness within the entire work force; checklists that help you plan, design, and execute an effective security program; and much more. (431 pages)
ISBN: 1-55623-875-4

EVERYONE'S SUPPORT SYSTEMS

A Complete Guide to Effective Decision Making Using Microcomputers
Edited by Dr. Robert S. Snoyer and Glenn A. Fischer
Co-published with Chantico Publishing Co., Inc.

Discover how to use information technology to meet your strategic goals! This handbook is filled with proven methods for selecting and building support systems that empower employees and improve decision making at all levels. (405 pages)
ISBN: 1-55623-874-6

Available at fine bookstores and libraries everywhere.